The Queen Has Been Pleased

The Queen Has Been Pleased

The British Honours System at Work

John Walker

Secker & Warburg
London

To Mum and Dad, with thanks

First published in England 1986 by
Martin Secker & Warburg Limited
54 Poland Street, London W1V 3DF

Copyright © 1986 by John Walker

British Library Cataloguing in Publication Data

Walker, John
  The Queen has been pleased: the British honours
  system at work.
  1. Decorations of honour—Great Britain—History
  I. Title
  929.7′2′09   CR4801

ISBN 0-436-56111-5

Photoset in 11/13pt Linotron Plantin
and printed in England by
Redwood Burn Limited
Trowbridge, Wiltshire

Contents

Examine the Honours List and you will know exactly how a government feels in its inside. When the Honours List is full of rascals, millionaires, and er – chumps, you may be quite sure the government is dangerously ill.

Arnold Bennett *The Title*

Honours, like impressions upon coin, may give an ideal and local value to a bit of base material; but gold and silver will pass all the world over without any recommendations other than its own weight.

Laurence Sterne *Tristram Shandy*

Preface

This book started as an article for *Labour Research* in December 1983. That work was generously promoted in *The Times* by Peter Hennessy and in Parliament by Austin Mitchell MP, both of whom I would like to thank for their assistance and encouragement. Thanks are also due to my former colleagues at the Labour Research Department, particularly Neal Moister, for forbearance when I was researching the book.

It has not been an easy book to write because so few people have been prepared to discuss a section of what Bagehot called 'the dignified part of the constitution'. I have been particularly obstructed in my endeavours by officials from the Conservative Party Central Office, to whom I offer no thanks. The failure to put their side of events is not through want of asking on my part.

The staff at a number of libraries were most helpful as I demanded more and more from them. I should like to thank especially those who gave assistance to me at the Guildhall Library in the City of London, the British Library, the Library at the London School of Economics, the Public Record Office and the British Library's Newspaper Library, Colindale.

I have had to rely on an enormous number of secondary sources for much of the information in this book and am particularly indebted to two biographies of Maundy Gregory: Gerald Macmillan's *Honours for Sale* (Richard Press, 1954) and Tom Cullen's *Maundy Gregory, Purveyor of Honours* (Bodley Head, 1974). Andrew Roth's biography of Harold Wilson, *Sir Harold Wilson: Yorkshire Walter Mitty* (Macdonald & Jane's, 1977), was also helpful on the 1976 resignation honours list, and I am grateful to Mark Boxer for permission to reproduce the cartoon used as a frontispiece.

I would also like to thank Audrey Phillips for deciphering my illegible scrawl and finally Edwina, Rose and Owen for their patience and understanding as I put this book together.

John Walker

September 1985

Introduction

This is a story of patronage, privilege and politics, with a common thread: power. The economic power held by those who have acquired almost anything that money can buy but who crave one last reward – the social status that comes from an honour – and the political power held by those who exercise control over the machinery that bestows such honours. Throughout the centuries the honours system has been a market place where the two meet. As with many markets the prices paid are often covered in secrecy as both vendors and sellers have a vested interest in keeping it that way. Sometimes the financial terms of the contract come to light, on other occasions barter, rather than cash, provides the means of transfer. But, in a status-conscious society, monarchs and prime ministers from the seventeenth century till the twentieth have found that the trade in honours has provided a handy way of replenishing depleted war chests.

'Corrupt' is a word that best describes many of the transactions from 1603 until the 1930s detailed on the following pages. 83 cases are cited where there is overwhelming evidence, actual or circumstantial, of an honours-for-sale deal. Heirs and successors, still bearing the title bestowed, can be traced in 29 of them. Monarchs and prime ministers commonly used intermediaries in order to stay at arm's length from the transaction, and allowed the agent to reward himself handsomely for performing the role of middleman. James I, for example, allowed his lover George Villiers (ennobled, naturally, to become the Duke of Buckingham) to sell peerages, in the early years of the seventeenth century, for £10,000 apiece. James later sold baronetcies for £1,000 each in order to raise funds for the subjugation of the Irish.

An early prime-ministerial honours salesman was Pitt the Younger. He at first dispensed peerages to gain control over the patrons of members of an unreformed House of Commons, but later went on to sell them for hard cash. (The present Lord Carrington's title was created at this time.)

Although Lloyd George is widely regarded as the villain of the honours-selling story, by the time he became Prime Minister he had a third of a century of recent practice on which to model his tactics. The extension of the franchise and the coming of the democratic era meant that large sums of money were needed to fight elections. From the 1880s both Liberal and Conservative parties engaged in large-scale honours-touting. Although the hands of the party leaders remained relatively untarnished by the transactions, the agents and managers, together with the party whips, supervised a colossal increase in party funds at the very time when large demands were being made on them. Over two dozen well-documented cases are cited where honours were either sold, or their sale seriously discussed, by prominent politicians in the thirty years before Lloyd George became Prime Minister. These were almost certainly the tip of an iceberg, with a scale of charges running at £50,000 for a peerage and £10,000 for a baronetcy widely quoted at the time.

When Lloyd George came to office he simply changed gear, from first to fourth. His need was as great as his cynicism. He became Prime Minister, without a party and the means to support an organisation, in 1916. If the sale of honours had been able to pay for the maintenance of the great parties of the nation there was no reason why it couldn't be used to keep him. He thus employed a number of middlemen, Maundy Gregory was only the most infamous, to sell peerages to the *nouveaux riches* and statusless – war-profiteers and crooks were among his clients. It was an expensive business and a whole edifice of gentlemen's clubs, exclusive social functions, prestigious magazines and elegant properties was built up around it. After all of these expenses were paid, Gregory made an estimated £30,000 a year from the traffic and Lloyd George himself is estimated to have left Downing Street £1½ million better off than when he entered it. He used the money to buy the *Daily Chronicle* and later to pay for his own political propaganda at the time of the Great Depression. Prices were negotiable, but peerages ran at £50–100,000, baronetcies £20–40,000 and knighthoods at about £10,000 each. Tory funds also benefited from Lloyd George's trading, and their coffers swelled as he offered them a tit-for-tat arrangement on honours' sales.

Nor did the trade cease with Lloyd George's demise. The Conservative Party continued to reap the rewards of this system throughout most of the 1920s, and Labour's first Prime Minister, Ramsay MacDonald, was involved in at least two very unsavoury incidents that bore the hallmarks of honours sales.

With the imprisonment of Gregory in 1933, as the only man found guilty of touting honours, interest in the system faded for over forty years. It was the Harold Wilson resignation list of May 1976 that rekindled widespread comment. Publication of the list was delayed, speculation about its contents mounted, and on publication *The Times* thundered, 'These are the very people whose lives are the contradiction of everything for which the Labour Party stands.' A detailed examination of the contents of the list followed. For over a year, more and more revelations tumbled out about the names on what came to be known as the 'Lavender Notepaper List'.

A thorough examination of Harold Wilson's earlier lists shows them to have been remarkable for the reforms that were introduced. But, as with so much of the Wilson era, almost all those changes have been overturned by the next-but-one Prime Minister, Margaret Thatcher.

The seeds of this book were sown when I noticed, after regular, but quick, perusals over the top names in the early Thatcher lists, that many of the private-sector industrialists directed companies which I knew to be prominent donors to Tory Party funds. I was blissfully unaware at the time of any significant honours-for-sale practices of previous times, and was intrigued by what I saw. But, no, I could not believe that a government of the 1980s could be so crude as to reward its party's paymasters with honours. This would be too obvious, too easily detected and too damning. So I decided to examine every Thatcher list in detail to test this absurd, unbelievable notion.

The facts are simple. Between Margaret Thatcher taking office in June 1979 and June 1985 there were twelve Birthday and New Year honours lists. In those lists 11 private-sector industrialists received peerages and 64 were knighted. Almost all of those 75 are extremely eminent, capable, trustworthy, successful, skilled and dynamic people; the very people that capitalist societies turn to for entrepreneurial vigour, commitment and drive, and without whom society would not be as it is today.

There is, in addition, a remarkable correlation between the names of the companies which these men direct and the names of the most generous funders of the Conservative Party. All 11 of the peerages went to men whose companies made total donations of £1.9 million to Tory funds between 1979 and 1984, representing one-seventh of all corporate funds traced as going to the party. Forty-four of the 64 awarded knighthoods direct companies that have given £4.3 million, or a third of the recorded donations to the Conservative Party over the period. Allowing for duplications, the companies that 55 of the honoured 75 direct account for £5.9 million in corporate donations to Conservative Party funds, or 44 per cent of the money traced over five years.

Looking at the figures from a slightly different perspective, 10 companies gave over £200,000 each to the Conservative cause between 1979 and 1984, all but one of them had a director honoured over that period and in total they received 6 peerages and 5 knighthoods between them. The next 10 most generous donors each gave over £150,000 in those five years, and 8 of them have had a director honoured during the Thatcher premiership to date.

These facts appeared remarkable enough to warrant a wider circulation.

Mrs Thatcher's other major contribution to the honours system is the persistence with which she has sought to reward her ideological supporters. She has reintroduced political honours and systematically sprinkled knighthoods among her long-sitting backbenchers and those outside Parliament who could clearly be identified as 'one of us'. When the honoured politically pure are added to the directors whose companies have funded the Tory Party, almost half of those to have received major honours since 1979 have provided the Thatcher government with ideological, electoral, or financial sustenance.

For the rest, the honours system is a mirror image of a class-conscious society. There lies, buried in Whitehall, a series of formulae which are rigorously applied to the honours list twice yearly – the same number and rank of honours goes to the same categories of people in each list. And there is a pecking order. No man (or woman) must be allowed to rise above his or her station – the gong you get depends not on the goodness of your deed, but on your position in society. Knighthoods for the nobs and BEMs for the bums; it would never do, would it, for the head of the Home Civil Service to receive an MBE when a clerk in a Social Security office in Newcastle received a peerage?

Around the edges of the system there are some oddities: trade-union officials lap up honours at a prodigious rate, despite disapproval from much of the movement, and the most honoured union is the National Union of Mineworkers. And it is not for nothing that we talk of newspaper barons – second only to a career in the Civil Service is a job in the newspaper world as the safest way to a gong; particularly for *Daily Mirror* staff in the days of a Labour government.

If conclusions are needed to this tale, and lessons are to be drawn, I can do no more than direct the reader to the quotations at the beginning of this book, they express them better than ever I could; heavy moralising seems a fatuous pursuit.

One

Honouring – the system

The Queen presides over the system, and publishes honours lists of up to 1,000 names at New Year and on the occasion of her official birthday in June. These names are submitted to her by the Prime Minister, who will have added to and amended lists already presented to her by a distinguished committee. That committee, the Main Honours Committee, consists of some of the most senior Civil Servants in Whitehall and is currently chaired by Sir Robert Armstrong, Secretary to the Cabinet. It sifts through lists submitted to it by numbers of sub-committees and ensures that a strictly defined formula is adhered to for the distribution of honours. The sub-committees themselves, with areas of responsibility like industry, agriculture, commerce and local services, whittle down lists of up to 5,000 names submitted to them by the Cabinet Office Ceremonial Office. These names will previously have been vetted by the police and security services after having been forwarded to the office by MPs, voluntary organisations, businesses and ordinary citizens.

This system, the honours system, is treated with near reverence by all the characters who play a part in the above sequence, except by some prime ministers. Monarchs are on record as having been angered at the way the system has on occasion been abused and Civil Servants fight jealously over 'the formula' (they themselves usually end up getting some of the honours that are dispensed). Those in receipt of honours usually regard the award as a highlight of their lives, and some who do not get honours, but who have been nominated, go to considerable ends to receive the public acclaim that honours accord.

For prime ministers, the true authors and manipulators of the lists, the honours system is simultaneously an irritant and a prime vehicle for patronage – rewards can be given for services rendered or for compliance, but oh what an enormous amount of pestering goes on by would-be recipients! The lists of disenchanted, by the testimony of prime ministers' biographies, are long.

The Honours

A brief run-through of the various degrees of peerage, chivalry and honour is perhaps in order.

The monarch, as the head of state, is followed in the pecking order of temporal social rank by his or her family and then the peerage. There are five degrees of peerage, in order of dignity: dukes, marquesses, earls, viscounts and barons. The first English *dukedom* was created in 1337, when the Black Prince was made Duke of Cornwall, and 25 of them survive today; but in the twentieth century their creation has been limited to members of the Royal Family. The first English *marquess* was created in 1385 in a title that implies land ownership; 28 remain today, of which only 6 have been created this century (the latest in 1936, although the only surviving one dates back to 1926). Next in the pecking order come *earls* and their female counterparts, *countesses* – the title predates the Norman Conquest and derives from the Old Norse word for 'chieftain'. 157 survive today and in the twentieth century this particular title has been regarded as the suitable reward for war-leaders and former prime ministers; it was an earldom that Harold Macmillan received in 1984. *Viscountcies* date from 1440 and the term means 'vice-' or 'deputy count' – a degree below the status of earl; 104 continue to exist today. The practice of awarding viscountcies, a hereditary title, was suspended by Harold Wilson in 1964, but resurrected nineteen years later by Margaret Thatcher with the elevation of Tory Deputy Leader, William Whitelaw, and former House of Commons Speaker, George Thomas. And finally there is the *barony*, the lowest degree in the peerage, introduced to Britain by William I; at the time of writing there are 842 of them of whom 345 are life peers, titles which fade away with the recipient.

The only other hereditary honour customarily bestowed in Britain is the *baronetcy*. The modern rank, as will be seen later, was a seventeenth-century creation designed to be a half-way point between a knighthood and a barony. Baronets are commoners, not peers, in the chivalrous pecking order, but are placed before knights in the order of precedence. Their title is that of 'Sir' with a suffix 'Bt' or 'Bart' at the end of the name. Although none have been created since 1964, about 1340 of these titles are still in existence – perhaps the most publicly prominent being Sir Keith Joseph and Sir Ian Gilmour (both inheritors of the title).

Next come the *knights*, but as befits the mysteries of honour, these come in a number of guises and they have their own hierarchy. As an institution, the Knighthood can be traced back to the time of Alfred the Great, who knighted his grandson in the ninth century. There are approximately 3,500 Knights Grand Cross, Knights Commanders and Knights Bachelor, together with over 200 of their female equivalents, Dames Grand Cross and Dames Commander. The seventeen-to-one ratio is a sign of quite how equal women are seen to be by the British establishment. Even this ratio, however, beats that accorded to women in the legislature – there are 59 in the House of Lords (1202 members, 20:1) and 23 in the House of Commons (650 members, 27:1).

The order of precedence, and therefore snobbish distinction, for the various orders of chivalry is: Garter, Thistle, Bath, Merit, St Michael and St George, Royal Victoria Order, Order of the British Empire, and most of these have a variety of ranks or classes within the order. Bringing up the rear are Knights Bachelor and Companions of Honour.

Most prestigious of them all is the *Order of the Garter*. The order was formed over 600 years ago by Edward III in an attempt to recreate the intimacy and camaraderie of the legendary King Arthur and his Knights of the Round Table. Lady Salisbury is supposed to have dropped her garter at a ball held by the King in 1348 and nobody would pick it up – except the King. He put it on his own leg and remarked *Honi soit qui mal y pense*, which became the motto of the order. For some reason St George, a Roman executed in AD 290 for protesting against atrocities committed on Christians, was stirred into the pot and a great British institution was born. The order is restricted to the most senior members of the Royal Family and twenty-four other prominent people. The fact that non-Christians are excluded is perhaps a suitable case for racial-discrimination prosecution in a multicultural society. There is only one rank of the Most Noble Order of the Garter and that is Knight

Commander, with the abbreviation KG. The members are nothing, if not decorous: the uniform is a dark-blue velvet garter below the knee for men, and between the elbow and shoulder for women, with a badge of gold and enamel – the Great George – and an eight-pointed silver star with a blue enamel garter in its centre and a St George's Cross in red and white in the centre of that. Then there is a blue-velvet mantle, lined with white taffeta, and a crimson-velvet hood (also lined with white taffeta) and a black-velvet hat with a plume of ostrich feathers and a black heron's feather. It's better than being in the Masons, or even in amateur dramatics. The Order consists, apart from leading members of the Royal Family and a few foreign monarchs, of prominent peers and distinguished commoners. Prime ministers are offered the Garter when they retire from office, and Harold Wilson took it.

Next in precedence comes the Most Ancient and Noble *Order of the Thistle*. This was founded originally in the fifteenth century and revived and reconstituted in 1687 in an attempt to cement the union of Scotland with England. It is the Scottish equivalent of the Garter and is restricted to the sovereign's family and sixteen others. In 1946, in an attempt to prevent the Order being abused by politicians (Lloyd George had offered one to the Marquis of Bute in his resignation honours, see p. 99), Attlee and Churchill agreed that, in future, conferment of the Thistle and the Garter should be solely in the hands of the sovereign. There is only one rank of the Thistle, Knight Companion, and its abbreviation is KT. Among the present batch is former Prime Minister, Lord Home of the Hirsel.

After the Thistle comes the Most Honourable *Order of the Bath*. This was established as a separate order of chivalry in 1725, although it has medieval origins and its name comes from the ceremonial bathing that formed part of the preparation of the candidate for knighthood. There are two divisions – civilian and military – and three ranks within each division. The numbers in each division and rank are fixed, with the military having about twice the allocation of the civil side; it is very much the career Home Civil Servant's order. Only the first two classes are knights. The ranks are: Knight (or Dame) Grand Cross, abbreviation GCB; Knight (or Dame) Commander, abbreviation KCB (DCB); and Companion, abbreviation CB. The awards in each class and division, as will be seen later, are strictly rationed each year and the ration allocated to each ministry or service is fiercely fought over. The Great Master and First (or Principal) Knight Grand Cross is the Prince of Wales.

The next most chivalrous order is the *Order of Merit*. The only rank is that of Member and the status does not entitle the possessor to the address of 'Knight'. The Order was founded by Edward VII in 1902 and membership is awarded on the personal recommendation of the monarch to people who have rendered significant service either in the armed forces or in the fields of art, literature and the Civil Service. Membership is limited to twenty-four, plus honorary members from overseas, and the Order's abbreviation is OM. Florence Nightingale was the only woman member of the Order's first seventy years of existence.

After the Order of Merit comes the Most Distinguished *Order of St Michael and St George*, established in 1818 and usually reserved for Civil Servants who have served in the Diplomatic Corps or have seen overseas or Commonwealth service. The Grand Master is the Duke of Kent. The Order has developed into a blue riband for long service, with the result that it has become almost a routine reward for those who have reached a certain position in the Civil Service – on what, in the parlance of the trade-union world, would be known as the 'automaticity principle'. There are three classes (in ascending order): Companion, which does not confer the dignity of knighthood, abbreviation CMG (widely known within the Civil Service as Call Me God); Knight Commander, KCMG (Kindly Call Me God); and Knight Grand Cross, GCMG (God Calls Me God).

The *Royal Victoria Order* is next in precedence. It was instituted in 1896 by Queen Victoria as a means of rewarding members of the Royal Household. As is appropriate for a status-conscious lady, she felt that five classes of the RVO were required – every man and woman to their status. The honour accorded was not to reflect the excellence of service, but the position of the recipient. The current Grand Master of the Order is the Queen Mother, and the ranks of the Order are: Knight (or Dame) Grand Cross, abbreviation GCVO; Knight (or Dame) Commander, KCVO (or DCVO); Commander, CVO; Member, 4th Class, MVO; and Member, 5th Class, also MVO. Only the first two of these classes have the status of knight attached to them. Willie Hamilton in his book, *My Queen and I*, is particularly disparaging about this order:

The Queen's household is crammed to the gunwales with its variations of status among the royal camp followers, from the G.C.V.O. of the Lord Chamberlain, to the K.C.V.O of the Queen's Private Secretary, the C.V.O. of the librarian at Windsor Castle and the M.V.O.'s of a multitude of minor dignitaries, including clerks, secretaries and the Royal Bargemaker . . . When the Queen makes her sorties into the Commonwealth she hands out medals, usually the R.V.O., to every acolyte in spitting distance. Thus many overseas luminaries also glow with an R.V.O. – until their assassination. Rumour has it that the Victorian Order medals are made on a production line in Neasden – a West London suburb – out of used railway lines disposed of by British Railways. (p. 137)

Next in precedence comes the most common of them all – the *Order of the British Empire*, established in 1917 in the Lloyd George era. A pause to look at the state of the honours business immediately before its inception is worthwhile. All honours founded before then were the exclusive preserve of the well-born and well-established. According to Kenneth Rose in his biography of George V, at the time,

The Orders of the Garter, Thistle and of St Patrick [now ceased with Irish independence] were confined to the sovereign's family, the landowning nobility, elder statesmen, an occasional hero of the battlefield, or the war at sea. The Bath was reserved for senior officers of the army, the Royal Navy, the higher ranks of the civil service, a handful of politicians and other public men; the St Michael and St George for British officials overseas, particularly in the diplomatic and colonial services; the Order of the Star of India and of the Indian Empire [unreplenished since Indian independence in 1947] for those engaged in the civilizing mission of the British Raj; the Royal Victoria Order for personal service to the sovereign. Not until the present century, was it generally resented that the aristocrat should have a prior claim to the distribution of honours. (*King George V*, Weidenfeld & Nicolson, 1983, p. 256)

In 1886, for example, Queen Victoria wished to bestow a GCB (Grand Cross of the Bath) on Conservative Minister W. H. Smith. He declined the offer, since in his early years he had managed the family newsagency business, which he felt unworthy of 'a decoration which, until recently at all events, has only been given to men of his standing for very distinguished services'.

Victoria's successor, Edward VII, proved to be a mixed dispenser of honours: he expanded the Royal Victoria honour sixfold in the first three years of his reign and introduced in 1902 the completely new honour, the Order of Merit. His Secretary of War at the time, St John Brodrick, told a friend,

> The King is much troubled with Orders. He showers decorations right and left. There is to be a new 'Order of Merit' – limited to 24. I got it reduced from 60. It is for savants and soldiers. Its chief objects are that it is worn round the neck and it puts Edward on a par with Frederick the Great, who invented a similar one. (Rose, p. 257)

Six years later, however, Edward denied Asquith's request that the then Foreign Secretary, Sir Edward Grey, should be awarded the Garter. He said that not since Walpole's time had such an honour been bestowed on a commoner and that its award should be restricted to those who had at least attained the status of earl. Grey achieved the rank four years later, in the reign of George V – the man who really allowed the floodgates to be opened for commoners to achieve a wide range of honours.

The First World War brought with it fresh demands to reward the gallant. However, there was no suitable order, so, after some delay and discussion of a suitable name, insignia and statute, the Order of the British Empire was instituted in 1917, 'in recognition of the manifold services, voluntary and otherwise, that have been rendered both by British subjects and their allies in connection with the war'. By the end of 1919 there were 25,000 recipients of all grades (for details of this profusion see Chapter 3).

The Order is now the most widely conferred on civilian or service personnel for public service or other distinctions. Today's Grand Master is the Duke of Edinburgh. Following the carefully graduated ranking system adopted by the Royal Victorian Order twenty years previously, the Most Excellent Order of the British Empire has five grades, the top two of which confer the status of knight. They are: Knight (or Dame) Grand Cross, abbreviation GBE; Knight (or Dame) Commander, KBE (or DBE); Commander, CBE; Officer, OBE; and Member, MBE. About 150,000 orders of one rank or another have been distributed since the

Order's inception, and at any one time 30–40,000 holders must be living.

MBE is about as ordinary as things get in the honours stakes – unless you are a very lowly person already, like perhaps 90 per cent of your fellow citizens, and have performed your job as village postmaster, government office cleaner or local milkman diligently for forty years. In this case, what awaits you is not a place in the orders of chivalry, but a distinction that sounds as if it is closely related – the British Empire Medal. It is a medal of the British Empire Order, but as the official publication, *Honours and Titles in Britain*, stuffily puts it, it 'is awarded for meritorious service, to men and women who do not qualify *by rank* for the higher awards in the Order of the British Empire' (my emphasis). Never mind the deed or quality of service, measure the rank.

Trailing behind the Most Excellent Order of the British Empire proper come four groupings of status, one a dignity and three orders. The first of these are the *Knights Bachelor*, and it is perhaps surprising that they come so far down in the pecking order, since this is the status aspired to by many Conservative politicians and industrialists. The Knights Bachelor, however, do not comprise an order of chivalry, merely a status; an important point of note for all social climbers. Searching desperately for dignity, the Knights Bachelor can satisfy themselves that their position has its origins in Saxon times, that it was during the Middle Ages that the prefix 'Sir' came into common usage, and that James I introduced a register of knights in the seventeenth century. This, however, was soon discontinued. In 1908 a voluntary association now known as the Imperial Society of Knights Bachelor was formed, with the express purpose of trying to establish continuity for registers of knights that date back to 1257 and of obtaining uniform registration for every created knight. Struggling purposefully for due chivalrous recognition, the Society had its badge for knights officially approved and adopted. But it has not yet been accorded with the elusive status of an order of chivalry – how much longer must these fine people languish almost as outcasts, unrecognised by those who matter?

It may be small consolation that beneath them comes the *Order of the Companion of Honour*. This was established by George V in 1917 – a busy year for George in shoring up the British establishment when revolutionaries in Russia were equally busy dismantling theirs. The only rank is the Companion of Honour (CH). It is awarded for service of conspicuous national importance and is limited to sixty-five people. It must grieve former Transport and General Workers' Union General Secretary Jack Jones (awarded the CH in 1978) that he was joined in the order by ideological opponent Friedrich Hayek in 1984.

Trailing behind the Companionship of Honour comes the *Imperial Service Order*, created in 1902 and very much the wooden-spoon award for Civil Servants who have worked in the Commonwealth. The only rank is that of Companion and the abbreviation is ISO.

Almost fading into obscurity is the final Order of distinction: the Most Venerable *Order of St John of Jerusalem*. It was incorporated by Royal Charter in 1888 and is the parent body of the St John Ambulance Brigade – it doubles up therefore as a charity and a status. It is not a State award and recommendations for the Order are made by the Grand Prior, the Duke of Gloucester, to the Queen in recognition of charitable work done in the name of the Order. It maintains the dignity of status, having six ranks, but it is a status held under a bushel, for membership does not confer any title and members do not use the authorised letters after their names except in the context of their work for the Order.

As if this little lot has not been enough to grasp, the divisions and gradations of social rank and merit extend further into the horizon, for the Central Office of Information handbook on honours states,

> The grant of peerages and baronetcies, the creation of knights or dames, and the admission of individuals to orders are not the only ways the Sovereign recognises merit. The conferment of a badge may in itself constitute an honour. This is the case with medals and decorations (that is, badges other than medals). The list which follows shows, in order of precedence, the principal decorations and medals awarded for distinguished or gallant services.

The booklet then proceeds to list twenty-seven different medals or grades of medals in order of precedence from the Victoria Cross to commemorative medals, which 'are issued by the Sovereign to selected recipients on such occasions as coronations and jubilees'. Even this seemingly exhaustive list, however, as the booklet states, 'excludes campaign medals awarded by the Sovereign to participants in particular wars or campaigns'.

So there it is, the honours system of Great Britain: 5 degrees of the peerage and 1 of baronets; 14 knighthoods or orders comprising 11 different methods of securing a knighthood; and 28 ranks in all (excluding the two Indian and one Irish order, all lapsed since independence, accounting for 7 more ranks, including 5 of knights), plus 27 medals or decorations. Apart from the possessors of the medals and decorations, the recipients of these honours amount, in total, to about 50,000 people, a tenth of whom probably attract courtesy titles for their spouses and children. 55,000 chivalrous and dignified people head a population of fifty-five million in a highly status-conscious Britain. For every member of a dignity there's probably a hundred others who crave for one; it's that craving and the power that it gives to the dispensers of the patronage that holds much of the social order together. Political parties are funded by it, backbenchers remain loyal, the Press supple, industrialists and trade unionists compliant, and huge swathes of people continue to be respectful of the status accorded by honours. No wonder attempts to reform, change or enquire into the system are dealt with so sharply. The honours system remains one of the last vestiges of what Bagehot called 'the dignified part of the Constitution' – shrouded in secrecy. If too much daylight is cast upon it, the mystery disappears.

The Selection Procedure

The first stage in the honours selection procedure is carried out by the Cabinet Office Ceremonial Officer – currently a former Treasury official, Mrs Mary Hedley-Miller (a CB), who has been in the Ceremonial Section for over thirty-five years – and his/her assistant (at present Miss Ruth Gardner). They are directly under the control of the Principal Private Secretary to the Prime Minister and keep an index of everyone who has ever been suggested or nominated for an honour from whatever source (including the 2 per cent who refuse an honour on each occasion). They divide the names suggested into a number of categories and submit them to a large number of official sub-committees of specialists – mainly Civil Servants, topped up by distinguished outsiders brought in to advise on the more technical subjects (Joe Haines, for example, when he was Harold Wilson's Press Secretary, sat on the committee recommending awards for journalists). Each sub-committee has a strict ration of awards to make at each rank and it submits its list to the Main Honours Committee, which operates under the direction of the Home Civil Service. The current Head of the Honours Committee and Secretary of the Cabinet, Sir Robert Armstrong, has been reported by *The Times* (5 December 1983) to be 'a great believer in honours, who, despite his other formidable duties takes a passionate role in its work'. He received a CVO in 1975 (he was Secretary of the Board of Directors of the Royal Opera House and on the management committee of the Royal Philharmonic Society at the time) and progressed through the ranks of the Bath within a decade; becoming a Commander in 1974, a Knight in 1978 and a Knight Grand Cross in 1983. He clearly is concerned to preserve the integrity of honours. This Main Honours Committee acts as the final quality-control mechanism before the lists reach the Prime Minister. More checks and balances come into operation at this stage, to ensure that the quotas for the various awards are not exceeded, that there is a correct regional balance (in the press ballyhoo that follows the publication of a list every local newspaper must have its own home-grown stars to write about) and that there is a fair sprinkling of women and perhaps, increasingly, that there is the odd Asian name on the list.

All of this takes time. To be seriously included, names need to be with the Ceremonial Office by the beginning of February for the June Birthday list and by mid-September for the New Year list.

Once sifted, searched, perused, checked and nurtured by the 'system', the lists are forwarded to the Prime Minister's Office. Ninety-five per cent of these will be accepted unchanged, if for no other reason than that nobody at Number 10 has the faintest idea who the people are. The Prime Minister can and does make changes, particularly at the Commander level and above in the various orders, and adds what Joe Haines refers to as the 'stardust' to complete the list. Sportsmen and -women and popular entertainers are sprinkled on the list to give it a wider appeal and Harold Wilson, who, particularly in his first years as Prime Minister, had a great empathy with public feeling and moods, developed this to a fine art.

Until 1923 the lists, thus suitably prepared, were then submitted to Buckingham Palace for formal approval. Occasionally the monarch resisted a nomination, but, as will be seen later, that resistance often only amounted to a delaying tactic and the nomination went through on a later list. However, following the 'honours-for-sale' scandals of Lloyd George's premiership, a Royal Commission was established to recommend ways of cleaning up the system. One of its main suggestions was the creation of a Political Honours Scrutiny Committee to consist of three Privy Councillors who would examine the names of all people nominated for 'political' honours. The names submitted to the Committee were to be accompanied by a declaration from the Chief Whip that there was 'no payment or expectation of payment to any party or political fund directly or indirectly associated with the recommendations contained within the attached list'. The Committee's comments were to be sent, however, not to the monarch, but to the Prime Minister, who could if he wished ignore them and forward the original nominations unchanged to the monarch.

This system seemed to work without any great problems and did not appear to provoke much controversy for the following fifty-three years – until the resignation list of Sir Harold Wilson. (The details of this affair are considered in Chapter 6.) Following this incident, the Committee was reconstituted by Wilson's successor, James Callaghan, and now consists of Lord Shackleton (Labour) in the Chair, Lord Franks (Liberal) and Lord Carr (Conservative). An early task was to recommend new, tightened-up procedures to be adopted before lists reached them. Under the new arrangements the Prime Minister or Chief Whip must give the full personal details of individuals proposed for honours, for *any* reason (not just 'political services'), whose firm has contributed to the Conservative or any other party, in cash or in kind. The Committee is supposed to receive a signed certificate containing the reasons for the nomination plus any details of any gifts or financial contributions. When in possession of the full facts, the Political Honours Scrutiny Committee is then in a position to make a judgement on the suitability of the potential recipient.

Shortly after becoming Prime Minister in November 1979, Mrs Thatcher told the Commons that she was going to extend the scope of the Honours Scrutiny Committee's remit:

I have asked the Committee to examine any names that I add to the recommendations at C.B.E. level and above which are submitted to me
through the official honours machinery in respect of services in all fields
other than that of political services. The Committee has readily agreed to
do so. This further extension of the Committee's function will, I believe,
help to maintain the integrity of the honours system.

Whether the honours lists issued over the subsequent six years continued to maintain that integrity is a matter for debate.

A 1979 Order in Council also redefined the role of the Committee
in a way that effectively gave it more bite by allowing the Committee
access to police files and security-service material, as well as day-to-
day Whitehall information, in order to investigate the names of
people nominated to them. The Committee is further empowered to
report to the Prime Minister if 'the past history or general character
of a person renders him unsuitable to be recommended. In the event
of the Committee reporting against any name and the Prime Minister determining still to recommend such a name, a copy of the report
of the Committee will be submitted to Her Majesty with the recommended actions'.

Once vetted, the entire honours list goes to the Queen for infor-
mal approval. She may, as her predecessors have done, raise objections to some of the names on the list. Once approved, the list is then
returned to Downing Street where the Prime Minister's Principal
Private Secretary supervises the dispatch of about 1,000 white
envelopes bearing the message 'Urgent Personal and Confidential'.
The envelopes contain the following letter:

I am asked by the Prime Minister to inform you that she has it in mind on
the occasion of the forthcoming list of Birthday [or New Year] Honours
to submit your name to the Queen with a recommendation that she may
be graciously pleased to approve that you be appointed a Member of the
Order of the British Empire [or whatever the honour is].

Before doing so, the Prime Minister would be glad to be assured that
this mark of Her Majesty's favour would be agreeable to you.

Fifteen to twenty people per list will turn down the offer, either
because they disapprove of the system, or because they feel they
have not been offered a high enough dignity.

Now that the limit has been finalised, by a multiplicity of layers of approval and an opportunity for self de-selection, it is sent to the Central Chancery of the Orders of Knighthood, behind St James's Palace. The staff of twelve then prepare the list for its publication in the *London Gazette*, order the insignia that accompany the awards, issue instructions to recipients, draw up the warrants, organise the Palace investitures and issue the invitations to the fourteen or so ceremonies each year at which about 2,000 orders, medals and decorations are awarded. Simply organising the gongs that go with the honours is itself an expensive business. The full Garter regalia, described earlier, costs well over £1,000; the silver-gilt breast star of the Order of St Michael and St George costs many hundreds, requiring, as it does, 8,000 separate chippings to produce the sparkling facets. A Knight Bachelor's neck badge, a gold filigree oval suspended from a vermilion and pale-gold ribbon, costs over £100, while the accompanying breast badge is nearer £200. Even the humble MBE badge costs over £40 a throw.

So much for the mechanics of the exercise. Who actually gets the goodies? The key is to be found in the all-important 'formula'. Among the Public Record Office files opened for scrutiny in 1985 was an Air Ministry one covering the period 1946–54 which is concerned exclusively with the Ministry's dealings in the honours game. Much of the file consists of the records of the Committee on the Grant of Honours, Decorations and Medals – and a high-powered Committee it was too. It had accumulated 446 meetings' documents by January 1947, most concerned with the distribution of honours between the different ministries. The men on the seventeen-strong Committee included the Permanent Secretary to the Treasury (then Head of the Home Civil Service, with his eye on the Order of the Bath), the Private Secretary to the King, three permanent Under-Secretaries dealing with Commonwealth relations (keeping an eye on the Indian awards, and those of the Order of St Michael and St George), a Permanent Under-Secretary from the Home Office (Order of the British Empire), a Permanent Under-Secretary from the Foreign Office (St Michael and St George), senior Civil Servants from the Air Ministry, Admiralty and War Office (military division of the Orders of the Bath and British Empire), all topped up and supervised by the Secretary of the Central Chancery of the Orders of Knighthood, who would be responsible for implementing the arrangements that they were to recommend.

These men were clearly in a strong position to consider the requirements made of potential honours recipients, for the Committee shared 41 honours, including 13 knighthoods, themselves. At this time the Committee's task was to examine the current distribution of honours and make recommendations for the future scale of awards. They listed, in a very detailed fashion, the number of awards eligible, in total and per annum, for each rank.

The maximum numbers allowed by statute for each category of the Order of the Bath were as follows: GCB – 27 for civil appointments, 59 for military; KCB – 92 for civilians, 14 for territorials and 167 for the armed forces; CB – 286 for civilians, 60 for territorials and 724 for the armed forces. The civil side of the Order of the British Empire's position was: GBE – 3 UK civilians per year (with a maximum total establishment of 38), 1 Foreign Office, 1 India Office and 1 Colonial Office nomination per year (with a maximum overseas total of 30 and a total military establishment of 16); KBE – 18 civilian appointments per year (with a maximum establishment of 172); CBE – 200 civilian appointments per year (with a total establishment of 772); OBE – 380 civilian appointments per year (with no maximum establishment); and MBEs – 630 civilian appointments per year (with no maximum establishment).

As far as Knights Bachelors were concerned, the annual maximum was 46 of which 15 were for political service, 8 for State service, 5 for local service and 18 for other services.

The same Committee, on 24 June 1948, gave a detailed breakdown of how it came to decide the number of honours available in each category on the military side. It provided a snapshot that speaks volumes for the operation of the honours system. The deliberations show how finely tuned was the establishment's view of the seniority of the various orders of chivalry, how meticulously the formulae for honours distribution were calculated. To be blunt, in the last analysis, honours were awarded not so much on merit as on Buggins' Turn.

The Committee report revealed the existence of a ratio of honours to holders of military posts which indicates that honours were not awarded for particular distinction but because the recipient happened to be at the top of a class of people who were thought worthy of honours because of their status.

Also, and most damningly, the Committee revealed a quadruple jeopardy that the honours system confirms on the British social system. This is made clear in two tables which appeared in the Committee's report and are reproduced here. One is a list of awards felt suitable for the different ranks in the armed forces and the other is a calculation of how many awards per year should be made to people in these categories (the two tables are merged as Table 1).

The quadruple jeopardy that the tables invoke is simple. The ranks in the armed forces themselves tend to reinforce social inequalities. In 1966, for example, C. B. Otley found that 83 per cent of army lieutenants-general, generals and field marshals had been to public schools – over half of that number to the ten leading public schools. The services' ranks therefore reinforce existing social division by their promotions pattern. This gulf is further widened by the honours felt suitable to each tier of the services. The higher you rise the more important the honour accorded to your rank; not for major-generals the lowly MBE, or for lieutenants a CBE – that might upset a preordained hierarchy. The final confirmation of social inequities is the ratio of honours to post-holders. A rear-admiral, simply because of his status, is thirteen times more likely to be honoured than a lieutenant in the navy, and that honour is itself likely to be three ranks higher in the social order. An 'average' rear-admiral could expect a thirty-five-year wait to pick up a Companion-ship, admittedly a rather long time when translated into reality, so the odds are 2:1 against him being so honoured. But an army captain would 'on average' have to wait 475 years for an MBE – or more realistically the odds are 40:1 against him receiving it.

The note that accompanies the tables indicates the fineness of distinction between the orders:

The categories do not necessarily show the exact limits of eligibility. Vice-Admirals, for instance, are eligible for the K.C.B., but the number of awards for K.C.B. would be considered by reference to the number of Admirals and so forth. Colonels without higher acting or temporary rank would ordinarily be eligible for the C.B.E. [i.e. Commander of the British Empire] rather than the C.B. [i.e. Companion of the Bath], but to avoid complexity the C.B. and the C.B.E. ranges are shown as equivalent.

The ratios that are indicated in the tables were those that it was

Table 1
Distribution of Honours Between Ranks of the Armed Services, 1948

Honour	Navy — Ranks to be honoured	Navy — Ratio of honours per year to holders of rank	Army — Ranks to be honoured	Army — Ratio of honours per year to holders of rank	Air Force — Ranks to be honoured	Air Force — Ratio of honours per year to holders of rank
KCB (Bath) KBE (Empire)	Admirals Vice-Admirals		Generals Lieutenant-Generals		Air Chief Marshals Air Marshals	
CB & CBE	Rear-Admirals to Captains	1:70 1:109	Major Generals to Captains	1:121	Air Vice-Marshals to Group Captains	1:135
OBE	Commanders to Lieutenant-Commanders	} 1:374	Lieutenant-Colonels to Majors	1:507	Wing Commanders to Squadron Leaders	} 1:359
MBE	Lieutenants to Warrant Officers	} 1:920	Captains to Warrant Officers	1:950	Flight-Lieutenants to Warrant Officers	} 1:857

proposed should be implemented for the New Year's honours list of 1949 and, with slight amendments, were those that were recommended to be applied to the honours lists over the succeeding five years.

Unfortunately, the deliberations of the Committee on the Grant of Honours, Decorations and Medals, as released to the public, do not extend to spelling out the formula to be applied in the Civil Service and other areas of non-military life, but undoubtedly one exists. The Permanent Secretary is almost guaranteed his 'K' along with his £52,000 annual salary, Index-linked pension and possible lucrative post-retirement position advising or directing a company that will find his contacts with former colleagues, who award the lucrative government contracts of the future, worthwhile. The Companion of the Bath is the Under-Secretary's gong – about 32 men and women of that or equivalent Civil Service rank a year can expect their CB. That is a ratio of about one for every fifteen holders of the post. For some, of course, their CB is a 'top-up' award coming, as it does, after an already awarded OBE. Not content with monopolising the Order of the Bath, senior Civil Servants receive about a sixth of the 95 or so Civil Commander of the British Empire honours (CBEs) awarded in each list. This is regarded as a suitable reward for Assistant Secretaries and their equivalents and is awarded on a ratio of 1:160 to the post-holders in each of the bi-annual lists. Then come the OBEs – the station regarded as most appropriate to Principal Officers and their equivalents in the specialist government offices. About 11 of them, from the total OBE list of about 175, will be honoured in each list; that is a ratio of about one for every 370 Civil Servants of that rank. Then come the MBEs – an honour felt most suitable for Higher and Senior Executive Officers and their equivalents. A typical list will see 47 of the 312 MBEs awarded going to Civil Servants of that rank – a ratio of one for every 700 currently serving higher grade Executive Officers.

Then there are the 'also rans', the entire industrial Civil Service, with about 100,000 employees who receive roughly 20 British Empire Medals on each list. They nestle in with village postmen, school-crossing-patrol ladies, bus-drivers, craft-workers and almost anyone else from the manual working class that is to be honoured, because, as the Central Office of Information reminds us, the British Empire Medal 'is awarded for meritorious service, to men and women who do not qualify by rank for the higher awards in the Order of the British Empire'. About 500 of these lowly ranked people get a medal each year.

The Committee on the Grant of Honours, Decorations and Medals, having reviewed the allocation of honours in 1948, made recommendations for the 1949 lists which it hoped would suffice for five more years, after which time it wanted a further review of the distribution pattern. The report said, in July 1948,

> We recommend that the annual Civil C.B.E. allocations should be increased by 12 to provide for a few additional awards for services in the larger departments of State, for the Arts, Science and Literature and for Commerce, Industry and Local Authority Services. We consider that the annual M.B.E. allocation should be increased mainly to provide more awards for Trade, Industry, Education and Voluntary unpaid service of various kinds and that the B.E.M. quota should be increased, mainly for awards in Trade and Industry.

The finely adjusted allocation considerations came up with new recommendations for total establishments and annual awards for each rank. A sample of the Committee's suggestions, for civil honours only, follows. Order of the Bath: Knights Grand Cross, new maximum 27 (no change) at the rate of 2 per year; Knights Commander, 113 (from 106) at the rate of 9½ per year. Companion: 446 (from 346) at the rate of 42 per year. Order of the British Empire: Knights Grand Cross, new establishment 40 (from 38) at the rate of 3 per year; Knights Commander, 172 (no change) at 18 per year. Commander, 1,572 (1,483) at the rate of 212 per year. Officers, 381 per year (380) and Members, 730 per year (630).

Quite how the members of the Committee arrived at the ratio of awards per rank to the annual distribution of these awards is not made clear, but it would appear that they believed not only that the higher status people deserved the best awards, but also that they deserved, or at least should be expected, to live longer. It would take 13½ years of regular honours lists to fill the complement of Knights Grand Cross of the Bath before the rank became full up and potential recipients waited for dead men's shoes. It would take less than 7½ years at the normal rate of distribution to fill the ranks of the Commanders of the British Empire.

The Committee did, in its most humble fashion, however, have one further point to make:

> It has come to our notice that there is much disappointment among the recipients of the O.B.E., M.B.E. and B.E.M. because they have not the honour of investiture by the King . . . We wish humbly to put on record in this report our view, should the King be graciously pleased to undertake the investiture of those awarded the O.B.E., M.B.E. and B.E.M. in such further lists, and subsequently, an immense amount of pleasure would be given to the recipients and the value of the awards greatly enhanced.

Table 2
Distribution of Honours Between Different Areas
of Public Life, June 1982

Category	Peers(%)	Kt(%)[1]	CBE(%)[2]	OBE(%)	MBE(%)	Total (%)
Civil Service	4(66)	4(13)	26(25)	20(12)	53(17)	103(17)
Industry	1(17)	4(13)	12(11)	23(13)	44(14)	84(14)
Political service		8(26)	11(10)	13 (8)	19 (6)	51 (8)
Medicine/Health		3(10)	8 (8)	10 (6)	24 (8)	45 (7)
Education		0	8 (6)	13 (8)	16 (5)	37 (6)
Sport/Entertainment/ Culture		0	5 (5)	13 (8)	16 (5)	34 (5)
Local government		1 (3)	5 (5)	8 (5)	19 (6)	33 (5)
Charities/Voluntary organisations		0	0	10 (6)	23 (7)	33 (5)
Nationalised industries		1 (3)	6 (6)	9 (5)	10 (3)	26 (4)
Quangos		1 (3)	5 (5)	9 (5)	9 (3)	24 (4)
Law and order		0	2 (2)	7 (4)	13 (4)	22 (4)
Societies/Associations		0	1 (1)	10 (6)	8 (3)	19 (3)
Agriculture		1 (3)	4 (4)	4 (2)	7 (2)	16 (3)
Youth		1 (3)	1 (1)	4 (2)	8 (3)	14 (2)
Press		1 (3)	3 (3)	3 (2)	5 (2)	12 (2)
Law and professions		2 (6)	2 (2)	3 (2)	3 (1)	10 (2)
Academics		3(10)	2 (2)	1 (1)	0	6 (1)
Trade unions	1(17)	0	0	1 (1)	1 (0)	3 (0)
Other public service[3]		1 (3)	4 (4)	11 (6)	31(10)	47 (8)
	6	31	105	172	309	619

1 Includes Knights Bachelor, plus knighthoods awarded in Orders of Bath and British Empire
2 Includes Companions of the Bath
3 Includes water authorities, 'community work', 'public service' citations

Within three years the King began to undertake the investiture of those awarded the OBE and MBE. Thirty-seven years later the King and his successor have still not found themselves 'graciously pleased' to undertake the investiture of the British Empire Medal. The horny-handed sons and daughters of toil presumably continue to experience the 'disappointment' noted in 1948 from the royal snub; they are still denied 'an immense amount of pleasure' and, of course – as is perfectly correct for a section of society that does not 'qualify by rank for higher awards' – they do not find 'the value of their awards greatly enhanced'.

Table 3

A Points Total for Honours Awarded in June 1982
(Weighting: Knighthood = 10, CBE=3, OBE=2, MBE=1)

Areas of service	No. of honours awarded (%)
Civil Service	211(17)
Industry	166(13)
Political service	158(12)
Medical/Health	98 (8)
Other public service	75 (6)
Education	66 (5)
Local government	60 (5)
Sport/Entertainment/Culture	57 (4)
Nationalised industries	56 (4)
Quangos	52 (4)
Charities/Voluntary bodies	43 (3)
Academics	38 (3)
Agriculture	37 (3)
Law/professions	35 (3)
Law and order	33 (3)
Societies/associations	31 (2)
Press	30 (2)
Youth	29 (2)
Trade unions	3 (0)
	1278

Since neither the formula that is applied to the award of honours nor the subject responsibilities of committees that make recommendations to the Main Honours Committee are publicly available, it is difficult to know exactly how honours are distributed. But an analysis of recent honours lists gives a rough indication of how this might be done. Table 2 is a breakdown of the June 1982 list, picked from the middle of Mrs Thatcher's first eleven lists. There is obviously some arbitrariness in the selection of categories and the way in which individual awards are allocated to these groupings, but it does provide a rough map of the distribution of awards for different areas of public life. As some categories, like 'political service', have more success in obtaining the higher honours, and others like 'charities and voluntary organisations' fare better with the lower awards, simply totalling the numbers of awards allocated to each category would be rather meaningless. Table 3 therefore presents a weighted total of awards. The basis of the weighting is that knighthoods are clearly more prestigious than MBEs – as ten times as many MBEs were awarded, each knighthood is therefore given a weighting of 10. Similarly CBEs are given a weighting of 3 and OBEs a weighting of 2, with each MBE receiving one point.

A number of comments are worth making. First, Civil Servants supervise the operation of the entire system, and do very well out of it! They get a sixth of the honours although they constitute less than a sixtieth of the population. Many of the honours, probably a quarter, go to volunteers, or members of authorities who are either unpaid or only paid expenses for their efforts. The rest go to people for doing the job they are paid to do – on that basis the Civil Service gets about a quarter of the honours going to people paid for doing their job, yet constitute only about one-thirtieth of the workforce.

It is the higher-echelon members of the Civil Service who make the selections of people to be honoured, and their own prejudices and social backgrounds largely shape the kinds of people honoured – probably 99 per cent of the people on any list are rewarded for their efforts in pushing pieces of paper about, either at work or in committees outside work. There is usually a token potter, boxing champion etc. in the list, but half the working population, by the nature of their jobs, are excluded even for consideration on this basis.

The 'gong-for-the-job' formula that was so graphically expressed in the minutes of the Committee on the Grant of Honours, Decorations and Medals in 1948 is still at work today. Your occupation determines the type of honour you will receive. No matter how wonderful you are as a youth-club leader, the most you can hope for is an MBE. Meanwhile, remote from the day-to-day needs of youth, administrators sit on vague national bodies who with careful time-

Table 4
Typical Positions Occupied by Those Honoured in Different Categories

Areas of service	Awards			
	KT	CBE	OBE	MBE
Civil Service	Permanent Secretary of major Department of State	Assistant Secretary	Principal Officer	Higher Executive Officer
Industry	Chief Executive of major UK company	Chairman of company ranked 500–1000 in UK, or divisional director of larger company	Export manager/ executive of large company, chairman of small, fast-growing company	Draughtsman/designer/ accountant/public relations manager, etc. of large company
Medical/Health	Chairman of regional health authority or professor in major teaching hospital	President of Royal College of Nursing, midwives, radiographers, etc.	Senior surgeon in non-teaching hospital	Member of area health board, GP or area nursing officer
Education	University Vice-Chancellor	Chairman of county education authority	Head teacher of large comprehensive school	Head of department in comprehensive, or head of primary school
Local government	Chairman of national association of local authorities	Leader of a city council	Chief officer of a county or metropolitan authority	Member of a district council, or senior officer in local authority
Sport/Entertainment	Prominent serious actor	Former England football/cricket captain	Popular family television entertainer	Olympic gold medallist
Nationalised industries	Chairman of major nationalised industry	Regional or divisional director of large nationalised industry	Head of a BBC department/manager of a large factory	Divisional manager of a regional gas or electricity board

Quangos	Director-General of major quango, e.g. Central Arbitration Committee or Ports Authority	Member of major quango like Monopolies Commission or director of minor one	Member of a development corporation	Member of minor quango board, or executive officer (e.g. harbour master)
Agriculture	Director of major agriculture research body	President of regional farmers' union or chairman of NFU sub-committee	Senior figure in Forestry Commission or agricultural college	Organiser of Young Farmers clubs or simply 'farmer'
Law and Professions	President of Law Society	'For services to architecture'	Solicitor with a large city practice	Head of administrative services for large firm of professionals
Press	Editor of a national newspaper	Director of national newspaper group, or editor of a regional paper	National newspaper correspondent, or editor of a local paper	Assistant editor of a local newspaper, or national newspaper photographer
Youth	Founder/chairman/director of major youth organisation in important anniversary year	Chairman of Scottish/Welsh/Ulster youth association	Chairman of a county association of youth clubs	Youth-club leader

serving can aspire to a CBE for their services. A world-beating national hero or Olympic champion must content her- or himself with an MBE, while there's a CBE for a Civil Servant who spends forty years simply keeping his nose clean, and a knighthood for a man who cultivates a dirty Page 3.

Table 4 looks at some of the main areas of activity that are rewarded with gongs and gives an indication of the rank for the job. It would never do, would it, for a preordained social order to be upset by the appearance of a name in the wrong list?

Two

The first 500 years

The sale of honours and titles by hard-pressed rulers can be traced back to the Roman Empire when Marcus Didius Julianus paid handsomely for the Imperial crown in AD 193. More locally, the Norman Conquest of 1066 provided the invading William with an opportunity to repay his debts by the distribution of earldoms and baronies to those who followed him. Periodic financial and political crises may well have led to a trade in titles over the following half-millennium – but it was small-scale stuff. Even allowing for the extinction of dynasties by failure to produce male heirs, few British titles pre-date the seventeenth century. Only one of today's duke-doms, Norfolk, was created before the end of the Wars of the Roses, and that was in 1483; indeed, only twenty of the noble titles which grace the red upholstery of the House of Lords today are more than 500 years old.

In the aftermath of the Wars of the Roses a number of *nouveaux riches* and victorious camp-followers were elevated to the nobility, but the extent was limited. Henry VII and VIII were poor dispen-sers of that kind of patronage, and Elizabeth I was positively mean – her reign ended with fewer peers (59) than it started with (62), and in the course of her forty-four years on the throne only four com-moners were ennobled.

The Stuarts

The modern profligate trade in honours starts very firmly with the Stuarts. The process began within months of James I's ascent to the throne in 1603. As with many innovations, the prototype for profit from honours required considerable modification before the model exploited during the last hundred years was developed. James I started off by raising money from *not* giving knighthoods! As soon as he became king he summoned all the people possessing Crown lands worth £40 a year or more to present themselves for knighting, an investiture which brought with it obligations to the throne. This was a device he had learned from Edward II. Those who refused to accept the honour paid a heavy fine in lieu! The result was that 906 knights were created in four months, including 46 at one breakfast sitting. On coronation day (23 July 1603) alone, 432 new knights were created. The average rate for James's first three months on the throne was one knight every four hours – a feat not equalled even by Lloyd George, the most profligate of twentieth-century honours-dispensers. In his twenty-two regnal years, James dubbed over 2,600 knights.

If knighthoods could raise money, why not baronies? Between 1603 and 1629, 72 citizens became peers, a twenty-six-year ferment of activity that doubled the number that had been created and survived during the preceding 537 years. James raised over £600,000 from the sale of peerages in this period and middlemen picked up about £100,000 in brokerage fees.

A fickle Parliament and financial hardship made sales an easy solution for the Stuarts in troubled times – and frequently it was Court favourites who came out best. George Villiers was James's lover and was rewarded with the dukedom of Buckingham for his services. According to his contemporary, Sir Roger Wilbraham, Villiers subsequently sold peerages to Sir John Roper (who became Lord Teynham) and Sir John Holles (who became Baron Haughton) for £10,000 apiece. (The 20th Baron Teynham – John Christopher Ingham-Roper-Curzon, an Old Etonian land agent – is still entitled to a seat in the Lords 370 years later on the basis of that deal.) In 1623, the new Lord Teynham paid a further £5,000 to become the Earl of Clore – an inferior earldom as there was no royal dignity attached to Irish titles – and in the following year Baron Haughton paid an additional £5,000 to be similarly upgraded.

1616 was a good year for the royal coffers – Sir Philip Stanhope was transformed into Baron Stanhope of Shelford for the going rate of £10,000, and five years later his progression through the peerage saw him emerge as the Earl of Chesterfield for an undisclosed sum. And in 1623, the then Duke and Duchess of Richmond picked up

£12,000 for ensuring that the widow of Sir Moyle Finch, Bart, was elevated into the Viscountess of Maidstone. So pleased was Lady Finch with her noble progress that five years later she further advanced in rank to become the Viscountess Winchilsea. The deal cost her £7,000, a set of tapestries and her Essex country house; but the sixteenth earl survives today to benefit from the transaction.

Between 1615 and 1628, £200,000 was raised from the sale of peerages. Sir John Roper, for example, at the age of eighty-one paid £10,000 for a barony in 1616, having bought a baronetcy and a lesser barony for the same sum a year earlier. He was to emerge as Lord Dormer. The present (sixteenth) incumbent still sits in the House of Lords, as a Conservative.

Richard Robartes suffered a fate that would have sounded familiar to some of those honoured by Lloyd George 300 years later. Plain Richard was knighted in 1616, became a baronet five years later and developed into the fully fledged Baron Robartes of Truro in 1625 – but at considerable cost. Contemporary accounts vary in the level of extortion involved in this case, but all are agreed on its presence. One version has it that Robartes had made a fortune in tin and 'was squeezed by the court in King James his time of £20,000'. Another records James taking £12,000 at the time of his knighthood in 1616 in return for no prosecution for usury. And when the Duke of Buckingham was impeached in 1625, one of the charges against him was that he had compelled Robartes to pay £10,000 for his peerage. Poor Richard – the strain on the family must have been great, for the line is now extinct! The articles of impeachment against Buckingham declared: 'The sale of honours deflowers the powers of the Crown for it makes them cheap to all beholders.'

Anxious for funds for the conquest and suppression of the Irish, James I turned to a ploy used by Edward III – the establishment of a mid-way house between the hereditary peerage and the too-temporary knighthood: the baronetcy. It was perfect. A hereditary title, and so worth more than a knighthood, but without the troublesome potential of future membership of the Lords. (Edward III had conferred such a title on William de la Pole and his successors in return for money to keep the army.)

James had re-invented the wheel. He established the Order of Baronets in 1611. Recipients had to undertake to support thirty soldiers in Ulster at 8*d* a day for three years, to protect the English settlers. The price: £1,095. At first James offered to keep the order select by putting a limit of 200 on the number, but as he was in danger of exceeding his limit he changed the rules. In 1619 the Baronetage of Ireland was created – with the same financial consideration and a limit of 100 members – thus overnight turning the 200 maximum promised into 300. What a good game. In 1624, to assist in the settlement of Nova Scotia, the Baronetage of Scotland was to be created with similar provisions, but James died before it could be put fully into operation. However, his two opening gambits in the baronetage game had by then raised over £250,000 for an activity that 300 years later must be profoundly regretted by most people on both sides of the Irish Sea.

As the currency became devalued, James took steps to encourage reluctant takers by stipulating that the only way to progress to the peerage was via the baronetcy. None the less the fact of devaluation remained. By the 1640s the price was down to £400 and at least one was obtained for £350. Market forces took over – at the lower price there were more takers – and the first two kings Charles ignored James's upper limit on the number of baronets. (By the accession of George III in 1760 there were 500 of them; George himself created a further 500 and by 1860 850 were still in existence. Although none has been created since 1964 over 1,300 still survive, 6 of them gracing the Conservative Party benches in the House of Commons.)

Charles I began his reign on a high moral plane as far as the sale of honours was concerned, referring to Buckingham's impeachment as an argument against the practice. But he soon fell under the persuasion of the financial argument and lived to outdo his father. He started gingerly by selling the less-prestigious Irish and Scottish titles, at lower sums than his father and his favourites had received for the real McCoy.

James I had created the Earldom of Cork in 1620 and Charles sold the incumbent an Irish viscountcy for one son, an Irish barony for another and the promotion of his son-in-law to another Irish earldom for a total of £3,000. (The current 13th Earl of Cork is also entitled to the first two of these honours bought from Charles I – Viscount Kinalmeaky and Baron Boyle of Brandon Bridge – in addition to the splendid list of eight titles he already possesses.) Charles, at the same time, sold to Sir Thomas Fairfax the Scottish barony of

Fairfax of Cameron for £1,500. (The fourteenth and current baron is a barrister and Conservative peer and hence current legislator.)

As financial pressures increased, Charles resorted to selling the more prestigious and lucrative English peerages. In 1642, at the start of the Civil War, Sir Richard Newport was elevated to become Baron Newport of High Ercoll for a consideration of £6,000. And in a last desperate bid to buy support for the Royalist cause Charles created 128 new baronets in the year before the outbreak of hostilities.

The later Stuarts also sold honours and distributed patronage to supporters on a similar scale. In a tactic employed to considerable personal advantage in our own times, Charles II openly employed honours touts to hawk baronetcies on his behalf – they travelled the country with blank forms to be filled in by anyone willing to pay the price. He created 68 knights at his coronation, and even managed to create 19 peerages while he was in exile. Twenty-nine further dukedoms were also inaugurated in his reign – two of them being conferred on his mistresses and eight more on six of his bastard sons. Four current British dukes owe the origin of their titles to that bastardy: St Albans out of Nell Gwynn, Richmond out of the Duchess of Portsmouth, Buccleuch from Lucy Walters, and Grafton from the Duchess of Cleveland.

Descent from Charles II is not the only thing the current holders of these titles have in common. All four went to Eton followed, in the cases of the 9th Dukes of Richmond and of Buccleuch, by a period at Christ Church College, Oxford and, in the cases of the 11th Duke of Grafton and the 13th Duke of St Albans, by time at Magdalene College, Cambridge. Before assuming his title, the 9th Duke of Buccleuch had a spell as the Conservative MP for Edinburgh North between 1960 and 1973. Now, weighed down by ten hereditary titles, he is doing good deeds of a charitable nature. The 13th Duke of St Albans manages to combine his splendid post as 'Hereditary Falconer of England' with his residence in Monaco. Family concern with regal nocturnal activity seems to prevail among the Graftons. The current Duchess was Lady of the Bedchamber to the Queen 1953–66 and has subsequently been Mistress of the Robes to the Queen.

The Hanoverians

Trading in dukedoms became the major concern of those concerned with the dignity of honours over the next century. Following Charles's creation of 29 of them, William and Mary added 12 more (including 5 in a fortnight), Queen Anne, 13, and George I, 18. In addition to Charles's 29, therefore, 38 were created in the following three reigns. But worst of all, only eight of the holders were royal personages – a veritable debasement of the currency!

Royalty since the Hanoverians has jealously guarded its ranks and kept out those who aspire to it. The only non-royal dukes created since George II have been those of Northumberland and Cardigan in the eighteenth century and six others in the nineteenth century. None has been created since 1874, so today there are only 26 non-royal dukes. Thank God that abuse has been stamped out!

The Hanoverian era distinguished itself not only by preserving the integrity of the status of duke but also for presiding over the emergence of the effective post of 'prime minister'. While royalty concerned itself with fostering ducal dignity, it received a grant to maintain itself. It no longer needed to engage in the sordid trade of honours. The brokerage vacuum was filled by the new breed of prime ministers and their immediate entourage, who bestowed peerages on political patrons in exchange for crude voting support in both Houses of Parliament.

The final spasm of regal sales came in 1742 as part of George II's pay-off to one of his mistresses, the Countess of Yarmouth. She sought from him a gift of £30,000 but he refused; instead he offered her the right to extract money from the creation of two peers. Henry Bromley stepped forward to become Lord Montford and Stephen Fox to become Lord Ilchester. The Ilchester barony was upgraded to an earldom in 1756 and the ninth and current earl is a director of the Nottingham Building Society.

The more normal trade in Hanoverian peerages was in return for political favours. The unification with Ireland presented problems for the English in the closing years of the eighteenth century. At that time there was a separate house of peers for Ireland. It was used in a blatant way for acquiring the 'acquiescence' of the Irish for the Union. George III, at the prompting of his English ministers, increased the number of Irish peers from 86 in 1775 to 157 a quarter of a century later. The ennoblements came in waves as fresh deals were struck; 18 barons created on consecutive days in 1776 with a further 12 existing peers being promoted; 8 more barons created in two months in 1783, 8 more creations and 12 promotions in 1789; and in 1798, shortly before the Act of Union, 13 more creations. Finally, to ensure the passage of the Act, the biggest wholesale package of bribery by these means was delivered with 24 further creations and 22 promotions.

A similar, though less dramatic, series of elevations and promotions took place in the English Upper House in order to swamp the Whig majority. Thus 7 peerages were created in 1771, 11 in 1776 and 8 in 1780, with the result that between 1760 and 1783 43 peerages were created in all – accounting for about one-fifth of the membership of the 1783 House of Lords. Such is the extinction rate of noble families that, although 143 commoners were created peers in the eighty years before 1783, the net increase in the membership of the House was only 18.

However, it was Pitt who brought youth and increased tempo to the honours game when he became Prime Minister in 1783. During his first ministry he increased the size of the Lords by 50 per cent with the creation of 95 peers, quite apart from Irish appointments. In the seventeen years in which he was in office he created over 140 peers.

Pitt's creations were for both political and financial considerations. By 1792 it was calculated that nine of his ennoblements were of men who between them through patronage and nominations controlled twenty-four members of the pre-reformed House of Commons. Among them were the forefathers of the present 7th Baron Lonsdale, Old Etonian and a director of Cannon Insurance, and the 7th Earl of Harewood, cousin to the Queen and also an Old Etonian. Halevy, the distinguished French recorder of English history, notes:

> Other creations, however, sufficiently numerous to excite contemporary imagination, had been frankly purchased with hard cash or political services by men devoid of merit or birth. The great creation of 1797, when 16 peerages were conferred, excited particular scandal. (*History of the English People in the Nineteenth Century*, Vol. I, Benn, 1949, p. 193)

Among those elevated in 1797 and specifically referred to by Halevy was Mr Robert Smith, a London banker. He had discovered that the original family name of a seventeenth-century peerage that had fallen into extinction had been Smith – what better than to take as a title that of the now extinct Smith line? Thus was created the first of the current Lords Carrington. Smith had, in fact, taken an inferior Irish peerage as Lord Carrington in 1796 but converted it into the more prestigious English peerage the following year. The present and 6th Lord may well have mused on the origin of his peerage when he was Chairman of the Conservative Party between 1972 and 1974 and a member of the Thatcher Cabinet as Foreign Secretary, 1979–82. After a period as Chairman of GEC he is now exercising his good services as Secretary-General of NATO.

The eighteenth-century Robert Smith was not the only one who found refuge in a title of grandeur. When the old Duke of Bolton died without heirs, Mr Thomas Orde, who had married his illegitimate daughter, adopted the name in 1797, so although there would no longer be a Duke of Bolton there would be a Baron Bolton. The seventh Baron (Eton and Trinity, Cambridge), survives today as a director of the Yorkshire General Life Assurance Company and Chairman of current Trade Secretary Leon Brittan's Constituency Conservative Association in Richmond, Yorkshire.

Halevy cites contemporary records which suggest that 71 peerages created in the final decade of the eighteenth century and the early decades of the nineteenth were attributed to the wealth of the peer. Of the 71 he cautiously names 12. Seven of those 12 survive today. In addition to Lords Carrington and Bolton there is the present sixteen-year-old Lord Oxmanton; his title, created in 1792, was upgraded to the Earl of Rosse in 1806, a position held by the minor's father. The current and seventh earl was educated at Eton and Christ Church, Oxford, resides in Ireland and is the stepbrother to Lord Snowdon – estranged brother-in-law to the Queen.

Another Old Etonian heir to a eighteenth-century *nouveau riche* creation is the 8th Baron Rendelsham. Stowe and Trinity, Cambridge provide the educational background of two other descendants, both of whom have ended up in the diplomatic world: the 8th Baron Henniker and the 6th Baron Huntingfield. The 7th Earl of Caledon, meanwhile, went to Gordonstoun.

Pitt had thus established strong precedents for his successors –

the liberal allocation of peerages for both political and financial gain. Like Lloyd George after him, he encouraged the creation of new awards and honours in an effort to increase the spheres of patronage. In the first year of Pitt's premiership, 1783, George III founded the Irish Order of St Patrick as a counterpart for the English Order of the Garter created 450 years earlier and the Scottish Order of the Thistle established in the seventeenth century. When in 1786 his sons were invested with the Garter, he enlarged the Order and prescribed that it should have twenty-five knights exclusive of the King and his sons.

With the end of the French Wars came a reorganisation and extension of the orders of chivalry. The Order of the Bath was reorganised, the maximum number of knights considerably extended, and within the Order iself a hierarchy of Grand Crosses, Commanders and Companions was created. Just as the explosion of honours under Lloyd George was to provoke public ridicule a century later, so did these manoeuvres. The reorganisation and expansion was denounced as an imitation of the honours distributed on the Continent and a copy of Napoleon's methods. The reformed Order received the nickname 'The New Legion of Honour'.

George III's reign, which ended in 1820, had seen the creation of no less than 388 additions to the peerage of Great Britain and the United Kingdom as well as this reorganisation and extension of lesser honours. Large-scale creation continued in the reign of George IV until the end of the Earl of Liverpool's fifteen-year premiership in 1827. The pace began to slacken the following year when the Duke of Wellington became Prime Minister.

Wellington created only 7 peerages in 28 months and, although rather more were created over the next three or four years by Viscount Melbourne and Earl Grey, once the 1832 Reform Act was passed one of the principal reasons for their creation on a large scale disappeared. With the abolition of the pocket and rotten boroughs, brought about by the Act, there were fewer patrons who had to be appeased and pandered to by the award of peerages.

The 1832 Reform Act reduced the need to award peerages as a political pay-off; ironically, as we shall see, it was later Reform Acts that, in extending the franchise, made the award of peerages for direct monetary consideration much more pressing.

The Victorian Era

The Victorian period began with commendable restraint. Peel, particularly in his second ministry (1841–46), tried to establish a high moral tone in regard to honours, and felt that they should only be awarded in order to strengthen the administration. Rather than use the system for his own personal or political advantage, he despised it. But he was lucky: he lived in the limbo period between the pre-democratic patronage era which expected rewards and the era of the democratic electoral machine that required lubricating.

Peel's disdain of the system and his detachment from it can be gleaned from some of his correspondence. On one occasion he informed the Duke of Wellington, 'It seems to me that the distinction of the peerage has been degraded by the profuse and incautious use that has been made of it.' On another occasion he was to anticipate Balfour with the remark, 'I wonder people do not begin to feel the distinction of an unadorned name.' When his offer of a baronetcy to Hallam the historian was rejected, Peel was delighted and asked him to allow his portrait to be painted so that it could be added to a collection he was forming of pictures of the most eminent men of the day.

Peel was succeeded by a couple of other pre-democratic moralists as Prime Minister. Palmerston rebutted one approach for ennoblement with the remark, 'The throne is a fount of Honour; it is not a pump; nor am I a pump handle.' Disraeli, although slightly freer in distributing the honours favours, felt guided by the principle that he would do what was in the interests of the party. He was, however, quick to point out that 'there is nothing more ruinous to political connection than the fear of rewarding your friends'. Between 1874 and 1880 he recommended 26 new peerages and 9 promotions.

The mid-Victorian pattern of honours was a simple one, even if the recipients were undistinguished. Peerages went to people of landed interest who continued to have some electoral influence or who had served in the Commons, or to Scottish or Irish peers whose presence in the Lords (not automatic for them in their own right) was felt to be useful to the government. Former ministers, generals, admirals, judges, ambassadors or other public servants would receive their share.

The number of peerages awarded to industrialists was tiny, although Gladstone gradually reintroduced the practice and also gave peerages for the first time to distinguished retired Civil Servants. They were each, apart from the politicians, expected to have an income or estate valued at more than £5,000 a year. Baronetcies went to well-off backbenchers or to businessmen with a notable record of public service or to lesser public figures like Lord Mayors of London, top soldiers, sailors, ambassadors and colonial governors. Potential recipients were expected to have an income exceeding £2,000 per year.

It was Gladstone who returned to the task of honours proliferation and salesmanship after a fifty-year lull in the tale of sales. His periods in office resulted in the creation of 67 new peers and 14 Scottish and Irish additions to the House of Lords. He justified the speeding-up process on two grounds: first, as a Liberal he set out to overcome the persistent Toryness of the House by improving its balance and composition; and secondly, he called to his aid an odd form of proportional representation. By a selective use of statistics, he was able to show that in 1840 there were 17 peers for every million people in the population, by 1869 the figure had fallen to 14 and so remained until 1880. A topping-up process was therefore in order. Had he looked a little further back in history, to the time of Henry VII, he would have discovered that the ratio was 15 to a million – about the same as it was in his own time when the power of the peerage and Second Chamber was much stronger. No matter, the case was made and the peers were created. Other less noble reasons for the honours bestowed are not difficult to find.

With the extension of the franchise and the development of a party system in Westminster the process of election began to replace that of nomination as the means of entering the House of Commons. Elections, not run on a national basis as today, were expensive affairs for the constituency caucuses, or more often than not, the candidates. In the 1870s, however, with the creation of central offices and organisation, the parties were beginning to merge into a more recognisable form. And with this arose a feeling that, for reasons of credibility, if for no other, it was important to contest as many parliamentary seats as possible. But there were few wealthy and philanthropic men in either of the two parties who were willing to fight and finance some hopeless seat if there was no prospect of reward – and an election could have cost a candidate £4,000 a century ago. Thus wealthy industrial patrons and sponsors were sought and offered inducements in the forms of peerages and other honours.

The Conservatives took an early lead in this practice under Sir Stafford Northcote, Leader of the Commons. H. J. Hanham quotes one letter from Northcote dated 1885 to a would-be election-funder, 'I know I am asking a great deal from you; but I trust you may be willing to make the sacrifice; and it will be felt a great addition to the claims you already have upon the gratitude of the Conservative Party' (*Elections and Party Management*, Harvester Press, 1959, p. 375). Northcote empowered David Plunkett, a former Conservative minister, to accompany the letter with a verbal promise of a baronetcy.

Both major parties' funds were hit by the depression of the 1880s, but the Liberals faced a further blow. Their support for Irish Home Rule in 1886 saw many of their wealthy landowners desert the ranks. 1886 also saw a general election only a year after the previous one. Gladstone wrote to Carnegie, 'While we have $9/10$th or indeed $10/10$th of the operations to carry on, our wealth, except perhaps $1/10$th, has absconded.'

The mid-1880s saw not only a dramatic decline in the Liberal Party's traditional wealth base but also a noticeable change in the composition of the newly elevated peers. Up to 1885 the number of commercial and industrial peers remained small – only 4 had been created in the previous ten years. In the decade beginning 1886 the number shot up to 18. This increase was accompanied by a nearly threefold increase in the number of baronetcies awarded (48 between 1875 and 1884, 116 between 1885 and 1894), the great majority of which, according to Hanham, were given to businessmen and manufacturers. The expansion was largely the result of economic changes and the social emergence and domination of plutocratic industrialists over the relatively decaying landed aristocracy. The craving for acceptability by these industrialists, who were treated by the nobility as little more than tradesmen, knew no bounds. A peerage signified respectability. Few things have changed over the last century.

Lady St Helier, in her memoirs published in 1909, revealed how Bishop Magee of Peterborough was offered £50,000 for the diocese funds if he would secure a baronetcy for the donor. Lord Suffield, a member of the household of the Prince of Wales (later Edward VII) was offered a sea-wall round his Norfolk estate by one man and £250,000 by another in return for peerages. The Duke of Devonshire was Leader of the Liberal-Unionist Party and his secretary, Sir Almeric FitzRoy, was approached by the wife of an invalid who claimed that her husband's invalidity was the result of the Duke's refusal to make him a baronet.

However, perhaps the most outrageous case of the sale of honours centred around Ernest T. Hooley. Until his bankruptcy in 1898, Hooley was the promoter of a number of very prominent public companies – among them Dunlop, Schweppes, Bovril and Singer – and by paying for the services of peers to sit on their boards he bought favourable coverage in the financial press. He also promoted himself – into the Prince of Wales's entourage – and achieved landed respectability by purchasing estates in six counties. He then lavished money on St Paul's Cathedral and ingratiated himself into the Conservative Party by fighting a hopeless seat and joining the prestigious Carlton Club with an extravagant £1,000 opening membership subscription. However, when he attempted to buy himself a baronetcy in the 1897 jubilee honours by offering Captain Middleton, principal agent of the Conservative Party, £50,000, he was rejected. He was still dreaming of schemes for his elevation when bankruptcy proceedings were initiated against him the following year.

Although there is no firm evidence of any honours for money deals being struck in the Victorian era until 1891, it is difficult to believe that the people quoted above would have gone to the lengths that they did had they not had some sign that activity of that kind paid dividends in the honours stakes.

The Liberal Party, meanwhile, was destitute and was encouraged in the mid-1880s by Northcote's practice in getting wealthy men to fight unpromising seats. If honours could be offered for this assistance to the party, why not for straight cash transactions? There was no shortage of potential takers as party leaders were plagued by requests for honours; almost a quarter of the 4,460 letters Gladstone sent to the Queen concerned the question of honours.

The Liberal Party certainly encountered an improvement in fortune from the early 1890s on – very soon after Gladstone had complained that 90 per cent of the party's wealthy supporters had deserted it. The size of its general-election fund grew from £30–50,000 in 1880 to £60–80,000 in 1895 and to £80–120,000 in 1906. At the same time the regular annual expenditure of the party grew from about £10,000 in the 1860s to about £100,000 by 1912.

By 1891 Arnold Morley, the Liberal Chief Whip, and Francis Schnadhorst, the party's chief organiser, had concluded that the only way to build up the Liberals' war chest was to offer honours directly for sale. There are two well-documented cases of the transaction – those of Sidney Stern and James Williamson.

Sidney Stern had been a Liberal candidate since 1880 but had not entered Parliament until a by-election in 1891, when he became the Member for Stowmarket. He came from a well-known family of bankers who specialised in Portuguese finance – indeed, he inherited a viscountcy of the Kingdom of Portugal from his father. When he died in 1912, *The Times* obituary recorded the fact that 'he was a lavish contributor to Party funds'.

James Williamson had been MP for Lancaster since 1886 but was virtually unknown outside the town, where he was one of two leading employers. He had made a fortune from the production of oil cloth (also known as 'American cloth'), but had made no great mark in Parliament. The circumstances surrounding his controversial elevation to the Lords in 1895 were such that he became the subject of ridicule in his home town and he had to wait two years before taking his seat. As he grew older (he died in 1930, without heirs, at the age of eighty-eight) his behaviour became more and more eccentric. His first move was to shelve plans to build a new factory in Lancaster, in revenge for the rumours that circulated about him there. In 1911 he withdrew his patronage from the area to such an extent that whenever he drove past the Town Hall, which he had paid for, he insisted that the blinds of the carriage be drawn. He gradually became a recluse and built his own golf course on which he would allow nobody to play except himself and his professional coach. As a final eccentricity he offered £50,000 reward to anybody who could cure him of taking snuff. His obituary in *The Times*, from which these foibles are taken, does not record whether the offer was ever taken up.

Fascinating as these two characters may have been, their public deeds by 1895 hardly merited the distinction associated with a

peerage. Details of the transaction emerged in correspondence following Gladstone's retirement from the premiership in 1894.
Arnold Morley and his successor as Chief Whip, Lord Tweed-
mouth, called upon Rosebery to complete the bargain by nominat-
ing the two men for peerages. Rosebery baulked at the prospect
until he received written confirmation of the deal from Gladstone.
The correspondence survives in the British Library and makes it
clear that Stern and Williamson were offered peerages during the
period of the 1891 election in return for giving 'financial help in
those cases where a contest could not effectively be carried on
without such assistance'.

Once Rosebery had received confirmation of the transaction from
Gladstone the names of Stern and Williamson duly appeared in the
resignation honours list of July 1895. Rosebery went to some
trouble to distance himself from the awards by having their announcement in the *Daily News* accompanied by the statement that
they were Gladstone's responsibility. Stern became Lord Wands-
worth and Williamson Lord Ashton – both died without heirs and
the peerages became defunct in 1912 and 1930, respectively. The
Spectator allowed itself a caustic comment on the peerages, 'There is
no allegation that either Mr Stern or Mr Williamson has ever done
anything worthy of reward but supply the party war chest.' The radical journal, *Truth*, confined itself to the quip, 'It is obvious that in
these cases [Stern and Williamson] the transaction has been a monetary one, for politically they are mere zeros.'

Much more vitriolic was *Truth*'s condemnation of the Naylor-
Leyland baronetcy conferred in the same year, 'I do not hesitate to
say that whoever was "concerned" in granting this "honour" to
Captain Naylor-Leyland is as much disgraced by it as the Captain is
in accepting it. I estimate that this Baronetcy and the peerages of
Messrs Stern and Williamson will cost the party more seats than the
money they may have brought into the parliamentary chest will do
good. "It does not smell," said Vespasian of the money that he
acquired from a tax on the latrines of Rome. But the money brought
in by this trafficking in hereditary legislatorships reeks of corruption. It stinks!'

Naylor-Leyland was twenty-eight when he entered Parliament as
a Conservative in 1892, three years later he resigned his seat and
announced his conversion to Liberalism, virtually assuring victory

to the Liberal candidate at the by-election. Four and a half months elapsed between the Liberal victory and Naylor-Leyland's elevation to the baronetcy. Like the cases of Stern and Williamson the Naylor-Leyland affair firmly established the precedent that honours could be bought for either money or party advantage. The present and third baronet, Sir Vivyan Naylor-Leyland (Eton and Christ Church, Oxford), resides in the Bahamas.

Perhaps because of the response to the 1895 resignation list, Lord Salisbury in his third administration, dating from that year, was considerably more cautious in his approach to honours brokerage. He rejected a suggestion from Richard Middleton, head of the Conservative Central Office, that a peerage should be sold to an Indian rajah in return for a donation, but he did encourage Middleton and Lord Abergavenny (then one of the trustees of Conservative Party funds) to accept large sums of money from men whose only objective in donating it was to receive honours. As a result the party became consciously indebted to men like William Waldorf Astor for a gift of £20,000 in 1900 (£500,000 at today's prices) for the election fund. Astor, who became British in 1899, put pressure on the Conservative Party for a peerage in 1909, but did not receive it until 1916 (see Chapter 4).

Another man similarly encouraged to donate to Conservative Party funds, according to Hanham, was the ironmaster, William Henry Armstrong. But he had to wait until the year after Salisbury's departure in 1902 to receive his elevation. The present and 3rd Lord Armstrong is an Old Etonian and Member of Lloyd's.

Salisbury was thus able to play the honours game quite deftly – he exploited people's craving for honours by accepting their money but denied them their wishes. However, for this tactic to be successful it had to be played at arm's length, and so intermediaries were required. At least two well-placed and plausible touts operated during the Salisbury years. The first was Sir William Marriott, an MP for Brighton during the 1800s who had had two spells as the Judge Advocate. It was Marriott who acted as an intermediary for the notorious Ernest T. Hooley. Marriott introduced him to peers to use as directors and obtained business for him on a commission basis. And it was Marriott who helped him jump the waiting list to join the Carlton Club, who gave money on his behalf to the Conservative Party fund and who offered Captain Middleton a cheque for £50,000 (or, according to Hooley's account, £10,000) in exchange for a baronetcy in 1897. The baronetcy was not granted and £10,000 was returned to Hooley at the time of his bankruptcy proceedings in 1898. The second tout according to Hanham's research in the Salisbury papers was another ex-Minister, Ellis Ashmead-Bartlett, who offered a knighthood for sale in the City of London as early as 1895.

Salisbury's successor as leader of the Conservative Party and Prime Minister, Arthur Balfour, had fewer scruples about awarding honours to those who funded the party. Correspondence in 1905 between the Conservative Chief Whip, Sir Alexander Acland-Hood (later Lord St Audries), and the Tory premier's Private Secretary, Jack Sanders, makes it clear that honours were sold by the Conservatives during the weeks before the resignation of the government in 1905. Balfour's government (1902–05) created 18 peerages, including 5 businessmen. The five were, William Armstrong (see above), A. J. Forbes-Leith (created Baron Leith of Fyvie) and three bankers: M. Biddulph, (Baron Biddulph), A. B. Faber (Baron Faber) and Herbert de Stern.

Herbert de Stern, created Baron Michelham, is particularly interesting. He was a senior partner in the finance house of Herbert Stern & Co, although his obituary in *The Times* in 1919 said that he never played any great part in the City's financial affairs. He had inherited £2 million from his father and passed £1 million on to his daughter-in-law at her wedding four days before his own death. He was created a baronet in 1905 and six months later was elevated to the peerage proper. The *Saturday Review* commented, in December 1905:

> A peerage has just been conferred on Sir Herbert de Stern, who a year or two ago was made a baronet [it was in fact six months earlier]. When we remember that in 1895 Lord Rosebery created Lord Wandsworth, the near relative of Sir Herbert de Stern, we may well ask what are the claims of the family upon the public that within ten years two of its members should be given the right to sit and vote with the hereditary aristocracy of Great Britain? Why have they been made peers? The answer is money.

The 1st Lord Michelham died in 1919 leaving £14 million – the present and 2nd Lord is his eighty-four-year-old Malvern College-educated son.

The Edwardians

Although they lost the 1906 general election, the Conservatives continued to benefit from the sale of honours during the next sixteen years of Liberal and Coalition government. Opposition parties are given a portion of the honours list to distribute and the Conservatives, following the patterns adopted both by themselves in the 1902–05 period and by the Liberal government of the day, exploited the honours system for all its financial worth in the succeeding years.

In a 1910 memorandum to the new Leader of the Conservative Party, Andrew Bonar Law, Party Chairman Sir Arthur Steel-Maitland paid tribute to the departing Chief Whip: 'He started [in 1902] without any invested funds, and left a nest egg of over £300,000. A year's peerages are hypothecated, but it is still a very fair performance.' He acknowledged that the ability of the party to collect a central target of £120–140,000 a year would depend partly on agreements about 'future honours'. John Ramsden, in his account of the organisation of the Conservative Party at the time, indicates how successful Steel-Maitland was in raising money. In the three years between becoming Party Chairman and the outbreak of the First World War, he doubled the invested funds to £671,000 and set up a special cash deposit of £120,000 in preparation for an election expected in 1914 or 1915. In that three-year period, therefore, Steel-Maitland was able to add, on average, more than £160,000 a year to party funds, after paying the running costs of the party. These sums are considerably higher than the money he had hoped for in 1911, even given the agreements about honours.

After some painstaking work, T. O. Lloyd has managed to trace the sources of major donations to Liberal Party election funds in both the 1900 and 1906 elections, revealing the source of £60,000 donated in 1900 and £228,000 contributed in 1906. Though the great bulk of the money in 1906 was in sums of over £1,000 donated by twenty-seven individuals, Table 5 makes interesting reading (from 'The Whip as Paymaster' in *English Historical Review*, Vol. 89, 1974, pp. 804–13).

Only eight men in Lloyd's list gave the Liberal Party more than £10,000, and all were honoured (or, in Horniman's case, were about to be honoured). The donations of the eight accounted for at least a third of the money raised by the Liberal Party at each election and totalled more than £130,000 (over £3 million at current prices). Although Lloyd goes to considerable length to justify the honours on grounds other than donations, the correlation is a striking one and, in terms of percentage of funds accounted for, bears comparison with the association of donations and honours recorded under the Thatcher administration in Chapter 7.

Table 5
Donations to Liberal Party Central Funds
and Award of Honours, 1900–06

Name	1900 Election (£)	1906 Election (£)	Other occasions 1900–05 (£)	Title awarded	Date
Wills	—	20,000	—	Barony	1905
Whiteley	—	20,000	—	Barony	1908
Lever	5,000	10,000	100[1]	Baronetcy	1911
				Barony	1917
Williamson	10,000[1]	5,000	—	Barony	(1895)
Langman	—	—	15,000	Baronetcy	1906
Horniman	10,500	2,625	—	Baronetcy agreed	1906
Joicey	2,000	10,000	—	Barony	1905
Robinson	—	10,000	10,000	Baronetcy	1908
McLaren	2,000	2,000	—	Baronetcy	1902
				Barony	1911
	29,500[1]	79,625	25,100[1]		

1 At least

A brief note on each of the recipients is in order here. William Henry Wills was the tobacco magnate who came to be Chairman of Imperial Tobacco. He had been an MP for ten years in the last two decades of the nineteenth century and was a public benefactor – in particular to Bristol University. He had been created a baronet in 1893 and was ennobled as Lord Winterstoke in 1905. When he died in 1911, without a male heir, he left over £1 million.

The Rt Hon. George Whiteley was the director of a textile company in Lancashire and had been first a Conservative MP (1893–1900) and then a Liberal MP (1900–08). He was a Whip for the last three years. On elevation to the peerage he assumed the title Lord Marchomley.

William Lever, the soap baron, had been a Liberal MP from 1906–10, was raised to the baronetcy in 1911, and under Lloyd George became first a baron (1917) and then a viscount (1922). The 3rd Viscount Leverhulme (Eton and Trinity, Cambridge) is currently Chancellor of Liverpool University.

James Williamson, the Lancashire linoleum magnate, has already been referred to above (see pp. 44–46).

Sir John Lawrence Longman was reticent about himself in his *Who's Who* entries, confining them to the fact that he had equipped and maintained a field hospital named in his honour during the Boer War. It is for this that Lloyd feels he was awarded his baronetcy – seven years later.

Frederick Horniman was the tea tycoon. Correspondence about his baronetcy, between Herbert Gladstone, the Chief Whip, and Campbell-Bannerman survives. Gladstone wrote to Campbell-Bannerman: 'Horniman. He is quite keen to rise to the bartcy, the equestrian condition is not enough. His health is not good and I should like to have some adequate assurance. He has served in two Parliaments and has given an immense sum to the public in his museum. He has supported us handsomely and is in all these ways up to the mark.' Campbell-Bannerman replied: 'As to old Horniman, he seems to me, though quite an eccentric and a fossil, perfectly qualified by his good deeds for the baronetcy.' Horniman died early in 1906 before he could receive the anticipated baronetcy.

James Joicey had been a Liberal MP from 1885 to 1906 and was the managing director of the two largest collieries in Durham. Like William Wills he was created a baronet in 1893 at the time of an earlier Liberal phase of converting honours into party funds. The present and 4th Baron Joicey (Eton and Christ Church, Oxford) is a north-eastern landowner.

The final large donor in the table, Joseph Robinson, was a South African businessman who attracted considerable unfavourable publicity later, in 1922, when he was nominated for a peerage in the Birthday honours list. Such was the furore over his nomination that, after considerable pressure, he rejected the offer (see pp. 62–63).

McLaren was a Liberal MP in 1880–85 and later 1892–1910. He was a nephew of Liberal reformer John Bright and director of a number of companies including John Brown & Co, Harland & Wolff and, according to his obituary, owner of 'the seaside watering place of Prestatyn'. He received his baronetcy in 1902 and was created Baron Aberconway in 1911. The present and 3rd Baron Aberconway (Eton and New College, Oxford) has taken not only his grandfather's title but also his directorship in John Brown & Co. To this he has added directorships in English China Clays, Sun Alliance, London Insurance, Westland Aircraft and the National Westminster Bank (this latter he has recently vacated).

Once the Liberals returned to office in 1906, their ability to cash in on the trafficking of honours increased. The booming nature of party funds and the explosion in the rate of honours awards both bear testimony to the fact. Whiteley, the Liberal Chief Whip between 1906 and 1908, told Asquith that the party's reserves stood at £20,000 after the 1906 election, but had risen to £500,000 within two years. The pace of awards began to quicken. In the period 1905–14, 99 peerages were bestowed, almost doubling the number awarded in the previous decade and the number of baronets increased by 50 per cent to 203 – a rate only surpassed in the following, Lloyd George-dominated, decade.

There are considerable difficulties in trying to establish which of the people honoured during this period paid for their titles, as both the recipients and the effective donors of the honours had every incentive to conceal the transaction. As a consequence, the number of confirmed cases of direct sales is very limited. But public and parliamentary concern at the practice was certainly aired, and in a study of the 1910 general election, Neal Blewett quotes the case of the Liberal retailer Hudson Kearley. He was created a baronet in 1908 and announced that while he 'wasn't going to buy' a peerage, if he became a peer 'he would like to voluntarily help the party by £25,000 or so'. Kearley became Lord Devonport in 1910 and was further elevated to Viscount Devonport under Lloyd George in 1917. The present and third viscount is a North Country architect.

In the decade before the First World War, the Liberal and Conservative parties between them had raised over £1¼ million (over £30 million today) more than they could spend, and much of it came through the sale of honours. One consequence of this overabundance of funds is that parties sought places to invest the money – and turned to a considerable extent to financing national and local newspapers. This relationship is explained more fully in Chapter 4.

Considering the scale of the trafficking of honours in this period, public and parliamentary comment was particularly mute. In May 1894 there was a brief debate in the Commons when a wild attack was made on the Rosebery administration's handling of honours, but there were only three speeches and the government had no difficulty in handling the criticism. There was little more excitement about the system until the *Saturday Review* attack on Sir Herbert de Stern, referred to above. The article, entitled 'Adulteration of the Peerage' also had a few choice words to say on the elevation of *Daily Mail* and *Daily Mirror* proprietor Sir Alfred Harmsworth into the first Lord Northcliffe: 'We say advisedly that he has done more than any man of his generation to pervert and enfeeble the minds of the multitude.'

Hugh Cecil Lea, a Radical MP, launched two attacks, in parliamentary debates in July 1907 and the following February, on the way in which the honours system was being used. In 1907 he revealed that a knighthood had been conferred on the director of a company which had been admitted by the Treasury bench to have been guilty of a gross fraud on the Admiralty, which had endangered a first-class battleship and its crew. He concluded that, 'The honours are bought and sold, the proceeds going principally to the war chests of the party in office at the time these so-called honours are conferred.' In the course of the parliamentary exchanges a letter from G. K. Chesterton to the *Daily News* was quoted: 'So long as the mass of money [i.e. party funds] remains unaudited, that mass of money remains omnipotent. Rich men pay into it and are made peers . . . But the thing is not written down anywhere, so we cannot prove bribery.'

Sporadic and unspecific attacks were made in Parliament on honours sales over the next two or three weeks leading to a parliamentary question. The Attorney-General replied that since the charges were flimsy, speculative and merely expressions of opinion the government had decided not to take any action. Seven months later Hugh Lea returned to the attack: 'Political corruption during the regime of the present leader of the opposition [Balfour] from 1903–05 had reached such a stage that the tariff for titles and decorations was well-known in the City of London and the percentage of commission allowed to the introducer of the customer was equally well-known.' He went on to point out that the market price for these honours went as high as £150,000.

In the period between the two elections of 1910 – dominated by discussions on the powers and fate of the House of Lords – Ramsay MacDonald, Leader of the Labour Party, attacked the Liberal's recent choice of seven new peers and the financial transaction involved. MacDonald was reported as saying that if the Liberals were to have men of title holding even the limited power in the Constitution which the veto resolution gave, he wanted men whom he could respect, not men who had bought their way into the upper chamber by liberally subscribing to party funds.

In February 1914, the first issue of a radical political journal, *Candid Quarterly Review*, launched a blistering polemic entitled 'The New Corruption' on the sale of honours, in which it declared: 'The head whip's office has been turned into a huckster's shop for the sale and purchase of peerages, baronetcies and knighthoods after bargaining that would become Petticoat Lane.' The author gave a number of examples of the traffic at work. One person, he said, gave £50,000 to a party fund and was subsequently made a baronet. Another, £150,000, another, £200,000 and yet another, £400,000 for a peerage. Brokers in the City, he went on to note, had gone touting for buyers of baronetcies, £4,000 down and £6,000 to be lodged in a bank in two names with 10 per cent commission to the first introducer of a customer. The article asserted that even a person who on merit 'deserved' honours had been forced into paying £10,000 for a baronetcy.

The attack was aimed particularly at the premierships of Balfour and Campbell-Bannerman, saying that it was impossible to scan the honours lists since 1902 without perceiving that they contained the names of many men who had never attained eminence or shown ability of any kind or had been known to do any public service of any kind. Good reasons are always apparent for the honours, it stated, when poor men (like Lords Roberts and Kitchener) are the recipients. In too many instances this was not the case with rich men. The way to conclusively deny the charges that honours were bought and sold, the article argued, was for the parties to open their books and 'to publish an account of the receipts and expenditure during, say, the last 12 years of the party funds'. In a crescendo of outrage, from a style of radical journalism now lost, the article exploded: 'This sort of corruption is the most cankerous and fatal that can exist in the State. It blasts with shame and ignominy those very honours which have been instituted for the reward of well-doing. It brands the Minister with the false mintage of false coin. It is loathsome and detestable beyond all usual Ministerial misdeeds, dishonouring and dangerous to the State beyond all ordinary offences.'

After the appearance of the *Candid Quarterly Review* article there was a day-long debate in the Lords on a resolution proposed by Lord Selborne to the effect that a contribution to party funds should not be a consideration when claims for an honour were being weighed. In the course of a fairly tedious debate, calls were made for a Royal Commission to examine the honours system and for citations or reasons to be attached to the names of each person honoured. These were rejected by the government.

Candid Quarterly returned to the subject in its second issue in May. Their Lordships, it noted, had great advantages when discussing the subject: 'Many of them know by recent experience what is the market price for a peerage, or rather what have been the fluctuations in the market.' The *Review* gave more, admittedly unsubstantiated, information on how it saw the honours-sales system operating. There are agents for the sale of these baubles, it declared, especially of baronetcies and knighthoods, who have a commission which, perhaps, has to be added. A baronetcy has been known to cost as much as £25,000, it continued, and as little as £6,000. A knighthood has been sold for £4,000 and another as low as £1,250, but there was much haggling over the latter deal, so the new knight must have been a capital bargainer. A number of variables determine the price: the wealth of the aspirant; the amount of service (if any) to the party; the aspirant's bargaining skill and above all the health of the party's funds. £40–50,000 is probably the going rate for a peerage, the article suggested, but 'we can never know for certainty because both parties to the contract have the utmost inducement to conceal it'.

Over the past fourteen years, the article noted, 104 peers had been created. No doubt some were for real service, but: 'There must certainly have been a great many created, to put it in the most delicate way imaginable, contemporaneously with a munificent contribution to the party fund.' This was the system that Lloyd George inherited when he became Prime Minister in December 1916.

Three

Lloyd George's maundy money

When Lloyd George became Prime Minister in 1916 he inherited a well-developed and lucrative honours-for-sale business in Downing Street. Over the next six years he exploited it for all it was worth, increasing the number of honours awarded and introducing new ones that were distributed on a profligate scale. In the process he picked up widespread condemnation and millions of pounds for his own personal 'political fund'. Honours-touting became a profitable business and the most notorious of its practitioners, Maundy Gregory, was later to become the only man convicted of it. The offence itself was first established in an Act of Parliament passed to remove what were seen as Lloyd George's abuses of the honours system.

The Lloyd George era and its aftermath (until 1934) provide a fascinating insight into the way in which rich men craved for the respectability that honours brought. Lloyd George exploited that craving. Between 1880 and 1908 an average of just over 7 new peers were created a year. Asquith increased the rate to 11 in his nine years in office and Lloyd George to 14 in his six. If he doubled the turn-of-the-century going rate for the bestowal of peerages, he changed into an even higher gear when awarding the lesser honours. Asquith averaged an award of 20 baronetcies a year in his period in office, Lloyd George increased that average to 43; Asquith averaged 154 knighthoods a year, Lloyd George 354. The biggest growth areas for the conferment of honours, and those that provoked most comment, concerned awards distributed to businessmen and newspaper proprietors – the former were to provide the money for the Lloyd George era and the latter the publicity.

As has already been shown, Asquith was no mean exploiter of the *nouveaux riches* in the honours trade but Lloyd George's activities put him in the shadows. The war had thrown up a number of very rich men and Lloyd George set about imposing a war-profiteering tax – except the money went to his own political fund and not the Exchequer. Of Asquith's 89 peerages, 12 went to business-men and only one to a newspaper man. Of Lloyd George's 87 peerages, 26 went to businessmen and a further 5 to pressmen. Thus only 13 per cent of Asquith's peerages went to business and the press, whereas over 35 per cent of Lloyd George's did. Forty-five per cent (90) of the baronetcies created in Asquith's premiership went to businessmen and none to pressmen. Fifty-five per cent (130) of Lloyd George's baronetcies went to businessmen and two per cent (5) to pressmen. Similarly with the knighthoods – only 18 per cent (158) of Asquith's knights were businessmen and one per cent (8) pressmen. For Lloyd George's era the figures were 25 per cent (481) and two per cent (37).

In both percentage terms and absolute numbers, Lloyd George's bestowal of honours on the business community was much greater than that of Asquith, but it is when the figures are expressed in absolute numbers per year of premiership that the contrast is great-est. On average 29 businessmen and one pressman per year were awarded a peerage, baronetcy or knighthood during Asquith's premiership, whereas under Lloyd George the annual rate was 106 businessmen and 8 pressmen.

Lloyd George often defended the length of his honours lists by referring to the need to reward those who had served during the First World War. In fact only 10 soldiers and sailors became peers during his premiership compared with 26 businessmen, 14 became baronets compared with 130 businessmen and 372 were knighted compared with 481 businessmen. Thus, fewer than 400 soldiers and sailors received major honours in the Lloyd George era compared to rather more than 600 businessmen.

Harold Laski, writing in 1922, looked at the rate at which minor honours, including OBEs, were awarded during the premiership of Asquith and Lloyd George and concluded: 'The average of Mr Asquith for each of the years of his premiership is 640: that of Mr Lloyd George for the first four years of his administration is 3,644 creations annually' (*Nations & Athenaeum*, 15 September 1922). The rate at which Lloyd George distributed the OBE turned the award into a music-hall joke. By the end of his term in office 25,000 of them had been awarded – more than enough for every man, woman and child in his Caernarvon constituency. The honour became disparagingly known in France as 'L'Ordre Britannique Embusque' and in England as the 'Order of the Bad Egg'. The Duke of Northumberland quoted a letter from one honours tout in 1922, who was offering a knighthood for sale: 'not the British Empire, no nonsense of that kind, but the real thing'. The wholesale distribution of awards meant that little or no check was made on the suitability of the recipient for the award and totally bogus citations were attached to the names of the individuals granted them. One batch of OBEs filled sixty quarto pages in the *London Gazette* – nobody could check them all and so the most unlikely names appeared. Richard Williamson, for example, was given the CBE in 1920 for 'his untiring work in connection with various charities'. Most worthy – except that his main claim to fame was as a Glasgow bookmaker with a criminal record.

Honours had been sold to aid party funds for the thirty years preceding the Lloyd George premiership, but the circumstances surrounding his entry to 10 Downing Street made the transaction a more personal affair. In ousting Asquith as Prime Minister, Lloyd George split the Liberal Party and found himself without a secure party base. Support was needed to ensure his own political future, so he set about acquiring it through the establishment of a political fund under his own direct control. That fund was a source of his political strength for years to come and was financed by the sale of honours.

Parliament expressed an early concern at his practices. Within eight months of Lloyd George becoming Prime Minister, the House of Lords debated the sale of honours. A second debate was held three months later, when two resolutions were carried. These sought public statements citing the reason for the award of honours and an assurance that the Prime Minister, before recommending anybody for an honour, should satisfy himself that no payment to party funds was connected with the award of any honour or dignity. In replying to the debate, Lord Curzon, speaking on behalf of the government, specifically undertook that Lloyd George and his colleagues would be bound by the terms.

Following the publication of the next honours list, in New Year

1918, there was a further debate in the Lords in which the Earl of Selborne complained that the reasons given in the *London Gazette* for the award of honours had been too vague.

In August of the same year, *The Times* published a letter signed by twenty-five peers specifically complaining about corrupt practices surrounding the bestowal of honours. In part it read:

> We think it necessary to point out in public the serious danger which may arise from a continual bestowal of honours without real safeguard from abuse ... Our feeling is that unless the bestowal of honours and titles is protected from this sort of cheapening and is unmistakably cleared from the danger of a peculiarly mean kind of pecuniary corruption and reserved for real merit, honours may come to be regarded as dishonours, leaving no way out except their entire abolition.
>
> It is an additional and very grave evil that the money obtained by the disgraceful traffic in honours has gone to swell, and if rumour is true, has mainly constituted, the large party funds which are at the service of party leaders and are used for party purposes.

In November 1918, the Earl of Selborne returned to the subject in the Lords, proposing that a committee of the Privy Council should be established to review the names of people recommended for honours and that their statements about the would-be recipients should be published in the *London Gazette*. The proposal was rejected.

The matter was raised in the Commons six months later in a debate on a Private Member's Motion which sought the publication of details of party funds because of their alleged link with the award of honours. It was left to Conservative Party leader and Coalition Member, Bonar Law, to lie the government's way out of the matter:

> The Prime Minister has made, and will make, no recommendation to His Majesty as a reward for contributions to party funds. I wish now to say, not only do I not know of any such bargain, direct or indirect, but I have asked the whips, and they have told me that there has been no such bargain.

Attempts were made intermittently in Parliament to seek the establishment of a Committee of the Privy Council that would examine and review the names of those to be honoured. The attempts were all rebuffed and it was not until the publication of the Birthday honours list in 1922 that the matter once more assumed widespread public significance. But the close association of honours with party funding continued – both parties in the Coalition benefited from it. The papers of John Davidson, later Chairman of the Conservative Party, give details of 56 men who provided £156,000 for the Conservative election fund in 1929. Seventeen of them received honours from the Lloyd George Coalition government. In many cases it is difficult to see from their entries in *Who's Who* and obituaries what qualities they had that deserved an honour; in all cases, however, they were wealthy men, as a brief survey shows.

Sir Abe Bailey was created a baronet in 1919; he was a Transvaal mineowner and speculator who owned two South African newspapers. Leonard Brassey, a Conservative MP between 1910 and 1920 was a generous donor to party funds and a keen racegoer. He was created a baronet in 1922 and raised to the peerage in 1938. Another racing enthusiast and Tory funder was George Bullough; he was created a baronet in 1916, but his *Who's Who* entry gives no details of any of his activities, public or private.

Robert Waley-Cohen was the first Managing Director of the Shell Transport and Trading Company and received a knighthood in 1920. He was also a Tory Party funder. The present Chairman of Shell, Peter Baxendell, was honoured with a knighthood in 1981.

Leading industrialists from heavy engineering companies who were honoured included Arthur Dawson, Managing Director of Vickers, who received a baronetcy in 1920. He had a penchant for collecting honours, for he also received the Grand Cross of the Order of Naval Merit of Spain together with the Orders of the Rising Sun and the Sacred Treasure of Japan. He became Vice-Principal of the Council of the Imperial Society of Knights Bachelor.

British-American Tobacco Vice-Chairman and Conservative financier, Sir Hugh Cunliffe-Owen, also received a baronetcy in 1920. And in the same year Babcock & Wilcox Chairman and founder, John Dewrance – another Tory Party funder – was knighted. The Babcock funding tradition survives today, as the company continues to give £7,500 a year to the Tory Party. Its present Chairman, Lord King, received his peerage during Mrs Thatcher's premiership in 1983 and is also Chairman of the City and Industrial Liaison Council, a front for Conservative fund-raising based at Conservative Central Office.

Arthur Dorman, creator of Dorman Long, disclosed few other details about himself. He was a Tory funder who was knighted in 1918 and created a baronet in 1923. Part of what Sir Arthur created became subsumed in Redpath Dorman Long, which in turn was taken over by Trafalgar House – a firm that also continues the Tory funding/honours tradition. They presently give £50,000 a year to party funds, and two of their senior directors have received honours during Mrs Thatcher's premiership: Victor Matthews (Chief Executive of the company 1977–83) was created a peer in 1980 and Nigel Broackes, the present Chairman, received a knighthood in June 1984.

Other Conservative backers honoured by Lloyd George in this period included: George Dolby, director of several tea companies, knighted in 1920; William Dupree, brewer and mayor of Portsmouth, created baronet in 1921; William Garthwaite, underwriter and shipowner, created baronet in 1919; Richard Gorton, Deputy Chairman of Watney Combe Reid, a director of Gortons of Battersea and erstwhile Conservative candidate, knighted 1918; and Ernest Jardine, lace-machine builder and President of the Nottinghamshire Football Association, created baronet 1918.

Samuel Ernest Palmer, one of the founders of Huntley & Palmers biscuits and Conservative funder, received his baronetcy in 1916. In 1933 he was elevated to the peerage in what was described as the 'first peerage conferred for services to music'. James Readhead, President of the South Shields Conservative Association and shipbuilder, became a baronet in 1922 and was openly financing the Tory Party some years later. His successor, the third baronet, chooses not to use the title.

Finally, a mention should go to Charles Wakefield, Director of C. C. Wakefield & Co. and an oil company. He was, according to his obituary, a prominent freemason, and seemed to go to considerable lengths to acquire honours, titles, dignities and distinctions. He became successively a knight in 1908, baronet in 1917, baron in 1930 and viscount in 1934. In addition he had picked up the status and handles of Colonel, Alderman of the City of London, Order of the Legion of Honour, Order of the Crown (Belgium), Grand Cross Order of Leopold (Belgium), Knight of Justice of St John of Jerusalem, Order of the Sacred Treasure (Japan), Order of the White Lion (Czechoslovakia) and the Order of St Savia (Serbia). It seems a pity that such an evidently distinguished man did not produce an heir to inherit the honour – when he died in 1941 the line became extinct.

The subscription lists of the Lloyd George fund are not publicly available – it is therefore not possible to provide details of who gave money to it and received honours in exchange – but the correspondence of the Conservative Chief Whip of the time, Sir George Younger, provides some insight into the trade. Younger complained: 'These damned rascals come to me demanding to be made Knights and when I refuse go straight to Lloyd George's whip's office and get what they want from him.' Frederick Mills was a Conservative and Chairman of the Ebbw Vale Steel, Iron and Coal Company who was looking for a seat in Parliament. He was created a baronet in 1921 and Younger wrote to the same Bonar Law who four years previously had strenuously denied that there was any link between donations and honours, that: 'There must be a stop to Freddie [F. E. Guest, Liberal Chief Whip] poaching our men. I haven't a doubt that if I had got Mills a seat, and got him into the House he would have proved a generous annual subscriber, and it was for us and not Freddie to give him something more later on' Tom Cullen, *Maundy Gregory, Purveyor of Honours*, Bodley Head, 1974, p.102). Presumably Mills's donations went to Lloyd George's political funds, although he did eventually become a Tory MP between 1931 and 1945. The present and third baronet, Sir Peter Mills, is a member of the Zimbabwe Civil Service.

The Mills baronetcy was only one example of the increasing recklessness of Lloyd George's approach to honours in his later years in office. Another, in the same year, concerned Rowland Hodge. Hodge was a shipbuilder from the North-East, Chairman of Eltringhams Ltd and the Northumberland Shipbuilding Co. He was subsequently to become a director of the Canning Town Glass Works – a company later associated with Lord Brayley, a man whose own honour in the mid-1970s led to some controversy (see p. 152).

Hodge had sought an honour for some time. He had contacted Maundy Gregory in 1912, when Gregory was starting his touting business, and had secured a flattering profile in his journal of the time, *Mayfair*. (This was one method by which Gregory tried to advance the claims of those for whom he was seeking honours, as will be shown later.) By 1918, Hodge was making overtures to the Conservatives and had offered Winston Churchill £5,000 for a baronetcy. However, Sir George Younger recorded that, 'his over-tures were so brutally frank that I had made up my mind to have nothing to do with him'.

Hodges' endeavours received a second, and what at any other time would have been a terminal, setback in 1918. He was convicted of hoarding food under the Defence of the Realm Act and fined £600 plus costs. He was found guilty of possessing: 1,148 lb flour, 333⅓ lb sugar, 148 lb bacon, 29 lb sago, 19½ lb split peas, 32 lb len-tils, 31 lb rice, 25 tins sardines, 10 jars ox tongue, 19 tins salmon, 85 lb jam and marmalade and 61 tins of preserved fruit. Yet, less than three years later, in the New Year's honours list of 1921, he was made a baronet. Although George V did not know of the conviction, he was still horrified at the choice. In an attempt to restrain Lloyd George's excesses, Lord Stamfordham, the King's secretary, wrote to the Prime Minister: 'the King ... said he perfectly recollected the man [Hodge] as the only individual of a personally unattractive (to say the least of it) character that he met on that tour [of Tynes-ide's shipyards in 1917].'

The elevation provoked comment in the Commons. Henry Page Croft MP, without naming Hodge, asked Lloyd George whether he knew of the conviction and whether he intended doing anything about it. The Prime Minister said that he did know of it but that although Hodge had accepted technical responsibility for it, it was done without his knowledge.

Undeterred by the private rebuffs from Younger and the King and the public challenge from Croft in 1921, Lloyd George pro-ceeded to cause total outrage in the 1922 Birthday honours list. It in-cluded five recommendations for the peerage, the only one of which was not regarded with total horror being that to Lord Borthwick – a custard-powder manufacturer.

The first would-be peer was Sir Joseph Robinson, whose baron-etcy in 1908 was already associated with a donation to Liberal Party funds (see Chapter 2). He had made his fortune from diamonds and speculation in South Africa and in the 1880s had bought land for a total of £26,000 which was later valued at £18 million. In 1911, at the age of seventy-one, he returned to England and sought respect-ability; one method he chose was in purchasing a 'Man of the Day' profile in Maundy Gregory's *Mayfair*. His association with Gregory continued until, in 1922, Gregory offered him a barony for £50,000.

Robinson knocked him down and they settled on the price of £30,000.

Robinson's citation in the *London Gazette* said that he was to be granted his peerage for 'National and Imperial Services' and that he was 'Chairman of the Robinson South African Banking Company'. The banking company, however, had been liquidated in 1905 – seventeen years before – and his 'Imperial Service' had so impressed the Judicial Committee of the Privy Council just seven months previously (in November 1921), that they dismissed his appeal against conviction for fraud and subsequent fine of £500,000 imposed in South Africa. The South African Prime Minister was quick to announce that his government had not been consulted on the award and Lord Buxton, Governor General of South Africa between 1914 and 1920, denounced the recommendation in no uncertain terms:

> I will undertake to say that no single person in the Union, white or black, considered that either by his services or by his record he deserved this honour. When it was announced in the press, so far as I can learn, it was received with universal astonishment and mystification; I will not use a stronger or uglier word.

Such was the public uproar at the announcement that the government felt the need to retract. On 23 June, Robinson was visited in his suite at the Savoy and persuaded to sign a letter, said to have been composed by Lord Birkenhead, the Lord Chancellor, rejecting the offer of the peerage. Robinson was by now almost stone deaf, and when approached with the document he thought it was a demand for more money for his peerage. He agreed to sign it, and it was later read out by Birkenhead in the Lords. It included the sentence, 'I am now an old man to whom honours and dignities are no longer matters of much concern.' Whether he was concerned enough to have reclaimed the £30,000 he paid for his peerage is not recorded.

Obituaries in *The Times* can usually be relied upon to paint the recently deceased in the best possible of lights. With this in mind, the piece on Robinson at the time of his death in 1929 makes interesting reading. He was described as 'Always litigious, never forgot and forgave ... His intense egotism and a sort of rasping intolerance offered no invitation to friendship or sympathy ... His despotic egotism tolerated no partner or equal.' The present and third baronet, Sir Wilfred Robinson, is Financial Officer of the Society of Genealogists, a job which no doubt will give him time to ponder on the merits of his grandfather and the origins of his own title.

The second provocative peerage of the 1922 Birthday list concerned William Vestey, who had been created a baronet by Asquith in 1913. The *London Gazette* citation at the time of the announcement of the peerage stated that he was 'Managing Director of the Union Cold Storage Co. Ltd. He ... rendered immense services during the war to the country, and provided, *gratuitously*, the cold storage accommodation required for war purposes at Havre, Boulogne and Dunkirk.' An alternative version of Vestey's activities would have shown that, as the Secretary of State for War told the House of Commons, he had been *paid* for the cold-storage facilities in Le Havre and Boulogne and that William and his brother Edmund (a donor to Tory funds who received a baronetcy in 1921) had done extremely well out of the war. In 1914 they had food-processing plants in three countries and seven ships in their cold-storage business; by 1918 they had plants in fifteen countries and twelve ships.

In 1915, tax changes introduced in Britain to help pay for the war led the Vesteys to examine schemes of tax avoidance: they moved the company's base first to Chicago and then to Buenos Aires. But when, in 1919, William wrote to Lloyd George seeking personal exemption from UK taxes, the Prime Minister told him to refer his case to the Royal Commissioners on Income Tax. Vestey informed them: 'The present position of affairs suits me admirably. I'm abroad; I pay nothing.' Taking the business abroad meant moving £20 million of meat-packaging plant to Buenos Aires at a cost of £3 million and throwing between 3,000 and 5,000 people out of work in Britain.

Between July 1919 and April 1921 the Vesteys stayed abroad while their tax advisers devised a complex tax-avoidance scheme. George V thought that the Vesteys' attitude was disgraceful and objected officially and bitterly to making William a baron. Lloyd George resisted the protests and is reported to have accepted £20,000 from Vestey for the peerage. In his letter to the King defending the peerage, Lloyd George replied that 'the evidence which he [William Vestey] gave before the Commissioners of Income Tax was not brought to my notice, nor that of my advisers', despite the fact that he had received a long letter from Vestey dated 19 February 1919 summarising his case and that it was he, Lloyd George, who suggested that Vestey took his case to the Commissioners.

The Vestey family had been frugal, but ennoblement led to a splash of opulent behaviour: William bought a gold coronet, Edmund acquired an Italian-style castle on the south coast, and the family engaged a genealogist for forty years, at considerable expense, to trace their ancestry.

The Vestey family's history of tax avoidance and moving business premises to reduce labour costs continued into the 1970s and 1980s, although their relationship with the Royal Family has considerably improved over the last sixty years (in December 1984, Lady Cece Vestey, the second wife of the present Lord Sam Vestey, became a godmother to Prince Henry, second son of Prince Charles, heir to the throne). In 1972, when five dockers were jailed under the provisions of the Industrial Relations Act, it was for the action they took against a company called Midland Cold Storage. The firm was based outside the dock area but, through containerisation, was carrying out work traditionally associated with the docks. Midland Cold Storage was, according to the *Sunday Times*:

> owned, through nominees, by the millionaire Vestey family, dockland employers, who have been firing dockers. And as the Midland depot opened, Vestey's closed another of their Thames-side wharves, throwing dockers out of work.

In 1980 the *Sunday Times* further reported that the Vestey family were still using the tax-avoidance loophole that they had developed in 1921. The Inland Revenue had decided that six members of the family, including the present and 3rd Lord Vestey, were, over a four-year period, liable for income tax on £4.3 million and surtax on £7.3 million. But the Law Lords ruled, as they had done in earlier cases concerning the Vesteys' tax affairs, that the family need not pay a penny of it. In reaching this controversial decision, the Law Lords took the unusual step of overthrowing an earlier decision of their own House, which had stood for thirty-two years.

The third controversial recommendation for the peerage in June 1922 concerned Samuel Waring. He had already been created a baronet during Lloyd George's ministry – in 1919 – but this had aroused no public controversy. He had been Managing Director of

Waring & Gillow, a company which in 1910 underwent capital reconstruction. This meant in practice that the previous shareholders lost all their investment. Subsequently, during the war, Waring made a great deal of money for himself. He was accused in the Commons of having made a fortune out of wartime contracts for military equipment and having abandoned all those shareholders who had lost their money by investing in the old company. He caused a sensation by standing up in the Strangers' Gallery in the Commons and shouting, 'That's a lie.' When Waring died in 1940 the title went with him.

The fourth controversial peerage of 1922 concerned Sir Archibald Williamson, who had already received a baronetcy under Asquith in 1909. He had been a Liberal MP from 1906 until his elevation to the Lords, as Lord Forres, and a partner in the trading firm of Balfour Williamson. Ronald McNeil MP launched into the elevation with gusto in the Commons, claiming that during the war 'the laxity of the firm in dealing with the enemy was notorious – so notorious that the Foreign Office listed 24 charges against the firm'. The matter was referred to the Director of Public Prosecutions and although not actually prosecuted the company had its licences withdrawn for a period. McNeil also claimed that the company sold fuel oil to certain German nitrate factories in 1915 and 1916 at a time when the government was attempting to strangle trade with Germany. Although McNeil retracted some of what he said four days later – accepting that the trading with the enemy had been sanctioned by the government – people seriously questioned what it was that Williamson had done that had led to his elevation. The present and 4th Baron Forres (Eton) lives in Australia where he is a company director.

Such was the furore over the elevations to the peerage in the summer of 1922 that shipowner Sir John Drughorn's award of a baronetcy hardly merited comment. Sir John had been convicted in 1915 of trading with the enemy.

Although the Liberal Party had traditionally acquired the temperance vote and had shown itself hostile to the interests of the drink lobby, Lloyd George saw no problem in spraying honours around the boards of directors of major distillers. In 1920 he awarded a baronetcy to John Stewart who was a partner in Messrs Alexander Stewart, whisky distillers in Dundee; it was granted for unspecified 'public services'. Sir John was sufficiently modest about his public achievements that he chose not to refer to them in his *Who's Who* entries. It has now been fairly well established that he paid Maundy Gregory £50,000 for his baronetcy and that afterwards, when his financial position became precarious, he had the £50,000 repaid to him from the Lloyd George political fund. He soon ended up in the bankruptcy court, and in the course of the proceedings the counsel for the creditors suggested that he had paid £150,000 to Lloyd George's fund. When Sir John died of self-inflicted gun wounds in 1924 his debts amounted to £500,000. His successor, the fourth baronet, Sir James Watson Stewart, manages to combine his directorship of a textile company with membership of the Standing Council of the Baronetage – which ensures that the correct dignity is bestowed upon the heirs of those honoured by the distingushed title.

Stewart was not the only whisky-producer to be honoured by Lloyd George. The Dewars family and the Distillers Company figured prominently in his era. One of the Dewars, Arthur, became a High Court judge and received a peerage, but he died in 1919. His two brothers, Thomas and John, however, both did very well from Liberal patronage and proceeded to the peerage, together with yet another director within their distillery concern.

Thomas Robert Dewar was Managing Director of John Dewar & Co. and a director of both Buchanan–Dewar and the Distillers Company in the early years of the twentieth century. He was also, between 1900 and 1906, a Conservative MP. In admirable fashion, he achieved first a knighthood from Lord Salisbury in 1902 then a baronetcy from Lloyd George in 1917 and two years later a peerage, when he took the title of his recently deceased brother to become Lord Dewar. He spent so much of his time on social advancement that he omitted to get married and so the title died with him in 1930. His brother, John Alexander Dewar, was a Liberal MP for the first few years of the twentieth century and became Chairman of the family distillery, John Dewar & Co. He was created a baronet under Campbell-Bannerman in 1907 and then a peer, taking the title Lord Fortevoit, in 1917. His obituary notice in *The Times* declared that he came to London with his brother Thomas determined to create a demand for Scotch whisky, which at the time was considered inferior to Irish. That he was successful in this cannot be denied; that the temperance supporters of the Liberal Party would have felt that such success deserved ennoblement is a matter for some speculation. The present and 3rd Baron Fortevoit inherited both his father's title and his place on the boards of the Distillers Company and its subsidiary John Dewar & Co.

Yet another man associated with the same company, James Buchanan, had honours bestowed upon him in Lloyd George's time. James was Chairman of James Buchanan & Sons, a firm that at first merged with the Dewar business and then became an integral part of what is now the Distillers Company. James became a baronet in 1920 and was raised to the peerage, becoming Lord Woolavington, in 1922. His *Who's Who* entries and obituary notices do not show him to have been particularly public-spirited. He died without heir in 1935.

If it was pertinent for the *Saturday Review* to ask in 1905, 'What are the claims of the [de Stern] family on the public that within ten years two of its members should be given the right to sit in the House of Lords and vote with the hereditary aristocracy of Great Britain?', was it not equally pertinent to ask seventeen years later what were the claims of three directors of the same group of companies to receive two baronetcies and three peerages within five years? Perhaps the *Saturday Review*'s answer to its own rhetorical question, 'Why have they been made peers? The answer is money,' would have been equally appropriate.

The Distillers Company even today has a fascination for political funding: in the year of the 1983 general election it gave the Conservative Party £50,000. The following year, its former Managing Director, John Carter, received a knighthood.

The Honours (Prevention of Abuses) Act, 1925

The last few pages have provided little more than a glimpse at the lives of some of the recipients of honours under Lloyd George and the characters of the people involved. As has already been suggested, five years of general unease at Lloyd George's practices exploded with the publication of the 1922 Birthday honours: the public manifestation of which were parliamentary debates in June and July of that year. In a Lord's debate on 22 June, Lord Harris attacked the proposed ennoblement of Sir Joseph Robinson; a week later Lord Strachie criticised the Vestey peerage. The major assault, however, was reserved for 17 July, when there were simultaneous debates in the Lords and the Commons.

A blistering onslaught was made by the Duke of Northumberland in the Lords. The Conservative Party, he said, was having a job making ends meet, 'but the Prime Minister's party, insignificant in numbers and absolutely penniless four years ago, has in the course of these four years amassed an enormous party chest, variously estimated at anything between one and two million pounds. The strange thing about it is that it has been acquired during a period when there has been more wholesale distribution of honours than ever before, when less care has been taken with regard to the service and character of the recipients than ever before.' He then referred to documentary evidence in his possession. One of his correspondents had been offered a knighthood by a member of the government for £10,000, which could be paid off in instalments over four years. Another tout, whose letter he quoted in full, said, 'There are only five knighthoods left for the June list. If you decide on a baronetcy you may have to wait for the Retiring List ... which a retiring Prime Minister is allowed to recommend on a change of government. It is not likely that the next government will give so many honours, and this really is an exceptional opportunity, but there is no time to be lost if you wish to take it ... It is unfortunate that governments must have money, but the party in power will have to fight Labour and Socialism, which will be an expensive matter.'

Also on the 17th there was a debate in the Commons. The motion before the House was essentially a repeat of previous demands, that in this particular case a joint Commons/Lords committee should be set up to examine recommendations for future honours. Seconding the motion, Sir Samuel Hoare said that public uneasiness about the system had first been felt in 1905, and in the years that followed some shoddy characters had been honoured. He cited, but did not name, a man who was created a baronet one year and a Privy Councillor the next who was subsequently proved to be trading with the enemy. Then there was a man who was made a knight, when those who recommended him did not even know his Christian name. His citation in the *London Gazette* stated that he was an 'author and writer', whereas his sum contribution to western culture had been in penning a few pop songs. He went on to refer, without naming the people concerned, to those honoured in the Birthday list. The remedy he sought was not an enquiry into the past but a committee to safeguard the future.

Lloyd George's reply to the debate consisted for the most part of a stream of evasion and the adoption of the straw-man tactic, successfully demolishing arguments that had never been put against him. He did, however, finally concede to the demands for the establishment of a Royal Commission – which, although gratefully received by his opponents, has often been used as a means by which embarrassed governments get themselves out of a corner. Royal Commissions have the merit for governments that they are seen to be concerned about a topic without actually *doing* anything about it. Lloyd George reinforced this point of view when he said that he would not be bound in advance by its recommendation, but hoped that it would lay down a machinery that would keep unworthy people off future lists.

Labour's position in the seven-hour debate was put by its Leader, J. R. Clynes, who quoted from a recent speech by Lord Carson, a member of Lloyd George's own government between 1916 and 1921. He had said: 'I have had more than once in my chambers to advise on cases in which I have examined long correspondence which showed that there had been a regular brokerage, however conducted, for the purpose of carrying out and obtaining honours.' The debate was talked out without a division, thereby avoiding an embarrassing conclusion for the Prime Minister. The composition and terms of reference of the Royal Commission were announced by Lloyd George in August. It was to 'advise on the procedure to be adopted in future to assist the Prime Minister in making recommendations to His Majesty of the names of persons deserving special honour'.

However, Lloyd George was to have the last laugh in his honours saga – he resigned from office before the Commission reported and thus his resignation honours list escaped the scrutiny that the Committee was to suggest. The man whose endeavours had led to a scrutiny procedure had, until the very last, resisted external scrutiny of his choice. His resignation list had forty-five names, a number only equalled by Balfour's list of 1905. It was almost twice the length of Asquith's list of 1916, which totalled twenty-four names. Unlike other lists, which are officially published by Buckingham Palace, Lloyd George's final flurry was published by an official of the National Liberal Club. The final ironic twist was the appearance in the list of the name of Lord Farquhar, the Conservative Party Treasurer dismissed by Bonar Law in 1923. It later transpired that he was an undischarged bankrupt who had secretly diverted some of the large sums the Tories had acquired through the honours system into Lloyd George's political fund, most notably a sizeable donation of up to £200,000 given by Lord Astor, of which Conservative Party accountants and auditors were later to find no trace. Lloyd George's final list elevated the noble Lord to an earldom.

The Royal Commission was composed exclusively of members of the two Houses of Parliament and did represent a range of opinions on the subject. Although there was considerable public interest in the intrigue and corruption that had surrounded Lloyd George's lists, the establishment closed ranks on the matter. When the Duke of Devonshire was approached by Lloyd George to sit on the Commission he made it clear that he would be 'willing to serve . . . on the strict understanding that there is no retrospective enquiry into individual cases before giving a final decision'. Suitably assured, the Duke of Devonshire agreed to serve.

The Commissioners began their work in October 1922 and interviewed all living former prime ministers (except Lord Rosebery who was too ill to attend) and a number of Chief Whips and organisers from the two main parties. They also took evidence from the Duke of Northumberland and Lord Selborne, who had been particularly critical of honours bestowed in the House of Lords, and from a number of Civil Servants who described how the departmental system operated.

The Commission concluded its deliberations in early December and published its report at the end of that month. A modern-day media manipulator bearing embarrassing news could not have timed an announcement that he hoped would be lost better – after Christmas and before the New Year began, conveniently placed in a parliamentary recess.

Whether the date was deliberately chosen to minimise adverse publicity or not, everything else about the Commission reveals attempts to conceal from the public the degree to which honours had been sold. Despite the very eminent list of people interviewed by the Committee, its report was only nine pages long. Added to that was a one-and-a-half-page note of dissent from Arthur Henderson, the Labour nominee on the Commission, and a third-of-a-page reply by the rest of the Commission to that. The total cost of the report, including travelling and subsistence expenses and printing was £31 10s – hardly an in-depth investigation.

Even today, over sixty years later, most of the evidence submitted to the Commission has been weeded out by diligent Civil Servants and is not available for public inspection in the Public Records Office. The fragments of evidence that are available do not name names and give the impression that those most responsible for managing the trade in honours in Lloyd George's time sought to draw a discreet veil over their activities. Thus, Freddie Guest, Liberal Party Chief Whip for most of the Lloyd George premiership, who in 1921 had been accused by Tory Party Chairman of 'poaching our men', declared: 'each case was personally scrutinised by myself before submission to the Prime Minister and every effort made by confidential enquiry to verify the merits of the recipients'. He did not mention the sliding scale of fees for honours operated by his office. Neither did Sir George Younger, the man who in 1921 described his fund-raising efforts to Bonar Law: 'I haven't a doubt that if I had got Mills a seat and got him into the House he would have proved a generous annual subscriber, and it was for us and not Freddie to give him something later on.' His evidence reassured the Commission: 'I have therefore exercised the greatest possible care in making independent enquiries on my own account, after we have made a preliminary selection of those thought best entitled to a reward, and I have never submitted a name without satisfying myself by those enquiries that the standing, character and local position of the person recommended are in every way suitable for the class of honour to be bestowed upon him.'

Having provided whitewashed evidence to the Commission in November 1922, Sir George was suitably rewarded with his own peerage two months later. During the Lloyd George Coalition government Sir George, as Conservative Party Chairman, had doubled the party funds from £600,000 to £1,250,000, largely via contributions associated with honours. In a 1927 letter to Stanley Baldwin, Younger attempted to explain his financial successes: 'I never, so to speak, sold an honour, nor did I ever make any bargains', but he 'superintended the collection of . . . the contributions occasionally made by the medium of the Honours List'. The distinction is difficult to appreciate.

The Royal Commission report can be summarised briefly. While accepting that, formally, the bestowal of honours is the responsibility of the monarch, 'the whole true responsibility rests with the Prime Minister' (para 6). The report listed a variety of different types of honours:

- those that are given on what may be termed 'exceptional occasions', which do not often recur – such as coronation honours and honours in connection with a war;
- those that may be termed 'departmental honours', mainly Orders of the Bath given to Civil Servants in Home departments;
- those given in connection with the Foreign Office, fighting services and India office and to people connected with the Dominions;
- those honours given to members of the general public for service or distinction in literature, science and art, using these terms in the broadest sense, and honours given for political service.

As far as the departmental lists were concerned, a limited number were awarded in each list and departmental Permanent Secretaries submitted the names and records of potential recipients to the Prime Minister who selected the final list from the names submitted, with the help of the Permanent Secretary to the Treasury. The Commission found no problem with this procedure. The procedure with the foreign lists was similar, except that the names went to the Prime Minister via the Foreign Secretary. The Commission found no difficulties here, either.

However, bearing in mind the outrage that had accompanied the announcement of a peerage to Sir Joseph Robinson and the controversy surrounding the elevation to the Lords of Max Aitken (see Chapter 4) the Commission did have recommendations to make about the colonial lists. Usually, they noted, potential recipients have their names forwarded to the British Prime Minister by their State premiers,

But there is in addition the case of honours being submitted in respect of Imperial Service by the British Prime Minister without initiative from the overseas government. It would not, we think, be expedient that the power of conferring such honours should be interfered with. But we are strongly of the opinion that before submitting to the King the name of any person who is or has lately been domiciled in any of the overseas dominions, the Prime Minister should communicate his intention to the Secretary of State for the Colonies, who, in his turn, should pass on the name to the Governor-General or Governor concerned for his observations, it being understood that, in the case of a self-governing dominion, he should consult with the Prime Minister... We think it eminently advisable that overseas opinion as to the antecedents of a person whom it is proposed to honour should not entirely be disregarded.

Could this paragraph represent a slight criticism of what was regarded as the most flagrant example of an abuse of the honours system? Did the Commission come close to recognising that there was, indeed, a problem? They almost exceeded their remit with such unguarded comments.

Back to bland reassurances. As far as the awards of honours for the arts, literature and sciences were concerned, 'the selection of an unworthy recipient is, in view of public opinion, unlikely, and in any event is not open to any public abuse'.

Political honours, the Commission noted, have been continuously awarded since the establishment of party government. Nearly all the witnesses, it recorded, said they should continue. Considering who 'nearly all the witnesses' were and how well they had benefited by the manipulation of this particular form of patronage, their thoughts on the matter come as no surprise. Political honours fell into two categories: those awarded to MPs and the others. Those awarded to MPs were recommended by the Chief Whip, and the others by the head of the party organisation, who may also be the Chief Whip. 'We put the question to each Prime Minister in turn, whether he had ever been cognisant of any bargain or promise to the effect that an honour would be contingent on the contribution to party funds. We received the answer we expected, they had not.' Answers to the same effect were given by the patronage secretaries and party managers.

It is not clear whether the Commissioners expected denials from the prime ministers because they believed the prime ministers they saw were inherent liars or because the Commissioners themselves were naive.

The Commission went on to recognise the fact that honours touts existed and that the definition of 'political service' for which honours were awarded was a broad one: 'As to service, some are able to help in one way, such as, for instance, in speaking; some in others such as organisation, and organisation cannot be directed without funds.'

The Commission concluded by making a series of recommendations. A Scrutiny Committee of three Privy Counsellors, with a secretary, should be appointed. The Prime Minister should send the list, with biographical details, to the Committee together with a statement from the patronage secretary (whip) or the party organiser that no payment or expectation of payment to any party or political fund is directly or indirectly associated with the recommendation. The name and address of the original proposer of the honour should accompany the biographical details and statement. The list of names was then to be returned to the Prime Minister with any comments by the Scrutiny Committee. If names were then submitted to the King by the Prime Minister, despite an adverse report, the King was to be made aware of the report. The Commission made it clear that it felt the duty of the Committee, whose establishment it was recommending, was one of scrutiny and not nomination of honours. It also wanted an Act of Parliament to be passed that would outlaw honours-touting.

Finally, the Commission turned to the criticism that Lloyd George had devalued the honours system by the scale of awards issued during his premiership. With typical caution they felt that there should not be a restriction of awards imposed on any future premier but that 'it is, of course, open to any Prime Minister to restrict severely the number of recommendations and we think that this course has much to commend it on many grounds'.

The Commissioners had done the minimum consistent with their brief and proposed a series of mild reforms which ultimately would not change the system: prime ministers could still recommend who on earth they wanted, for whatever reason. The King was simply to be made aware of any misgivings that might be held about potential recipients. Although an Act of Parliament was suggested, the Commissioners made it clear that they regarded such an Act as a deterrent and did not expect many convictions. All the members of the Commission, except Arthur Henderson, the Labour nominee, endorsed the report. Henderson wrote a memorandum of dissent:

> Though the terms of reference were somewhat restricted I am of opinion that the Commission might with advantage have made a much more searching inquiry than they have done. I regret that, though the Commission were in possession of the names of persons who are conveniently and appropriately described as 'touts', none of them were invited to give evidence. Nor was any person who had been approached by 'touts' called to give evidence before us, though the names of such persons were also before the Commission. The omission of evidence from those who are alleged to have asserted that they were in a position to secure honours in return for money payments, and from those who have been approached by such persons, has left unexplored one of the gravest abuses concerning the nominations for honours. Had the investigation been pursued more thoroughly, I have no doubt that the evidence forthcoming would have led the Commission to realize the inadequacy of their recommendations.
>
> The proposals contained in the report of my colleagues would not, if put into operation, be sufficient, in my opinion, to prevent abuses or to allay the suspicion which undoubtedly exists in the public mind on the subject of honours . . .
>
> It cannot be doubted that honours have been conferred upon persons whose chief claim to recognition was party service, and it appears to be implied in the evidence of certain witnesses before the Committee, though it was not so baldly stated, that the financial exigencies of political parties were in themselves almost a sufficient reason for the conferment of political honours. This system whereby financial assistance rendered to a party is recognized by the conferment of an honour by the State is, in my judgement, deplorable, and discredits the honours system. . .
>
> . . . It is indisputable that public service of great value has been rendered by men and women whose thoughts have never dwelt upon titled reward, and in view of the difficulty of keeping the honours list pure, I do not believe that the abolition of political honours would in any way diminish either the volume or quality of the services given to the community by its citizens.

The rest of the Commission replied briefly to Henderson's criticism of their failure to call for witnesses on the touting of honours: 'In view of Mr Henderson's note of dissent, we think it right to state that we did not invite those who had been approached by touts because we were already satisfied that such advances had been made, and the gentlemen approached could tell us no more; and we did not invite the attendance of those who had behaved as touts because that would not have helped us in any way to make suggestions for the future.' They concluded by saying that Henderson's call for the abolition of political honours was both negative and outside their terms of reference.

The anodyne report's recommendations were quickly accepted by the new Prime Minister, Andrew Bonar Law, who, as a gesture of faith in its suggestions, established a scrutiny committee and delayed the publication of the 1923 New Year's honours list until they had a chance to cast their eyes over it. Within weeks Bonar Law moved to patch up the damage Lloyd George had inflicted on the Order of the British Empire. Lloyd George had created the order in 1917, but by the time he left office 25,000 of them had been awarded. Bonar Law amended its terms of reference to restrict the numerical membership of the Order.

Within six months of Lloyd George's departure the harm that he had inflicted on the honours system had been swiftly rectified. A Royal Commission had suggested minor reforms without publicity of previous abuses, the reforms had been accepted and added to, and a new Prime Minister had issued a short and uncontroversial New Year's list. In April 1923 the Honours (Prevention of Abuses) Bill was introduced to the Lords, incorporating the recommendations of the Royal Commission and laying down maximum penalties of a £500 fine and/or two years' imprisonment for attempting either to buy or sell honours. The establishment had thus acted quickly to perform a damage-limitation exercise. A year after the controversial 1922 Birthday honours list it was business as usual. The ruffled feathers were back in place. Except that the awkward subject would not quite go away.

Although the bill outlawing honours-touting had been introduced to Parliament in April 1923, it had not passed through all its stages by the time Baldwin, who had succeeded Bonar Law as Prime Minister in May, resigned in January 1924. The Bill thus fell and had to await reintroduction at a later date, therefore continuing to give attention to a subject that the establishment wanted to be quietly buried.

January 1924 provided further honours controversy when Baldwin's New Year's list was published without definite statements on the reasons for the award of each honour. A year after the publication and acceptance of the Royal Commission's rather tepid report, one of its few recommendations was being flouted. *The Times* was moved to comment that the omission was a bad precedent and particularly unfortunate.

Baldwin's resignation in January and the subsequent general election paved the way for Britain's first, minority, Labour government. There was some interest in how Ramsay MacDonald would deal with the subject of honours: his party was suspicious of them; his party's representative, Arthur Henderson, had called for the abolition of political honours in his note of dissent to the Royal Commission; and as recently as November 1923 Ramsay MacDonald himself had alleged that the Tory Party war chest was filled with gold derived from the sale of honours.

When his first list appeared, MacDonald explained that it was larger than he would have liked because he had inherited some promises given to Civil Servants which he felt obligated to honour. The list was, none the less, shorter than had been published for some time: it contained no peers (although his party was badly outnumbered in the House of Lords), 2 baronets and 13 knights. *The Times* applauded his restraint.

However, the circumstances surrounding the award of one of the two baronetcies was later to provoke considerable press concern and criticism. Alexander Grant was a biscuit manufacturer, Chairman and Managing Director of McVitie & Price. He was also an old friend of Ramsay MacDonald's, his father having worked on the railway with MacDonald's uncle. Wholly sympathetic accounts of MacDonald's relationship with Grant are to be found both in Grant's *Times* obituary (1937) and in David Marquand's long and official biography of Labour's first Prime Minister. According to *The Times*, 'When he [Grant] found that the then Prime Minister, being ill and overworked, was going about by underground railway, he persuaded him to accept a motor car with an endowment of 30,000 shares in McVitie & Price for expenses, the shares to revert to the Grant family if the car was given up.'

That was in February 1924, within a month of MacDonald entering Downing Street. In April 1924, Grant was recommended for a baronetcy 'in recognition of his many philanthropic services'. The baronetcy was awarded in June and on 11 September the *Daily Mail* revealed that MacDonald had acquired 30,000 McVitie & Price shares, making him the second largest shareholder. At the end of 1924, as he left office, MacDonald handed the Daimler and the shares back to Grant – but the damage had been done.

During the December election campaign, Katherine Bruce-Glasier wrote to MacDonald, 'Poor old baronet Grant's motor-car misery . . . is flung in our teeth at every village-green meeting just now' (David Marquand, *Ramsay MacDonald*, Jonathan Cape, 1977, p. 360). *The Times* obituarist of 1937 was clearly not at too many 1924 Labour Party village-green meetings, for he was able to write, 'The gift was connected by certain persons with Sir Alexander Grant's baronetage: the matter was even raised in Parliament, but needless to say the true position was universally felt to be nothing but honourable to both parties.'

It is true that Grant donated an estimated £750,000 to charity during his lifetime and that MacDonald handed back the car and the shares. It is also true that a Prime Minister's salary and expenses in 1924 were not great and that a poor working man may well have had extreme difficulty in managing. It may even be true, as Marquand has suggested, 'that neither he [Grant] nor MacDonald saw any connection between the baronetcy and the £40,000 [total estimated value of the loan]'. But it was, being charitable, the height of absurdity to expect that nobody else should see any connection, a mere two years after the public airing of Lloyd George's honours scandal.

Alexander Grant was a life-long Conservative and his name appears as a subscriber to the party's 1929 election fund. His son, Robert, succeeded him both as a baronet and as Chairman and Managing Director of McVitie & Price – he died without heir in 1947. McVitie & Price has subsequently become part of United Biscuits. That company's present Chairman, Sir Hector Laing, was knighted by a Labour government in 1978 and the firm has averaged a donation of £33,400 to Conservative Party funds over each of the last five years.

Between the Grant–MacDonald arrangements being developed in the early part of 1924 and their public exposure in September came the Parkinson affair – in July. Although the case did not concern the payment of money to party funds in exchange for honours, it did reinforce the widely held view that honours could be bought.

Lt-Col. Parkinson was a North Country industrialist who was prepared to pay for a knighthood. At the suggestion of a third party he went to the College of Ambulance where he met the secretary, Mr Harrison. Harrison told Parkinson that a donation of £20,000 to the College, a registered charity, would secure a knighthood. Parkinson haggled a little and they agreed on a down-payment of £3,000. However, when the knighthood was not forthcoming he pressed for progress and was given a letter of introduction to a Conservative Party whip who assured him that the honour was on its way. He then went to Conservative Central Office and was told that he had been conned by Harrison. Parkinson sued both Harrison and the College for the return of his money and, although the jury found in his favour, the judge ruled that it would be against public policy to allow him to recover his money. He therefore lost both his £3,000 and his knighthood.

While this case was still before the courts, the Sir John Stewart bankruptcy proceedings (referred to on page 67) were heard, in the course of which it emerged that Stewart had paid Maundy Gregory £50,000 for his baronetcy and his creditors suggested he had contributed a total of £150,000 to the Lloyd George political fund.

These two sets of court proceedings led to fresh questioning in the Commons and MacDonald was asked if he would appoint a Commission to enquire into the circumstances of recommendations for honours in recent years. He declined. Two months later the arrangements he had entered into with Grant were published in the *Daily Mail*.

In June 1925 the Honours (Prevention of Abuses) Bill was once more introduced to Parliament; it quickly passed through all its stages and received the Royal Assent in August. It was the same bill as had been introduced two years previously except that the maximum term of imprisonment for summary conviction (i.e. in the magistrates' as opposed to higher courts) was reduced from four months to three months. The maximum penalties were now £50 and/or three months on summary conviction and £500 and/or two years on indictment (higher court).

With the passage of this Act, controversy subsided temporarily. Eighteen months later, however, a Labour MP introduced a bill to Parliament to make it illegal for honours to be given in return for payments to party funds and also requiring political parties to publish periodic statements of their subscriptions. The Conservative government refused parliamentary facilities for the passage of the bill. Shortly afterwards, during an otherwise mundane court case, it was revealed that a North Country shipowner had paid £35,000 to the Lloyd George fund for the baronetcy that had been conferred upon him. In the course of the following eighteen months allegations appeared in the press, and political speeches about the sale of honours were made in Parliament, but the matter began to fade from public view.

Behind-the-scenes offers and payments were still made for honours, however. Robert Rhodes James refers to five cases in the late 1920s of individuals offering J. C. C. Davidson, when Chairman of the Conservative Party, considerable sums of money in exchange for baronetcies and peerages. A. J. P. Taylor in his biography of Beaverbrook says that, in December 1928, Beaverbrook approached Baldwin with the suggestion that Andrew Holt, a Canadian banker, should be knighted for his services to commercial aviation. Baldwin promised to give the matter his 'personal attention' and Beaverbrook made out a cheque for £10,000 to Davidson adding, 'I am sure you know the source of supply. I only scribble this note in case you think that I am the Good Samaritan myself.' Holt's name did not appear in the New Year's honours list or the resignation list that followed the end of the Baldwin government in the summer of 1929. On 12 June Davidson returned the cheque to Beaverbrook with the message, 'I have had no occasion to make use of the money.' It is not known why the transaction was not completed, but Taylor's summary of the events is clear. 'Money was paid. A knighthood was promised. Baldwin's claim to clean hands is hardly redeemed by the fact that the promise was not kept' (*Beaverbrook*, Hamish Hamilton, 1972, p. 258).

This failed transaction was not, however, a matter of public knowledge. Little media attention had been paid to honours scandals from 1927 until 7 February 1933 when the *Daily Sketch* published the dramatic headline 'Honours List Summons Issued'. The story told that a little-known figure called Maundy Gregory was to be charged by the Director of Public Prosecutions under the terms of the Honours (Prevention of Abuses) Act, 1925. Gregory's prosecution was the only one ever to have been made under the Act and the prospect of a trial must have filled a gossip-hungry public and a guilt-ridden establishment with whetted appetites and horror respectively, in equal proportions. Gregory was in fact the honours tout *par excellence* and hastily convened arrangements implicating and benefiting all three main political parties were set in motion to prevent Gregory revealing all. The public was to be disappointed and the establishment spared embarrassment.

Maundy Gregory

The Gregory story, painstakingly researched by two biographers, Gerald Macmillan and Tom Cullen, to whom I am indebted for much of the material in this section, is a fascinating one and bears some telling. It offers an insight into the elaborate and sophisticated art to which honours-touting had been developed, and provides a glimpse of the breadth of its coverage and the scale of finance involved.

Arthur John Peter Michael Maundy Gregory was born in July 1877. The son of a Southampton vicar, he was educated locally and went to Oxford as a non-collegiate student. He left in 1899 without a degree, spent a short period as an assistant master in a prep school in his native Southampton and soon drifted into a career as a professional actor. After a year on the stage, he progressed to managing theatrical companies and playing the part of an actors' agent. Gregory's activities in the decade 1909–19 are not well-documented but he seems to have spent a while pursuing a hotel-detective business in the plusher London establishments. His job was to collect information about guests, particularly overseas guests, whom hoteliers may have thought undesirable to have had on their premises. As a result he collected vast amounts of information on the European aristocracy.

This information opened up two further forms of activity for him, both of which provided ideal training for his future career as an honours tout. First, he went into business with J. C. Keen-Hargreaves and his brother Harry as co-proprietor of a magazine entitled *May-*

fair and Town Topics – the Society Journal. This later changed its name to *Mayfair*, not to be confused with today's soft-porn magazine of the same name. The magazine was essentially window-dressing for a feature article at first entitled 'Man of the Day', and later 'Men of the 20th Century'. Those featured paid between 50 and 500 guineas for wholly flattering profiles of themselves which subsequently circulated in 'Society'. Gregory also wrote 'At the Hotels' which dealt with the mighty and the hotels they stayed at on their travels. From this he later developed his second concern – a credit-rating agency.

Such were his contacts among the European aristocracy that when the First World War broke out he was recruited by MI5 to provide intelligence for the British government. According to the *Empire News* in 1950, Gregory soon put his selling talents to use:

> During the First World War, while acting as an agent for the government in counter-espionage work, Maundy Gregory set up a suite of offices in an hotel in Leicester Square. His business was selling import permits and various other trading facilities. At the same time, Gregory, unknown to his partners, was using a well-known solicitor as an intermediary for selling commissions in the services. Business prospered.

In later life Gregory claimed that Lord Murray of Elibank was the man who introduced him to honours-touting. Murray had been Liberal Chief Whip in 1910 and had had to raise money quickly to fight two general elections. In 1912 Murray was forced to resign the Whip and leave the House of Commons when it was discovered that he had invested £9,000 of Liberal Party funds in Marconi shares, a company that was doing well from a monopoly granted to it by . . . the Liberal government. A select committee was appointed to investigate the Marconi scandal and Murray conveniently slipped away – to Bogotá in Colombia. So short were memories, that by December 1918 Murray was regarded as a respected elder statesman in Britain. After the election of that month, Lloyd George emerged victorious, but he was a man without a party and without the financial or organisational means to sustain him in office. Only 136 of the 484 Coalition MPs were of his own faction. He needed money desperately if he were to survive.

It was at this point that Lord Murray introduced Maundy Gregory to Freddie Guest, Lloyd George's Chief Whip, and therefore patronage secretary, for most of the remaining years of his premiership. Sir Colin Coote, later an editor of the *Daily Telegraph* and an acquaintance of Gregory's, was after many years to describe Guest's relationship to Gregory as that of 'a sportsman [who] employs a retriever . . . to bring the game into the bag'. 'Freddie's only concern,' Gregory told Coote, 'was that he shouldn't get his hands dirty.'

Nine months after Gregory had been introduced to Guest, he reacquainted himself with the world of magazine publishing. The first issue of the *Whitehall Gazette* appeared in August 1919. It was an expensively produced monthly (although by 1931 it had slid to become a bi-monthly) which had all the appearance of an official publication, with its title in prominent displays advertising government stocks, and circulated freely (in both senses of the word) among the gentlemen's clubs of London. Few of its articles were signed, other than with *noms de plume*: 'Carfax', 'Vigilante', 'Sophist', etc. Its content was fiercely anti-Communist and anti-Labour and, in its latter days (in common with much of the rest of the British establishment), pro-Mussolini and pro-Fascist. ('The *Whitehall Gazette* has from the first given its full sympathy and wholehearted support to this emerging movement.' September 1932 edition.) Regular features were published on the Court of St James, the Empire, embassies and foreign affairs and the clubs (in which a club he controlled received outrageously favourable publicity – without the connection or interest being declared).

Two other features, however, stand out and were to provide much of the rationale and certainly the finance for producing the magazine at all. They were entitled, 'British Enterprise' and 'Officials I have Met', and did for the *Whitehall Gazette* what 'Men of the 20th Century' had done for *Mayfair* – they were the excuse for incredibly flattering profiles of individuals, each accompanied by an equally resplendent colour plate of the person concerned. A number of the people featured were figures like the Archbishop of Canterbury, the Assistant Commissioner of the Metropolitan Police, the King, the Prince of Wales and other distinguished British notables. Others were such European dignities as King Alfonso XIII of Spain, King Gustav of Sweden and Prince Peter of Montenegro. A third and sizeable chunk of the entries went to Imperial and non-European dignities – the Maharajah of Burdwan appeared three times and the Governor of Mecca and Prince of Satsuma twice each.

These were, according to Gregory's biographers, persuaded to part with sums of up to £500 in order to be well-advertised among British society.

The fourth category, however, was the interesting one. It consisted of wholly unexceptional British businessmen. Of the 150 or so profiles featured in the thirteen years of the magazine's publication, over a third were of this class. According to Tom Cullen:

> In reality the profiles were a useful means of sounding out prospects whether they would be willing to pay £25,000 to become a baronet, or maybe just £10,000 to become a plain Knight Bachelor. When an industrial or civic magnate approached him unsolicited, with a view to purchasing an honour, Gregory, while assuring the magnate that the matter could be arranged, would suggest a profile in the *Gazette* as a preliminary 'to get your name and face before the people who really matter'. The proof of Gregory's success is the number of people who, profiled originally as plain Mister, made a second appearance in the *Whitehall Gazette* as 'Sir So and So'. (p. 102)

Mr Cullen, delicately, decided not to dwell on the names of those successes. A very brief survey reveals sixteen men who received a knighthood or baronetcy around the same time as a flattering profile in the *Gazette*, or some years later. If Mr Cullen's scale of charges is accepted and these men did pay for their honours, Gregory would have netted £310,000 from these sales alone over a twelve-year period.

Albert Barratt was profiled in September 1921 under the inspiring title 'Development of the Sugar Industry'. He was a director of Barratt & Co., a member of the Sugar Confectionery Board and even within the terms of this flattering description seemed to possess few other qualities. He was knighted in 1927.

Edmund Fleming Buckley was profiled in March 1926, when his chief claim to fame was described as being 'Parliamentary Candidate for Wrexham'. He was never in fact elected. He was also a cotton merchant, which hardly seems justification for his knighthood in 1926.

William Butlin was profiled in August 1921 under the title 'Development in British Iron'. He was Chairman and Managing Director of T. Butlin & Co. Pig Iron for twenty-four years and was knighted in the same year as his profile.

James Calder was an interesting man. He was profiled in February 1921, when he was described as a landowner and distiller (he was Managing Director of James Calder & Co., distillers). At or around this time he must have held discussions with the Dewars and Buchanans (who received 3 peerages and 2 baronetcies from Lloyd George in a five-year period) for he picked up a tip or two. Four months later he received a knighthood and two years after that joined their lordships on the Distillers Co. board of directors.

Edward Mackay Edgar was profiled in February 1920 under the title 'Pioneer Finance'. He was a Moorgate-based merchant banker and financier and received a baronetcy in the year of his profile.

Mayor G. R. Hennessey was an MP who later became a government whip and so may have expected elevation as a result of his parliamentary activities. He was profiled in April 1920 and again in November 1927; he was created a baronet in 1927 and the first Baron Windlesham in 1937.

Joseph Isherwood was a naval architect profiled under the title 'Evolution of Shipping' in July 1921 – he was created a knight in the same year. Erik Ohlson was the Sheriff of Hull and a coal and timber merchant and exporter when his puff appeared in the *Whitehall Gazette* in July 1920 – he received his baronetcy within six months. Similarly John Priestman, a Durham JP and sole proprietor of the shipbuilding firm, J. Priestman Ltd, was honoured and profiled in the same year, 1923. Kynaston Studd, a London City Alderman, was also knighted and profiled in 1923. Arthur Wheeler, a provincial stockbroker, received both a baronetcy and profile in the same year, 1920. The present Lord Whitelaw's uncle, also called William Whitelaw, received two profiles – one in May 1926 as 'Chairman of the London and North-Eastern Railway' and another in April 1929 under the title 'Transport Development' – but received no honour. (Perhaps he fell foul of the Davidson–Bennett device constructed to thwart Gregory – see p. 89.)

Frederick Wise was profiled as the MP for Ilford South (which he had represented since 1920) in November 1922; eighteen months later he received a knighthood. He was profiled for a second time, in the form of an obituary, in January 1928. Three other men received knighthoods between their first and second profiles in the *Whitehall Gazette*; all three honours were bestowed in 1929. Alexander Nairne Stewart Sanderson first appeared in June 1923 under the title

'Industry and Empire' – he was a cotton and jute spinner who later became MP for Middleton and Prestwich. He received a knighthood in 1929 and a second Gregory profile the same July. Walter George Kent was profiled under the title 'British Enterprise' in June 1923. Chairman of George Kent Ltd, the Luton Conservative Association and the Mundakayom Rubber Company, he was knighted in 1929, the same year as he received a second profile under the heading 'The Progress of Inventions'. Finally, George Thomas Broadbridge was flattered under the heading 'An Imperial Romancer' in December 1925. He was Chairman of a group of Nigerian tin-mining companies and was created a knight in 1929, re-emerging in the *Whitehall Gazette* in a second profile under the heading 'Empire Resources'. One other profiled person later elevated was Julien Cahn – about whom, more later (see p. 91).

The *Whitehall Gazette* was only one of Gregory's ploys in the honours-touting business. At about the same time that he established the magazine he set up office at 45 Parliament Street. A year later he moved to number 38, nearer to the hub of the government machine and an impressive enough address to convince his clients of the closeness of his contact. When, a decade later, he moved his home address to 10 Hyde Park Terrace he told his staff to tell those who called at his offices when he was out that he was 'over at number 10'. Similarly he cultivated the acquaintance of a member of the staff at Buckingham Palace, whom he encouraged to telephone the Parliament Street offices when he was entertaining a prospective client. This meant that his interview could be interrupted with a member of his own staff telling him that 'the Palace is on the telephone'.

Gregory cultivated the acquaintance not only of senior members of the Lloyd George Coalition, notably Freddie Guest and Lord Birkenhead (the former F. E. Smith), but also exiled European royalty. He befriended the Montenegrin royal family, King Alfonso XIII of Spain and the kings of Portugal and Greece. He wrote flatteringly of them in the *Whitehall Gazette* and received status and gifts in exchange. All of this enabled him to cultivate an element of patronage from the British Royal Family which manifested itself in his prized possession – an inscribed gold cigarette case, presented to him by the Duke of York (later George VI).

He mixed with and lavishly entertained the mighty in London's gentlemen's clubs, all of which gave him conversation pieces and evidence of his good connections with which to impress those for whom he touted honours business. Eventually, in 1926, he acquired his own club, the Ambassador in Conduit Street, which attracted distinguished visitors including the Prince of Wales (later King Edward VIII). Here he was able to entertain prospective clients and impress them with his contacts.

His greatest coup at the club was to use it to host a significant occasion in the social calendar – the Derby Eve Dinner. Such functions are regularly covered in the society pages of the press, and the June 1931 edition of the *Whitehall Gazette* published a guest list which gave an indication of the significance of the occasion. Among the 167 guests were 2 dukes, 3 earls, 3 marquesses, 3 viscounts, 12 barons and 37 knights or baronets. At least seven of the number were men whose titles were associated with Gregory's puffs in the *Gazette*. Prominent political figures of all parties attended, including Sir Austen Chamberlain, Winston Churchill and J. C. C. Davidson from the Conservative Party, Jimmy Thomas and J. H. Clynes from Labour, and Viscount Elibank and Freddie Guest from the Liberals. Gregory himself sat on the top table of the feast with 21 others. Only 4 of the 22 were untitled – the other 3 were Winston Churchill, Jimmy Thomas and Dudley Ward, the Conservative Whip.

In 1930, shortly before this dinner, Gregory, still flush with the rewards of honours brokerage, indulged his obsession with social status further by his purchase of *Burke's Landed Gentry*. His control of the important social register could provide further evidence to those who required it of his involvement with dignity. The fact that, in the eight years since the fall of Lloyd George, Gregory's activities had expanded to encompass loss-making but prestigious projects like the acquisition of the Ambassador Club and *Burke's Landed Gentry* and that a year later he was hosting such distinguished occasions as the Derby dinner referred to above, is evidence that his trading position was little affected by the departure of Lloyd George. But his days were numbered. The fact that he was still *persona grata* with politicians and nobility alike suggests that, even if the excesses of Lloyd George's peerage sales had ended, there was still money and acceptance to be found as a tout for minor honours.

Fate and Conservative Party unease, however, combined to bring about his downfall a mere eighteen months after his greatest social coup: the 1931 Derby dinner. Although the Conservative Party's finances had benefited greatly from those who had been honoured, J. C. C. Davidson, Party Chairman between 1926 and 1930, ungratefully moved to smash Gregory's honours-touting racket. He persuaded Albert Bennett, a rich Conservative MP and Assistant Treasurer of the party, to befriend Gregory and show that he was well-placed to supply honours. Once accepted by Gregory, Bennett then got the names of his clients and passed them on to Downing Street to ensure that they were not honoured. Since Gregory's trade depended on delivering the goods, he was soon in trouble. Davidson himself continued to befriend Gregory, as his appearance at the 1931 dinner suggests. His diary records:

> Some weeks before an Honours List was about to be published, I used to be asked to lunch at the Ambassadors' Club [*sic*], which was owned by Maundy Gregory, and which he used for those purposes connected with his nefarious occupations... He would discuss the qualifications of his Honours List candidates and I would depart full of expressions of sympathy and of how difficult things were, and having made arrangements that the list of men and the honours for which they were suitable should be conveyed to me secretly by hand... (Robert Rhodes James, *Memoirs of a Conservative: J. C. C. Davidson's Memoirs and Papers 1910–1937*, Weidenfeld & Nicolson, 1969, p. 281)

Gregory's extravagances continued as the source of their funding, honours brokerage, began to dry up, and he was soon to fall financially pressed from an unexpected source: the death of Sir George Watson in July 1930. Watson had been the millionaire owner of the Maypole Dairy and had received a baronetcy in 1912. In 1923 he gave Gregory £30,000 in bonds in the expectation of a peerage. Although no peerage was forthcoming, Gregory managed to string Watson along until his death – finding an excuse twice-yearly for the non-inclusion of his name in honours lists (e.g. in June 1926 the General Strike was blamed: 'The Strike has butted in and caused the entire side-tracking of our collection of names, which was otherwise fully approved.'). But when Watson died in July 1930 his executors tried to redeem the money from Gregory. He held out till the last moment but eventually settled out of court in January 1932 rather than face the publicity consequences of a hearing. He agreed to pay £10,000 immediately with two further instalments of £10,000 six months and twelve months later.

After paying the first £10,000, Gregory was effectively broke: his clubs, magazine, Whitehall offices and expensive lifestyle were all proving a considerable drain on his now meagre resources, and he was also, according to Macmillan, being blackmailed over his homosexuality.

In increasing desperation, Gregory resorted to new ways of making money. According to Tom Cullen, in a period of nine months in 1932, Gregory progressed rapidly through the hierarchy of Roman Catholic honours – Knight Commander of the Equestrian Order of the Holy Sepulchre, Knight Commander of the Most Noble Order of Pius IX, and Grand Cross of the Holy Sepulchre Order – and began to engage in a brisk trade in selling Papal honours himself. He also renewed his acquaintance with a lady theatrical friend, Ethel Rosse, and in the space of four months persuaded her to change her will so that he became the only beneficiary of the £18,000 (£150,000 at today's prices) estate and presided over her death in September 1932. The circumstances of her death and burial brought about enough suspicion to provoke a police inquiry and exhumation the following April. Meanwhile, Gregory had run through Mrs Rosse's £18,000 by November and so once more began desperately to tout his honours business. It was one such clumsy approach – to Lt-Cdr Leake – that led to his court appearance as the only person charged under the terms of the 1925 Honours (Prevention of Abuses) Act, subsequent imprisonment and exile.

Gregory first approached Leake in December, through an intermediary called Moffatt. Why he should have chosen Leake remains a mystery – the man happened to be an associate of Lord Mountbatten and was well-connected enough already. Moffatt impressed Leake with Gregory's contacts, showed him a copy of the Derby Dinner issue of the *Whitehall Gazette* and indicated that a knighthood could be obtained from Gregory for £12,000. Leake went to the police, but kept in touch with Gregory in order to obtain evidence for the prosecution. Gregory was arrested on 4 February 1933 and charged with trafficking in honours. He appeared at Bow Street Court less than two weeks later, having used the twelve-day interval to visit a few former clients – receiving £2,000 from each to ensure his silence in the impending trial.

The case was heard by the Chief Magistrate, Rollo Graham-Campbell (who received a knighthood in the next honours list), the prosecution was conducted by the Attorney General, Sir Thomas Inskip, and the defence was conducted by one of the most eminent criminal barristers of the day, Norman Birkett (later a Lord Justice of Appeal). Gregory pleaded not guilty and sought an adjournment. The case was adjourned for five days; when Gregory returned he had changed his plea to one of guilty. The conspiracy of silence prevailed – no details, no names, no fees were mentioned. Gregory was given two months' imprisonment.

The establishment had two months to finalise arrangements to ensure Gregory's continued silence. Davidson's diaries explained the situation:

> Nobody knew to what extent Maundy Gregory would betray his part in his desperation and financial stringency. We accordingly organised someone to go and see him, who told him that he couldn't avoid a term of imprisonment, but that if he kept silent we could bring pressure to bear on the authorities to let him live in France after his sentence had been served.
>
> When this occurred he was met at the prison gates by a friend of mine who drove him in a motor car to Dover, took him to France, esconced him in previously arranged accommodation, gave him a sum of money and promised him a quarterly pension on condition that he never disclosed his identity or made any reference to the past . . . we kept him until the end. (Rhodes James, p. 288)

Some months after Gregory had left Wormwood Scrubs, Stanley Baldwin approached Prime Minister MacDonald and asked that Sir Julien Cahn should be made a baronet in return for paying Gregory off with £30,000. Cahn was an interesting character and had been an earlier client of Gregory's. In February 1927 he had received a profile in the *Whitehall Gazette* under the heading 'Master of the Hunt'. Gregory was clearly at some trouble to find much of worth to say about Cahn, but the height of his achievement was expressed in a way that later was to have an ironic air to it: 'Mr Cahn has not, until now, participated actively in the political world, but as vice-chairman of the finance committee of the Nottingham Conservative

Association, he has started on the tortuous road of politics, which may lead him who knows where.'

Two years later Cahn was knighted. He himself seemed to have difficulty in justifying his exalted position, for his *Who's Who* entries show him to have controlled the Nottinghamshire Furniture Co., but that his main achievements seem to have been in captaining cricket teams to: Jamaica (1929), Argentina (1930), Denmark and Jutland (1932), Canada, USA and Bermuda (1933), Ceylon and Singapore (1937) and New Zealand (1939). In his useful route through life Sir Julien also picked up the Knight Commander of the Order of George I – an honour bestowed upon him by one more of Gregory's associates, the King of Greece.

Ramsay MacDonald was shocked when Baldwin approached him with the request to further advance Cahn to the baronetcy, as his diary of 13 December 1933 records:

> Baldwin came into the Cabinet Room in the morning and sat down and straight away asked me what I had against Julien Cahn. I said he was one of the honours hunters whom I detested, that his friends and agents had beset me for a long time for a baronetcy for him, that he was not a commendable person . . . B [Baldwin] replied that I must yield and when I asked why he said that Maundy Gregory's papers and Maundy Gregory's presence here would stir up such a filthy sewer as would poison public life . . . that all parties were involved (I corrected him at once and said, 'Not ours'. He smiled and said that unfortunately friends of mine were. I replied that if they were I knew nothing about it. Then I remembered that Clynes and Henderson were mentioned at an earlier stage); that people like Winston Churchill, Austen Chamberlain, Birkenhead were involved; that Gregory had been used by Ll.G and Bonar Law . . . Gregory, as indeed I know, was a blackguard who netted innocent people who did nothing that was irregular or bad, but whose association with those who had, enshrouded them in a cloud. The dunghill had to be cleared away without delay and £30,000 were required to do it. So I *had* to give the honour. (Marquand, p. 795)

MacDonald resisted for six months but his diary on 19 May 1934 noted: 'Mr B . . . involves me in scandal by forcing me to give an honour because a man has paid £30,000 to get Tory headquarters and some Tories living and dead out of a mess.' Sir Julien became Sir Julien Cahn, Bart a month later. His son and heir Sir Albert Jonas

Cahn is an Old Harrovian who describes himself as a marriage-guidance counsellor and a marital and sexual therapist.

Meanwhile, back to Gregory. While he was in prison in March 1933, creditors started proceedings against him to recover their debts – his household goods were seized and sold for £400. He was released from prison on 12 April and went straight to France under the arrangements described by Davidson, and none too soon. Sixteen days later Mrs Rosse's body was exhumed, as foul play had been suspected, but not proved, concerning her death. Four days later bankruptcy proceedings were started against Gregory. One of the creditors, representing the executors of Cardiff shipowner Daniel Radcliffe, claimed that Gregory had taken £12,789 from Radcliffe without fulfilling his obligation. Radcliffe's executors did not get their money back, nor was the Receiver informed of the arrangements Davidson had made to pay Gregory his pension of silence – which continued to the end. He died in Paris on 3 October 1941, aged sixty-four.

Four

The press barons

Journalists and politicians are closely involved in a mutual fascination society: what they have in common is the belief that they can do the other's job better than the incumbent. There is considerable role-switching between the two occupations and the evidence seems to suggest that it doesn't matter too much who does what.

The press has always watched politicians but it was only with the growth, first of the mass electorate in the last decades of the nineteenth century, then the rise of the mass media in the early years of this century, that the fascination became mutual. And, though the first press barons had emerged some years before, it was arch-populist Lloyd George who developed the relationship and, as a man without a party, sprayed honours the length and breadth of Fleet Street in order to gain support for himself and his Coalition. Not content with this, he purchased newspapers with money gained from his peerages trade to amplify his message and became the first British Prime Minister to appoint a Press Secretary with a view to media management.

In the succeeding sixty years, politicians have moved with the changing media times. Successive waves of press owners have been ennobled, prominent journalists have received knighthoods and the news managers and manipulators have gained their own honours. The populism and press consciousness of Lloyd George has only been equalled (or surpassed) this century by Harold Wilson and Margaret Thatcher. The former liberally bestowed honours on press friends and foes alike, particularly those at the *Daily Mirror* (the one true friend Labour had throughout his term of office), and the latter has rewarded not just Fleet Street's Conservative proprietors and editors, but also TV personalities and those who have done so much to promote her image in the world of the new media.

Sir Algernon Borthwick was the start of it all. He was editor and proprietor of the *Morning Post* throughout most of the 1880s and 90s. He was knighted in 1880, received a baronetcy in 1887 and in 1895 became the first newspaper proprietor to enter the House of Lords, as Lord Glenesk. The paper reached its high point under his proprietorship; later it failed to meet the challenge of the popular press that came in the wake of the Northcliffe revolution and was eventually taken over by the *Daily Telegraph* in 1937.

It was the Conservative Lord Salisbury who began the press-baron process with Borthwick's peerage, and his successor, Arthur Balfour, continued it with the ennoblement, in 1903, of Edward Levy Lawson, the principal proprietor of the *Daily Telegraph*, as Lord Burnham. In the same year, Balfour ensured that a baronetcy went to his friend, Alfred Charles Harmsworth, and three years later that this, the greatest press baron of them all, emerged suitably ermine-clad. A somewhat jaundiced view of the new Lord Northcliffe's achievements was provided by the *Saturday Review* when his peerage was announced:

> With equal aversion, though of a somewhat different kind, we regard the peerage conferred upon Sir Alfred Harmsworth, the founder and proprietor of *Answers*, *Comic Cuts*, the *Daily Mail*, *Daily Mirror* and a dozen other newspapers. We say advisedly that he has done more than any man of his generation to pervert and enfeeble the mind of the multitude. By his numerous journals he has catered for their morbid love of the sensational and their vulgar taste for personal gossip, whilst his narrations, such as that of the Peking massacre, have trained them to prefer excitement to truth.

The popular press had arrived, and been recognised for its worth! Northcliffe went on to use his power and influence to great effect, particularly as far as his family was concerned. Francis Williams, in his history of the press, said, 'Not since Napoleon has any man enriched the nobility with so many of his relations as Northcliffe did; by the time he was done, he and Harold [his brother] were viscounts, another brother was a baron and the two youngest were baronets' (*Dangerous Estate*, Longman Green, 1957, p. 138).

His ability to gain honours for his family was simply a reflection on the control he had over the press. At one time he owned *The Times, Observer, Daily Mail, Evening News, Daily Mirror, Weekly Dispatch*, two provincial newspapers and a host of comics and magazines.

The lengths to which honours were bestowed on the most unlikely members of the Harmsworth family can be gauged by the baronetcy that went to his younger brother, Hildebrand, in 1922. Hildebrand's greatest claim to fame was that he was sole proprietor of an almost moribund paper called the *Globe* between 1908 and 1911, when he sold it to Max Aitken. None the less, eleven years later, by which time almost all the other living Harmsworths had been accorded honours, he was made a baronet, 'for public service'. His nephew, Cecil King, later recalled that since Hildebrand had never done a stroke of work in his life, the family responded to the announcement of the honour by inundating him with sarcastic telegrams, along the lines, 'At last a grateful nation gives you your due reward.'

The *Globe*, ditched by Hildebrand in 1911, provides the probable explanation for the knighthood that went to future press tycoon Max Aitken in the same year. The Canadian Max Aitken had won a seat in the House of Commons for the first time, along with forty others, in 1910. In April 1911 he received a call from Conservative Chief Whip, Acland-Hood, offering a knighthood 'for the purposes of rewarding me for services to come and to the Unionist party and not the Canadian party'.

'Services to come,' says Max Aitken's biographer, A. J. P. Taylor, might have meant a substantial donation to Conservative Party funds, but there is no trace of that in the Aitken papers. What it more probably meant was that Aitken was to provide a subsidy to various newspapers supporting the party. The subsidy was in the disguised form of an investment in the company's shares, via a third party. In this instance the vehicle was Sir Alexander Henderson of Glasgow, later to become Lord Faringdon. Through this, and other channels, papers like the *Globe, Observer* and *Pall Mall Gazette* received some of the money from Conservative Party coffers that had been obtained from honours trafficking – sometimes as much as £10,000 a year. The *Globe* was bought from Harmsworth for £40,000, Aitken putting up £15,000 and the party finding the other £25,000.

Aitken received his knighthood in 1911 under the arrangement by which Opposition leaders nominate people for honours in the twice-yearly lists. A year later, Bonar Law was lunching with William Waldorf Astor at the Ritz. Astor had been a heavy subscriber to Conservative Party funds and, under similar arrangements to those that Aitken had with the *Globe*, provided subsidies for papers that proclaimed the Conservative message, notably the *Observer* and the *Pall Mall Gazette*. Bonar Law was aware, too, that Astor was disappointed at not having received a peerage from Balfour and that the Conservative Party's allocation of peerages for 1912 had already been made. However, presumably Bonar Law was able to convince Astor of the party's long-term good intentions in fulfilling the *quid pro quo*, for Astor became a baron four years later in 1916 and a viscount the following year.

Michael Astor is perfectly candid about the origins of the family's viscountcy in his book, *Tribal Feelings* (John Murray, 1964). William Waldorf, Astor relates, had bought the Liberal *Pall Mall Gazette*, and turned it into a Conservative paper. He then bought the *Observer* from Northcliffe in 1911, which he handed over to his son four years later.

> In 1916, William Waldorf was made a peer for political and public services, an ambiguous phrase which is still employed in the bestowal of honours. What this phrase often means, and what in this case it meant, was that the gentlemen to be ennobled had contributed handsomely both to philanthropic causes and more particularly to the political funds of the party in power. William Waldorf had qualified on both these scores. There was plenty of precedence for purchasing a title. It had been done before and was to be done again many times. William Waldorf, without showing any marked propensities for public service, acquired two titles. He was made a baron one year and a viscount the next. (p. 19)

Thus, even before Lloyd George became Prime Minister, the press-baron habit had begun with men being offered or promised honours in return for financing a 'kept' press. As with his other manipulations of the honours lists, Lloyd George simply changed gear and rapidly built on established practice.

Towards the end of his six years in office, the Duke of Northumberland explained to the Lords just how generous Lloyd George had been to the press:

It is also remarkable how papers which have opposed the government, and then turn round and support them, are immediately rewarded with honours for their proprietors and editors. These things may of course be only coincidences, but still they are very curious. And yet can you really, when we go on to think about it, call them coincidences when we find forty-nine Privy Councillors, Peers, Baronets and Knights created since 1918, all of whom are either proprietors, principal shareholders, editors, managing directors or chairmen of groups of newspapers? This figure does not include a multiple of others who have been made Companions of Honour, C.M.G.s and the like, nor does it include certain gentlemen who have been similarly honoured and who without having this connection with the Press, have very obligingly provided the money to purchase a newspaper or a group of newspapers.

It subsequently transpired that the Duke underestimated the degree of Lloyd George's patronage of the press.

The first peerage announced by Lloyd George was to a newspaper man – Sir Max Aitken – who, after buying into the *Globe* in 1911, soon got the newspaper bug and acquired part of the share capital of the *Daily Express* in 1913, taking active control of it at the end of the First World War. According to Robert Blake, biographer of Andrew Bonar Law, 'seldom has the offer of a peerage caused more furore'.

Aitken's name was submitted to George V for a peerage in December 1916. The King replied that he did not 'see his way' to approve the peerage since he did not consider that 'the public services of Sir Max Aitken called for such special recognition'. Bonar Law had to tell the King that refusal would cause much embarrassment, since the title had already been offered and arrangements were under way to hold a by-election in Aitken's Lancashire parliamentary seat. The King gave way, but asked to be informally consulted in future before approaches about peerages were made – a point studiously ignored by Lloyd George in the succeeding years.

Lord Beaverbrook took his seat in the Lords in February 1917, introduced by two sponsors: Lord St Audries and Lord Rothermere. The former, as Sir Alexander Acland-Hood, had given him his first introduction to journalism by persuading him to invest in the *Globe*, and the latter became his adviser and rival when he embarked wholeheartedly on his career as a press tycoon.

If Lloyd George's premiership started off with a bang as far as press-baron creation was concerned, it raised itself to a crescendo by the end of 1922 when he left Downing Street. The full list bears some repetition here simply to give an indication of the comprehensive nature of his ennoblements (Table 6).

There were fifty-seven names on that list and, though it may not have been exhaustive, this is considerably more than the number that the Duke of Northumberland had been outraged at in the 1922 House of Lords debate and exceeds the number Harold Laski found when he did his head count and categorisation of honours for the *Nation & Athenaeum* magazine in 1922.

One name that isn't there is the Marquis of Bute, and in many ways the circumstances of his joining the Order of the Thistle in 1922 summarises Lloyd George's attitude to honours and the press. He had seen the power of the press under Northcliffe and in 1918 used £1.6 million from the political fund he had raised from the sale of honours in the business community to purchase the *Daily Chronicle*. Two men played a key part in that purchase: long-time Liberal MP Henry Dalziel, whom Lloyd George created a baronet in 1918 and a baron in 1920; and Charles Sykes, who was knighted in 1918. Henry Dalziel acted as chairman of the company after the acquisition, but the Marquis of Bute remained a large shareholder. On the day Conservative MPs were plotting Lloyd George's downfall at the Carlton Club in October 1922, Lloyd George received a letter from the Marquis saying that he was getting alarmed at the financial position of the company and felt that the time was right to replace the chairman (Dalziel) with 'some capable businessman'. Whether as a kindness to a backer in his newspaper company, or as a means of shutting him up, Lloyd George responded by offering the Marquis, who had almost everything, the one last gift in his possession. And the day he left Downing Street, he wrote to the Marquis: 'I had the honour to recommend your name to His Majesty for the vacant Thistle [i.e. membership of the Order of the Thistle] and he was graciously pleased to accept my recommendation. It is a pleasure to do that as my last act of premiership.' An honours-bestower to the end, Lloyd George's period at Number 10 began and ended with patronage to the controllers of the press.

However, there were, in the interim years, one or two not uncontroversial appointments and elevations. Lloyd George managed to

Table 6
Lloyd George's Press Honours, 1916–22

Viscounts

Baron Astor	Proprietor *Pall Mall Gazette* and *Observer*
Baron Burnham	Proprietor *Daily Telegraph*
Baron Northcliffe	Proprietor *The Times, Daily Mail, Daily Mirror, Evening News, Weekly Dispatch*, plus provincial papers, comics and magazines
Baron Rothermere	Proprietor *Sunday Pictorial, Daily Mirror* (acquired from brother, Baron Northcliffe)

Barons

Sir Max Aitken	Part-proprietor *Daily Express*
Sir H. J. Dalziel	Chief proprietor *Daily Chronicle, Pall Mall Gazette* and *Globe*
Sir Hugh Graham	Founder and proprietor *Montreal Evening Star*
Sir George Riddell	Proprietor *News of the World, Western Mail* and Vice-Chairman Newspaper Proprietors' Association
Sir Edward Russell	Editor *Liverpool Post*

Privy Councillors

Major Sir Henry Norman	'Several years London journalism'

Baronets

Gervase Beckett	Part-proprietor *Yorkshire Post*
W. E. Berry	Editor and part-proprietor *Sunday Times*
Davison Dalziel	Sometime proprietor *Evening Standard* and Dalziel's newsagency
Rt Hon. Sir H. J. Dalziel	Managing Director Reynolds Newspapers in 1918 (see above)
Hildebrand Harmsworth	One-time proprietor *Globe*
Edward Hulton	Bought *Evening Standard* 1915
E. T. Madge	Managing Director *People*
Sir George Riddell	Proprietor *News of the World* etc. (see above, created baronet 1918, baron 1920)
Sir A. Sutherland	Proprietor *Newcastle Evening Chronicle, Weekly Chronicle, Northern Mail* and *Sporting Mail*
G. A. Sutton	Chairman Amalgamated Press
Sir Charles Sykes	Shareholder *Daily Chronicle*

Companion of Honour

Sir John Ellerman	*The Times*
Mr Philip Kerr	*Daily Chronicle*
Sir W. R. Nicoll	Editor *British Weekly*

Knights

J. Coode Adams	Secretary *Pall Mall Gazette*
T. J. Bennett	Former editor *Times of India*
Henry Brittan	Ubiquitous journalist
R. Bruce	Editor *Glasgow Herald*
Andrew Caird	Manager *Daily Mail*
W. Emsley Carr	Editor and part-proprietor *News of the World*, Vice-Chairman *Western Mail*
David Davies	Proprietor *North Wales Times*
William Davies	Editor *Western Daily Mail*
David Duncan	Senior proprietor *South Wales Daily News* and President of Southern Federation of Newspaper Owners
Mr Fenwick	New Zealand Press Association
Cpt Malcolm Fraser	Formerly editorial staff *Evening Standard*, latterly Conservative Central Office
Philip Gibbs	*Daily Chronicle*
Charles Hyde	*Birmingham Post* and *Birmingham Mail*
Charles James Jackson	*News of the World*
Joseph John Jarvis	Director *Financial News*
A. G. Jeans	Editor *Liverpool Post*
L. R. Jones	Managing Director Reuters Newsagency
J. M. Le Sage	Editor *Daily Telegraph*
Sidney Low	One-time editor and special correspondent *St James's Gazette*
David Hughes Morgan	Chairman *Western Mail*
Maitland Park	*The Times*
J. C. Percy	Proprietor *Irish Motor News*
Percival Phillips	*Daily Express*
J. J. Radcliffe	Proprietor *Liverpool Courier* and *Liverpool Express*
Stanley Reed	*Times of India*
A. F. Robins	London correspondent *Birmingham Post*
Dr S. S. Spriggs	Editor *Lancet*
Arthur Spurgeon	Managing Director Cassell & Co. and member of Institute of Journalists
Alderman C. W. Starmer	Director of North of England Newspapers (including *Northern Echo* and *Northern Evening Dispatch*)
A. F. Stevenson	Director *Southport Visitor*, *Oldham Daily Standard* and *Preston Herald*
Campbell Stuart	General Director *The Times*
Charles Sykes	Acquired *Daily Chronicle* for Coalition
Arthur Willett	Formerly Washington correspondent *The Times*
D. Williams	Editor *British Medical Journal*

annoy the King in three successive honours lists with his recommendations for elevation to and within the peerage. In April 1918, following the resignation of Lord Rothermere as Secretary of State for Air, Lloyd George asked the King to agree to his promotion from baron to viscount. Explained thus, the request seems not unreasonable, but the reply of the King's secretary, Lord Stamfordham, makes the suggestion appear ludicrous:

> The King hopes you will not raise the question of Lord Rothermere's promotion in the peerage. The newly constituted Air Force, of which he was minister, had only been in existence twenty-four days when he resigned. Rightly or wrongly, his administration has been sharply criticised, and it is to be discussed in both Houses of Parliament. He has only just been made a Privy Councillor which, in itself, is a high distinction. (Rose, p. 247)

The proposal to promote Rothermere after twenty-four controversial days as a minister makes the 1911 attempt to gain a knighthood for Max Aitken after only six months in the Commons appear reason itself!

However, the Coalition was not to be shrugged off so lightly. A year later, Bonar Law repeated the request for a promotion in the ranks of the peerage for Rothermere:

> I earnestly hope that this recommendation will be allowed to go through. I must point out to you that, while I fully realise the difficulties raised in your letter, the Prime Minister undertook, at the time of Lord Rothermere's resignation, that he would support this recommendation to the King, and the Prime Minister, I think, would personally be placed in a very unpleasant position if His Majesty could not see his way to accept the recommendation. Although some criticism may be passed upon the success, or otherwise, of his short administration at the Air Ministry, his intense loyalty and assistance to the government during the later and critical days of the war, and also at the General Election, have considerably increased the obligation due to him. (Rose, p. 248)

The cat was out of the bag: Rothermere was being recommended for the propaganda support his papers offered the government at the end of the war and immediately afterwards. It is interesting that it still had to be dressed up in terms of his twenty-four-day stint at the

Air Ministry. They had spent fifteen times as long discussing the merits of his ministry than the ministry itself had lasted.

The 1919 New Year honours list was published four months late, on 29 April, and Rothermere's elevation was announced. Stamford-ham had explained to Bonar Law,

> His Majesty gives his approval, but with much reluctance. He cannot help thinking that it would have been better if the Prime Minister had not given an undertaking to Lord Rothermere at the time of his resig-nation that he would be recommended to the King for promotion. This is another case of a quasi promise and, what is worse, a quasi committal of His Majesty.

The next rebuttal to the King came barely six weeks later, in the Birthday honours list. Sir Edward Russell, editor of the *Liverpool Daily Post*, was to be elevated to the peerage. He was, however, eighty-five and the King objected to the ennoblement of one so old. The appointment went through and the new Lord Russell of Liverpool lasted eight months before dying and passing the title on to his son.

George Riddell had done well out of the Liberal Party. He was the owner of the *News of the World*, Arthur Pearson Ltd, the *Western Mail* and *Country Life* magazine. He received a knighthood from Asquith in 1909, a baronetcy from Lloyd George in 1918 and a peerage in 1920. The King had at first objected to the ennoblement, feeling perhaps that Sir George's attribution would have been better splashed across the *News of the World* than the red-leather benches of the Lords, for he had recently been found the guilty party in a divorce case. Regal morality, however, came second to appeasing the press, and the elevation of the first divorcee to the peerage occurred. The title died in 1934.

Such regal discontent was not uncommon – some of the great press barons of the century received their knighthoods, baronies and viscountcies against the better wishes of the King and leading aristocrats. The press naturally, was reluctant to criticise this whole-sale trafficking in honours, although the *National Review* was able to remind its readers in 1922 of Kipling's words – that to escape distinction in this company was indeed distinction.

The *National Review*'s summary of Lloyd George's achievements was, however, an overstatement of the case when in January 1922 it reported,

But on the whole Mr. Lloyd George has been extraordinarily successful in organising a mighty propaganda machine which will grind out whatever he wants, which is prepared to swear, as we have lately seen, that black is white and white is black, as Downing Street wishes.

The following month it returned to the theme: 'The boundless admiration of the press for our Prime Minister is only equalled by his enthusiasm for the press as registered in successive honours lists.'

But Lloyd George's luck deserted him – he didn't in fact manipulate the press to the end. By 1922, Northcliffe, Rothermere and Beaverbrook were all against him and even Riddell switched sides by the close of the year.

The press had learned to play the politicians at their game, for baubles. As the Conservative Party was considering withdrawing from the Coalition towards the end of 1922, Rothermere intervened. According to Robert Blake, in his biography of Bonar Law,

> Rothermere's son Esmond was an MP and Bonar Law intended to offer him a minor post in the Government. But Rothermere had higher ideas than this. He called on Bonar Law and demanded, as the price of his newspapers' support, an earldom and Cabinet office for his son. (*The Unknown Prime Minister*, Eyre & Spottiswoode, 1955, p. 472)

In the event, Bonar Law recorded the incident, called Rothermere's bluff, and threatened to publish the exchange if support was not forthcoming. Rothermere backed down.

Lloyd George's attempts at manipulating the egos of the press barons was not, however, the only way he sought a good press. He was also the father of modern methods of news management. Having acquired the *Daily Chronicle* in 1918 and awarded one barony, a baronetcy, the Order of the Thistle and two knighthoods to those connected with it, he ensured that his case was well-presented in its columns by the appointment of his former Press Secretary Mr Philip Kerr who, according to the *National Review*, 'having wearied of his mischievous activities in Downing Street now misdirects public opinion in the *Daily Chronicle*'.

Among Lloyd George's other techniques were arranging to have his cronies planted in various national newspapers and using Sir William Sutherland as an early disinformation man. Sir William

would be used as a go-between for the parliamentary lobby correspondents. He would invent damaging stories about Lloyd George's
opponents, on lobby terms (i.e. anonymously and unattributed) and
sit back and watch as the press published them as authentic information. Succeeding generations of politicians have learned much
from this early maestro of media manipulation.

If Lloyd George was the first British Prime Minister to fully appreciate the power of the popular press – by showering its principals
with honours, buying into it and adopting a variety of techniques to
influence its content – his experiences were not forgotten by his successors in Downing Street. Although this book is not the place for a
formal history of the press, a snapshot of the patterns of ownership
at the outbreak of the Second World War shows the degree of
patronage bestowed on the controllers of daily papers by subsequent
governments.

A 'who's who' of the press, published in 1939, identified eight
major national newspaper groups, seven of whom had boards of
directors or controllers honoured within the last couple of decades,
specifically for their influential positions in publishing companies.
The Beaverbrook Group, which published the *Daily Express*,
Sunday Express and *Evening Standard*, was actively and personally
controlled by Lord Beaverbrook (see above) with his son, the Hon.
Max Aitken, as general manager of the *Sunday Express*.

The Camrose Group published the *Financial Times* and the *Daily
Telegraph* and was run by Lord Camrose, another of the twentieth-
century newspaper giants. He was born William Berry in 1879 and
was the second of three sons, all of whom were ennobled (Viscount
Kemsley and Lord Buckland were his brothers). In 1915, he bought
the *Sunday Times*, which he edited for twenty-two years, and in
1919 the *Financial Times*. In 1924 he founded Allied Newspapers
(later Kemsley Newspapers) with Sir Edward Iliffe (knighted 1922)
to take over the Hulton Paper Group, which included the *Daily Dispatch* and *Sunday Chronicle*, from Lord Rothermere. By 1928 they
had also acquired the Amalgamated Press from the executors of
Lord Northcliffe, plus the *Daily Sketch*, *Western Mail* and *South
Wales Echo*. In 1927, they bought the *Daily Telegraph* from the 2nd
Lord Burnham, son of the second member of the press-barons club.
In 1929, by which time the group controlled twenty-six daily and
Sunday newspapers, Berry himself got his peerage to emerge as

Lord Camrose. In 1937, in the dog-eat-dog world of publicity, their rapidly expanding group devoured the *Morning Post*, incorporating it into the *Daily Telegraph*, thereby absorbing the product of the father of the press-barons club, the 1st Lord Glenesk.

In the same year, the Camrose (baron 1929) – Iliffe (baron 1933) – Kemsley (baron 1936) triumvirate split. All three had acquired peerages over the preceding seven years and in the process had consumed the products of three of the earliest of Fleet Street's Lords in this incestuous/cannibalistic publishing world. (Camrose took with him the *Daily Telegraph*, *Financial Times* and the Amalgamated Press, and was later to receive further honours. He was promoted to the viscountcy in 1941 and died in 1954 when both his title and influence over the *Daily Telegraph* were passed on to his eldest son. His younger son, Michael Berry, took over the reins at Amalgamated Press, but following its sale in 1959 reverted to the *Telegraph*. His position as Chairman and Editor-in-Chief of that Conservative paper was rewarded with a peerage (to become Lord Hartwell) by the then Prime Minister, Harold Wilson, in 1968.)

A third newspaper group identified in 1939 was Odhams, which published the *Daily Herald*, *People*, *Sporting Life* and *John Bull*. The key and central figure in this group was Julius Salter Elias. He had started his newspaper life by acquiring *John Bull* when its founder, Horatio Bottomley, had been sent to prison for fraud. He had also been instrumental in preserving the *Daily Herald*, a paper founded in 1912 and taken over by the Labour Party in 1923, at a time when the direct ownership of newspapers by political parties was commonplace. It experienced financial difficulties and Elias constructed an ownership arrangement in 1929 that gave Odhams 51 per cent of the shares and the TUC 49 per cent. Elias was rewarded with a peerage in 1937, and elevated to the viscountcy in January 1946, four months before his death without heir.

Another major group was Kemsley Newspapers. John Gomer Berry joined his brother William to found Allied Newspapers in 1924 (see above) and shared in the growth, acquisition and power that that partnership brought with it until its dissolution in 1937. In the process, he had acquired a baronetcy in 1928 and a barony in 1936 to become Lord Kemsley. By 1939, his share of the division, now renamed Kemsley Newspapers, accounted for the *Daily Sketch, Daily Dispatch, Sporting Chronicle, Sunday Graphic, Sunday*

Chronicle, Sunday Times (of which he remained Editor-in-Chief until 1954) and fifteen regional papers. Lord Kemsley was clearly a man of distinction, for in addition to his baronetcy and barony he was to become a Knight of St John in 1944, a viscount in 1945 and a GBE in 1959. The five British honours were topped by recognition from abroad in the form of the officership of the Legion of Honour (France), Grand Cross of George I (Greece) and the Commander Order of the Crown of Belgium before his death in 1968.

The next, and much smaller, company listed in 1939 was the Provincial Newspaper Group, controlling four regional newspapers. It had as two of its directors Sir Herbert Brent Grotrian, Chairman of the Argus Press, who received a baronetcy in 1934, and Sir Harry E. Brittan, KBE (1918), CMG (1924). Then there was the Rothermere Group – very much the rump of the great empire built up by Lords Northcliffe and Rothermere. Although the first Lord Rothermere, Harold, was still living, he had almost killed off the *Daily Mail* in the 1930s with his pro-Fascist anti-Semitic ramblings; control of the group had effectively switched to his son, the Hon. Esmond, who was left with the *Daily Mail, Sunday Dispatch, Evening News* and ten regional papers.

The seventh group mentioned in the report was the Westminster Press, which controlled 4 regional morning papers, 9 regional evenings, 1 Sunday and 30 weeklies. Its board included Earl Rosebery (a Scottish earldom dating back to 1703) plus Lady Denham (whose husband had been elevated to the peerage in 1937) and Viscount Cowdray (a generous donor to Liberal Party funds, who was created first a baron in 1910 then a viscount seven years later). Cowdray is estimated to have pumped £750,000 in subsidies into the loss-making Liberal paper, the *Westminster Gazette.*

Lord Camrose himself, in a pamphlet, identified other controllers and owners of London newspapers in 1939. There was first *The Times*, owned by Northcliffe until his death and subsequently purchased by Colonel the Hon. John Jacob Astor in 1922. Although he was the youngest son of Viscount Astor (created 1916) and brother of the owner of the *Observer*, John Jacob had to wait rather a long time for his own ennoblement – until 1956, when he became Lord Astor of Hever. He remained proprietor of *The Times* for the following decade and died in 1971.

The *News Chronicle* was the single most important newspaper whose controllers were not honoured or were not families of the peerage – and there is no little irony in this fact, since it was formed in 1930 from the merger of the *Daily News* and the *Daily Chronicle* (proprietor Lloyd George). The new company was three-quarters owned by the Cadbury family (which also controlled the London evening paper, the *Star*) whose Quaker origins would not welcome the social distinction created by elevation to the peerage.

The *Daily Mirror* and *Sunday Pictorial* of the day were formally independent of each other, although both had substantial holdings of the other's shares as well as a relatively widely distributed share-ownership. Lord Rothermere, who had controlled the papers until 1931, severed his connections with them, but his nephew, Cecil Harmsworth King, remained a significant shareholder and a direc-tor of both. Although controller of a number of major newspapers and a member of a much-elevated family, Cecil Harmsworth King remains to this day 'Mister'. Such are the stories about the press and the peerage that Andrew Roth was able to recount the tale of how King was offered a low-rank life peerage by Harold Wilson, but rejected it, allegedly insisting on a life earldom to reflect his emi-nence in comparison with Viscounts Northcliffe and Rothermere. Harold Wilson did not feel able to offer this. (The previous award of a life earldom, two centuries earlier, had gone to a mistress who served both George I and his father.)

The *News of the World* was founded in 1841 and changed hands in 1891 so that it came to be owned by a syndicate. By the 1930s its two largest shareholders, one of whom was also its editor, were two well-honoured Lloyd George beneficiaries, Lord Riddell (baronetcy 1918, barony 1920) and Sir Emsley Carr (knighthood 1918). The *Observer* of 1939 was still owned by Viscount Astor (see above, barony 1916, viscountcy 1917).

Outside of Fleet Street there was Edward Mauger Iliffe, the third member of the trio that had built up Allied Newspapers. His share of the spoils on the group's division in 1937 was Kelly's Directories, the *Birmingham Post* and *Mail*, the *Coventry Evening Telegraph* and the *Cambridge Daily News*. He went on to develop interests in the City, but not before he had raced through the ranks of honour, becoming successively a CBE in 1918, a knight in 1918, a baron in 1933 and a GBE in 1946. Just for good measure, he had also been declared an Officer of the Legion of Honour and a Knight of the Order of St John.

As this brief survey shows, newspaper magnates continued to have honours bestowed on them up to the Second World War and well beyond. Postwar Conservative prime ministers continued to dispense patronage at a steady rate but, being blessed with a naturally Conservative press and, for the most part, being slightly aloof from the hurly burly of Fleet Street's games, they did not feel the need to ingratiate themselves with the controllers of the press to such an extent. Perhaps this explains why the owner of the 'top people's paper' did not receive his peerage until 1956, and the *Telegraph*'s controller had to await Harold Wilson's premiership for his honour. Although Harold Macmillan tended to shower baubles on his own backbenchers at a much faster rate than he did the media, he was not unaware of the significance of getting a good press. He rewarded his Minister of Information, Lord Hill, with a life peerage in 1963 and, most unusually, his Downing Street Press Secretary, Harold Evans, with a baronetcy when he left office.

It was the arrival of Harold Wilson as Prime Minister, however, that saw the return of profuse patronage in Fleet Street. The man who always had an eye on the front page of newspapers was not slow in rewarding those responsible for producing them – particularly if there was a chance that they might support the Labour Party. The Canadian Roy Thomson, a latter-day Beaverbrook, came to Britain and bought newspapers and was the first on the Wilson press-baron list, receiving a peerage in 1964. (Two years later he acquired *The Times*. Wilson clearly felt this in itself merited further attention, for Lord Thomson was further honoured by the Labour leader in 1970 with a GBE.) Also in 1964, Charles Edward Leatherland, who had toiled so long at the Labour Party's greatest national daily ally, the *Daily Herald*, received his peerage. Eighteen months later, Jock Campbell, chairman of the company that produces the *New Statesman* – the only 'heavy' weekly of the political Left – was ennobled.

Towards the end of his first years in Downing Street, Wilson filled a missing gap in the Berry family by creating William, proprietor of the distinctly un-Labour *Daily Telegraph*, Lord Hartwell. Six months later another publication generally anti-Labour, the *Economist*, had its editor, then Chairman, Sir Geoffrey Crowther, ennobled.

The last of the six press barons to be created during Harold Wilson's first premiership was John Beavan, political adviser to the *Daily Mirror* from 1962 to 1976. He emerged as Lord Ardwick and was the symbol of a remarkable affinity that Harold Wilson developed with the *Daily Mirror* and its controllers. By now the *Mirror* was the only friend in Fleet Street that Labour could consistently hope to have. In Wilson's eight years as Prime Minister, four people associated with the *Mirror* received peerages, one a knighthood and lesser honours were bestowed on five more – a ratio of reward per person only surpassed in recent years by Mrs Thatcher's patronage of her back bench, ideologues and financial backers. John Beavan was ennobled in 1970, Ted Castle (one-time assistant editor of the paper) in 1974, and Sidney Jacobson and Don Ryder (both directors of IPC, the *Mirror*'s then holding company) in the following two years. William Connor, the *Mirror*'s famous 'Cassandra' columnist, received his knighthood in 1964, while agony aunt Marjorie Proops received an OBE in 1969. In the last six months of Harold Wilson's first period in Downing Street Donald Zec and James Beecroft of the *Mirror* received an OBE and an MBE respectively. Wilson's second premiership lasted only two years – but it was long enough for the three *Mirror*-related ennoblements already referred to, together with an OBE for Emily Bell (IPC) and a CBE for the paper's sports editor, Peter Wilson.

However, Harold Wilson's honouring of the press did not end with the *Mirror*. He conferred knighthoods on Fleet Street at an average rate of almost two a year throughout the period of his premiership, compared with a rate of less than one a year by his prime ministerial successors, Edward Heath, James Callaghan and Margaret Thatcher. A knighthood-a-year difference does not sound much, but when added to his bestowal of peerages on the press (10 in 8 years) he dished out 24 senior honours to the press in 8 years, compared with 3 in 4 years by Edward Heath, 2 in 3 years by Jim Callaghan and 8 in 6 years by Margaret Thatcher. Had he been as frugal as any of his three successors, up to 20 newspaper men receiving honours from him would not have received the knighthood or peerage they did.

The Wilson press knights included: William Connor (*Mirror*), Geoffrey Sandford Cox (ITN), Leslie Newton (*Financial Times*), Neville Cardus (*Guardian*), Trevor Evans (*Daily Express*), Alexander Jean (*Liverpool Daily Post*), George Pope (for newspaper management), William Richardson (*Sunday Citizen* and *Reynolds News*), Thomas Blackburn (Beaverbrook Newspapers), Osbert Lancaster

(*Daily Express*), Denis Hamilton (*The Times*), Francis Boyd (*Guardian*) and Henry Boyne (*Telegraph*) – who also received a CBE in January 1969.

In their book *Sources Close to the Prime Minister* (Macmillan, 1984), Cockerill, Hennessy and Walker refer to the then Mr Wilson's relationship with the then Henry Boyne. Put simply, the Prime Minister used the journalist to communicate with his Cabinet, via the newspaper's front page. For example, whilst attending the Commonwealth Prime Ministers' Conference in Jamaica in 1975, Harold Wilson summoned Boyne, the *Telegraph*'s lobby correspondent, and told him that he was intending to demote Tony Benn in the Cabinet hierarchy. 'Mr Wilson gave me permission to write a story about it, which I duly did,' reports Boyne (p. 127). Mr Benn was subsequently demoted and six months later Mr Boyne was given a knighthood.

Wilson did not only award knighthoods and peerages to supporters in Fleet Street. Like his predecessors and successors he was a generous dispenser of the minor honours. One of the standing advisory committees that recommends honours to the Main Honours Committee is exclusively concerned with newspapers and periodicals. In Harold Wilson's time, it regularly succeeded in getting fourteen of its nominees per year on the honours list. Edward Heath was very much less generous to the press – the awards dropped to eight per year – but the Wilson level was re-established in his second stay in Downing Street, and this was maintained by both James Callaghan and Margaret Thatcher.

Harold Wilson was followed at Number 10 by Jim Callaghan, a man who was extremely frugal in dispensing patronage generally, and did not give a knighthood or peerage to a single active journalist or proprietor. He was caring enough, however, to appreciate the importance of the Mirror Group to Labour's cause, and he honoured its employees at a rate unequalled by his treatment of any other newspaper group – six minor honours in three years. Hence an MBE went to *Mirror* caricaturist Ralph Sallon in January 1977, followed by MBEs to the paper's chief photographer, Frederick Reed, in January 1978, and to John Calder, a journalist on the *Mirror*'s sister paper, the Scottish *Daily Record*. A year later, OBEs went to sports writer Frank Taylor and to the deputy chairman of the IPC Business Press. Callaghan's final nod in the direction of the Mirror Group came with the CBE that went to the chairman of the *Daily Record* in June 1979.

Many of those appearing on the press list are journalists on the point of retirement or people who have written for many years on such relatively 'unpolitical' areas as agriculture, and so the claim that such honours are apolitical would appear to have considerable force. But a look at the honours distributed to those working on national newspapers in the decade 1974–84 – half Labour administration, half Conservative – shows a pattern of honours distribution that reflects, to some degree, the political slant of the papers (albeit that there have been changes in editorial direction in some papers over that period). The *Daily Mirror* and associates, for example, had 14 of their staff honoured during the decade, 11 by Labour and 3 by the Conservatives; at the other extreme the *Daily Mail* had 4 honoured – all by the Conservatives. The figures as far as other Fleet Street daily groups are concerned are: Press Association (Labour 4, Conservatives 0); *Guardian* (Labour 4, Conservatives 1); *The Times* and *Sunday Times* (Labour 4, Conservatives 2 . . . the times are a-changing); *Telegraph* (Labour 2, Conservatives 2); *Financial Times* (Labour 2, Conservatives 2); ITN/ITV/IBA (Labour 3, Conservatives 4); BBC (Labour 1, Conservatives 2); *Sun, News of the World* (Labour 1, Conservatives 2); Express Newspapers (Labour 3, Conservatives 5). There are sometimes problems of identifying which papers certain beneficiaries write for, but the above figures are those positively associated with the respective papers. Others may have been honoured, but it is not clear from their citations which paper they work for.

A number of interesting facts seem to emerge from all this. First, although journalists only account for a tiny percentage of the working population – less than a quarter of one per cent – they do consistently well in the honours game. Second, as with other areas of honours awards, the white-collar scribblers in the newspaper world do well – their blue-collar colleagues who operate the presses hardly get a look in. Third, there is a very broad and general relationship between the pro-Conservative nature of a news medium and the rate at which it has received honours from Mrs Thatcher, the converse is less so because of the lack of a wide number of pro-Labour papers. Fourth, Mrs Thatcher has moved with the media times – her appreciation of the IBA and BBC, compared with her two Labour predecessors, suggests an awareness of their importance even greater than that of Harold Wilson, generally regarded as a man with an eye for the media. It was Mrs Thatcher, indeed, who first gave knighthoods to TV news and current affairs presenters Robin Day (January 1981) and Alastair Burnet (January 1984).

The non-Fleet Street press has also done well from the honours system – the daily regional press has received honours at the rate of two per year over the last decade. The correlation between a paper's politics and the receipt of honours is nowhere near as marked as on Fleet Street, but the *Yorkshire Post* (5 honours over the decade), *Western Morning News* (3), *Belfast Telegraph* (2) and *Birmingham Evening Post* (2) have done well enough out of the system to know that honours are not one-off rewards that come out of the blue, but a regular event that can be expected by those who scribble for long enough on the nation's news sheets.

Local papers too receive their awards – the Journalism Committee distributes about three awards per year to local papers. But they exemplify, in a civilian context, the armed-forces formula for the distribution of honours. Local journalists outnumber national journalists by a factor of ten and yet receive rather fewer rewards, and those that they do receive are overwhelmingly MBEs – over two-thirds of awards traced going to local papers are of this lowest of honours, and none of the newspaper knights created over the period are from the locals.

The lesser fry of the profession are also not overlooked in the annual deliberations, for almost every year there is a token representative from the ranks of editors of obscure journals. January 1965, for example, saw an MBE for the editor of *Red Tape*, a Civil Service trade-union journal. And MBEs also went to the editor of *Adam International Review* (June 1966), the editor of *Outposts* (January 1978), the editor of the *British Dental Journal* (January 1979), the editor and Managing Director of *Bulldog* magazine (January 1982) and the editor of the *Guinea-Pig Club Magazine* (June 1982). All very worthy, and all in their places as Members of the British Empire.

The message from the press lists is that if you want fame and honour, get on to the *Mirror* and wait for another Labour government. No doubt Robert Maxwell's intention as the proprietor of Mirror Group Newspapers is different. I wrote and asked him about his ambitions in the honours stakes, but he did not reply. Neither did his arch-rival and other unhonoured newspaper 'baron', Rupert Murdoch, of *The Times, Sunday Times, News of the World* and *Sun*. However, he is the son of an Australian knight and has recently accepted the Companion Order of Australia. (Murdoch is widely and often reported to have turned down a UK honour from prime ministers of both political parties.)*

At the national level, journalists are more likely to be honoured by the party to which their paper's editorial line leans. At regional and local level, impending retirement is a definite plus for potential recipients.

Another trend is for premiers to adorn the names of their image-makers. Following Lloyd George and Macmillan's examples more recent prime ministers have rewarded their press secretaries and information ministers. Harold Wilson gave a knighthood to his Press Secretary, Trevor Lloyd-Hughes, in his first administration and offered one to Joe Haines, who performed the role in his latter days at Downing Street. George Wigg, Wilson's early Minister of Information, was ennobled. Edward Heath gave his Press Secretary, Donald Maitland, a knighthood towards the end of his period as Prime Minister and Jim Callaghan gave his Press Secretary, Tom McCaffry, a knighthood in his resignation list.

Margaret Thatcher's appreciation of the importance of modern media is not limited to the knighthoods conferred on Robin Day and Alastair Burnet and the patronage of the Saatchi and Saatchi advertising agency. Bernard Ingham, the present Number 10 Press Secretary, is as yet unadorned, but two other men in the Prime Minister's entourage responsible for her press image have received their due rewards. Her chief speech-writer is Ronald Miller, who has written for her since she became Party Leader and has taught her how to lower and project her voice. It was he who prompted her to quote St Francis of Assisi when she first entered Downing Street with words that must ring hollow in many places today,

> Where there is discord may we bring harmony,
> Where there is error may we bring truth,
> Where there is doubt may we bring faith,
> Where there is despair may we bring hope.

* Mr Murdoch has recently become an American citizen, so would now be ineligible for a British honour.

Having scaled new heights of political absurdity with this ironic message, Ronald picked up his knighthood the following year and later excelled himself by writing the campaign song for Mrs Thatcher in the 1983 election.

The Thatcher image-maker and projectionist *par excellence*, however, has been Christopher Lawson whose pre-Downing Street career illustrates the vacuous nature of modern political packaging. The admen do for Conservative politicians in the 1980s what newspapers have done for much of the rest of the century. Lawson became the Conservative Party's Marketing Director in 1982, having spent a working lifetime promoting pre-packaged foods and soap products for Mars Ltd, with a brief to 'advise on a more appealing presentational approach of the government's privatisation policies'. He soon brought another man on board with a feel for modern policies – Stephen Prendergast, whose previous experience included marketing Petal toilet rolls and Brown & Polson blancmange.

Soon after Lawson's appointment as image-maker, the London *Standard* commented, 'If Mr Lawson succeeds in selling Mrs Thatcher to an unwilling electorate, it will be an advertising triumph that would make selling ice-cubes to Eskimos like kids' stuff.' When comparing the differences between selling Mars bars and politicians, Mr Lawson had this to say: 'I think there is a slight difference . . . but apart from having less say about what goes into the product I think it's more or less the same. It's communication. It's getting the message across.'

Christopher Lawson was knighted in 1984, almost 100 years after a knighthood went to Britain's first newspaper baron. The first Fleet Street Lord entered the Upper House in 1895. Will the modern image-projectors and promoters – the admen – have to wait eleven more years for lordly recognition?

Five

Labour and the trade-union barons

When Len Murray's peerage was announced in the 1985 New Year's honours list, his public reaction to it summed up the ambivalence that trade-union and Labour movement leaders have to the honours system in general and the House of Lords in particular. Yes, he was honoured to receive it, and like all good Academy Award winners he was anxious to show that his peerage was a symbolic recognition of the work of many others, in this case the trade-union movement. But then there came the defensive side: he was expecting abuse, but he said he'd been called so many names in the past he didn't think any more new ones could be dreamed up. And, although he was a believer in a secondary chamber, 'I would be very happy to participate in voting a hereditary chamber out of existence', he said.

In almost every section of society, the craving for honours is only matched by the pride that is expressed when the gongs come along. Whether it's the Civil Service or show-business, the Health Service or big business, the voluntary sector or the football field that is honoured, gratitude and pleasure are universally expressed at the awards bestowed. The trade-union and Labour movement is the sole, rather large exception. Honours are accepted warmly privately, but apologetically publicly. Acrimony and accusations of collusion, class collaboration, selling out the workers and worse, greet every announcement of honours given to trade unionists. The trade-union movement has, however, been well-accommodated into the honours system. The establishment has been able to smother leading trade unionists with flattery and take some of the sting out of the formal threat that trade unions pose to its social and economic power. TUC General Secretary Norman Willis can expect to follow his predecessors Len Murray, Vic Feather and Walter Citrine into the Lords; a peerage is there for the taking on his retirement, unless he, like George Woodcock (General Secretary 1960–69), declines the offer.

Similarly the recently retired David Basnett, General Secretary of Britain's third largest union, the General, Municipal and Boilermakers' Union, can expect to follow his predecessor Jack Cooper and his erstwhile big-union contemporaries Frank Chapple and Joe Gormley into the Lords. Hinting at his expectations on retirement, Terry Duffy, President of Britain's second-largest union, the AUEW, said this of the peerages bestowed on Messrs Chapple and Murray in January 1985: 'I have never been opposed to the Lords. My two predecessors [Bill Carron and Hugh Scanlon] went there. It is a powerful body and the trade-union movement should be represented.' Other large union bosses to have found their way into the House of Lords over the past couple of decades have included Alf Allen, ex-Secretary of the shop-workers' union, USDAW, and Ted Hill of the boilermakers.

There are two major ennoblement omissions from the trade-union big league, one reflecting the inability of the establishment to come to terms with changes in trade-union structures and practices, the other to do with the integrity of the general secretaries of a major union.

No ex-general secretary of a major white-collar or predominantly public-sector union has been ennobled for almost two decades. Britain's fourth-, fifth- and sixth-largest unions – the National and Local Government Officers' Association, the National Union of Public Employees and the Association of Scientific, Technical and Managerial Staffs – have yet to see one of their general secretaries enter the Lords, although a general secretary of the almost miniscule Amalgamated Weavers Association, Lewis Tatham Wright, was elevated to become Lord Wright of Ashton-under-Lyme in 1968. The dearth of honours for white-collar unions generally is considered in more detail later in this chapter.

Britain's largest union, the Transport and General, has dominated the trade-union movement since its formation more than sixty years ago, and its former general secretaries – by a combination of the weight their union has given them and the force of their own personalities – have called the tune in Labour politics for much of that period. Two of its ex-general secretaries were thought important enough to be plucked from their trade-union roles and put directly into the Cabinet (Ernest Bevin in 1940, and Frank Cousins in 1964) and a third (Jack Jones) is widely regarded as architect of much of the industrial-relations legislation of the last Labour government. Moss Evans, now retired as the sixth General Secretary of the TGWU, will probably continue the honourable tradition of that union in declining to grace the House of Lords. Not a single one of his predecessors has gone there: Ernest Bevin, Arthur Deakin, Arthur Tuffin, Frank Cousins, and Jack Jones have each in their own way contributed much to British society, but nothing to the House of Lords. The tradition of the TGWU is a silent testimony to the adage that honours are for the second-rate. Bevin, Deakin, Cousins and Jones have not needed a peerage to distinguish them from their fellows, their achievements have done that. Also, the fact that the union, which because of its size has consistently been the largest trade-union funder of the Labour Party, has not had a single one of its officials elevated to the highest positions in the honours league in itself suggests that the money-equals-baubles formula that appears to have influenced the British system on other occasions does not affect the Labour Party to the same extent.

If the attitude of trade-union general secretaries to the House of Lords has been confused, some accepting membership, others declining, it is no more than the agony that has afflicted the Labour movement throughout this century on the subject of honours and the peerage. Labour has formally been in favour of the abolition of the House of Lords for much of the period since 1908 and yet, although victorious at eight subsequent general elections, it has failed to introduce a bill to abolish the House. The Labour Party in Parliament has done less to restrict the powers of the Lords, or reform it, than either the Liberal or Conservative parties. Labour's only significant statutory alteration of the powers of the Lords was to amend the Liberal Parliament Act, in 1949, to reduce the delaying powers of the Lords from two years to one. It was a Liberal government that introduced major legislation restricting the Lords' powers in the first place, in 1911, and a Conservative government whose 1958 Life Peerages Act affected the composition of the Lords most dramatically.

The Labour and trade-union movement, at a rank-and-file and conference level has been scornful of the Lords and the honours system, but at a leadership level has been happy to accept most of what the system offers. A brief survey of the divergence of theory and practice for seventy-seven years would seem in order.

At the 1908 Labour Party conference, Mr W. C. Robinson of the Textile Workers' Union moved the following resolution:

The Upper House being an irresponsible part of the Legislature and of necessity representative of interests opposed to the general well-being, is a hindrance to national progress and ought to be abolished.

The resolution was carried unanimously.

Two general elections were fought in 1910 and the role of the House of Lords was central each time. Labour's manifesto in both the January and December elections was unambiguous. In bold letters it proclaimed 'The Lords Must Go'. Labour policy was reiterated at its 1910 conference when a motion was amended to include the sentence: 'Further, this conference reaffirms its previous decisions in favour of the abolition of the House of Lords.' The amendment, which was accepted and passed, was moved by Will Thorne MP, one-time general secretary of the gasworkers' union which formed the basis of what was later to become the General, Municipal and Boilermakers' Union. In his speech he made it clear that his amendment had originated from a conference resolution passed by his union. Whether John Cooper was aware of the gasworkers' resolution of 1908 when he, as successor general secretary, took his life peerage in 1966, is not clear.

Labour's 1918 conference is a significant milestone in the history of the party, for it was then that the basis of its present constitution was adopted. Among the other business decided was a resolution on the nation's constitution which included the sentence: 'This conference calls for the abolition of the House of Lords without replacement of any second chamber.' That, too, was agreed to.

By 1922 there was evidence of some backsliding on the question by the Labour Party leadership. The election manifesto had no ringing calls for the abolition of the Lords, but simply a rather cautious phrase, 'there must be no restoration of the Lords' veto'.

1924 saw the first Labour government, but it had no overall Commons majority and lasted less than a year, so the opportunity was not there, even had the will been, to abolish or reform either the House of Lords or the honours system. Ramsay MacDonald faced more pressing problems, but as has already been seen with the case of Alexander Grant, he was not able to avoid honours controversy during his first spell in Downing Street.

In 1927 the Conservative government announced its intention to reform the House of Lords. The National Executive Committee of the Labour Party, in conjunction with the General Council of the Trades Union Congress, responded by passing a resolution which was 'of the opinion that the House of Commons should be the supreme authority in all matters of national legislation and finance, and that the hereditary Upper Chamber should be abolished'. That resolution went to the 1927 Labour Party conference where it was carried out. Seconding the motion was Lord Arnold. To rapturous applause he ended his speech:

> The House of Lords would never give the Labour Party a fair chance, because the House of Lords was blind to the signs of the times: it was callous, selfish, cynical, inconsistent, unscrupulous and utterly reactionary.

Sydney Arnold in many ways exemplified Ramsay MacDonald's approach to the Lords. Constitutionally, he was required to have two secretaries of state and two under-secretaries in the Lords, so when he became Prime Minister in 1924 he needed people to fill the jobs. His criteria for elevation were that the recipient should support Labour and be without male heirs, so that the title would not transfer. Sydney Arnold had been a Liberal MP with some ministerial experience when he changed parties and joined Labour in 1922, and he had no son. MacDonald ennobled him in 1924 and used him in both his Labour governments, as Under-Secretary for the Colonies in 1924 and Paymaster General 1929–31.

Labour was back in government, albeit without a parliamentary majority, in 1929. Sidney Webb became the first long-standing socialist stalwart to enter the House of Lords. MacDonald needed ministers in the Lords and, within a few days of moving into Number 10, offered office and a peerage to Webb. As a socialist intellectual, without heir, he was an ideal candidate. According to one biographer, Webb's elevation was distinctly distasteful to him, and he attached so little importance to it that he let his Private Secretary decide his title – Lord Passfield. He told Walter Citrine, General Secretary of the TUC, that he accepted the peerage just as he accepted court dress, 'because it was necessary for the work of the government'. He was unimpressed with the pomp and regalia, as have been later ennobled members of the Labour Party, and became the first peer created not to have a coat of arms.

The following year, MacDonald was still looking to strengthen the Labour benches in the Lords, and approached Walter Citrine and TGWU General Secretary, Ernest Bevin. Bevin consulted his executive committee before turning down the offer – Citrine simply rejected it. MacDonald then told the two of them that a trade-union official had approached him, offering his services for the House of Lords. This un-named man was described by Citrine as 'of excellent character and reputation'. The problem was, however, that he had a son who was an agricultural labourer. Although the bastard son of a domestic servant himself, MacDonald had due regard for propriety. He told Citrine and Bevin, 'I could see it was impossible because when this man died his son would succeed to the peerage, and the position of an agricultural labourer as peer would be impossible' (Lord Citrine, *Men and Work*, Hutchinson, 1964, p. 312).

1931 saw the Labour Party split in two in Parliament, but also provided further evidence of the theory and practice division within the party on the question of the Lords. The question of abolition was so uncontroversial that a resolution was moved and passed without debate at the party conference that year. It was very specific on what action was to be taken:

> This conference demands the speedy abolition of the House of Lords, affirms its belief in the efficacy of a House of Commons single-chamber government, and instructs the National Executive Committee to place the abolition of the House of Lords in the forefront of the Labour programme at the next general election.

The 1931 election manifesto, however, was less than wholehearted in accommodating this resolution; it simply said that the party would 'tolerate no opposition from the House of Lords'.

One man who had been very close politically to Ramsay MacDonald was his former Chancellor of the Exchequer, Philip Snowden.

As early as March 1931, before the break-up of the Labour government and the formation under MacDonald of the National government, Sidney Webb visited an unwell Snowden and gained the impression that he would soon be dispatched to the Lords. According to Snowden's biographer, Colin Cross,

> That Snowden should go to the House of Lords would have been a thoroughly agreeable arrangement. MacDonald, as Labour's prime minister, would confer peerages only on men who lacked male heirs and he continually complained at the lack of qualified candidates in the Labour Party. The childless Snowden would have made an admirable Labour peer. (*Philip Snowden*, Barrie & Rockliffe, 1966, p. 269)

In the event, Snowden joined MacDonald in deserting Labour, but did not stand in the general election of October that year. (MacDonald emerged from that election with a massive parliamentary majority but with even fewer National Labour supporters in the Lords than he had had before deserting the Labour Party.) Snowden became the first well-known, self-proclaimed socialist to be ennobled. He entered the Lords as Viscount Snowden of Ickornshaw, named after the small village of his birth, and became Lord Privy Seal in the Coalition government. Churchill called the peerage 'the surrender value of his socialist policy'. According to Colin Cross, 'The transformation of "Philip" into "Lord Snowden" largely destroyed the influence he had held for over 40 years over working people of the North of England.'

It is customary that when a new peer is introduced into the House of Lords there is an audience of the new peer's political friends, but only one Labour MP came to watch Snowden's elevation and the occasion was boycotted altogether by the few Labour peers that there were. The extremity of this reaction had as much to do with Snowden's desertion of the Labour Party as with his ennoblement, of course, but the autobiography of Harry Snell, who had gone to the Lords earlier the same year as a Labour peer, gives a flavour of the reaction that ennoblement provoked among Labour supporters. Snell had been a Labour MP from 1922 to 1931 and was elevated to the Lords to hold one of the constitutionally required ministerial portfolios there, as Under-Secretary at the India Office, in 1931. He recalled in his autobiography,

Attendance at Labour meetings became for the first time an unpleasant experience, and on more than one occasion I was cut, or snubbed, by my old associates, regardless of the fact I had gone to the Lords not for personal reasons, but to satisfy the party as well as constitutional requirements. (Quoted in Cross, p. 322)

Labour was badly defeated in the 1931 election and, shorn of its old right-wing leadership, was back in the business of committing itself to abolition of the Lords. The 1932 party conference unanimously passed a resolution which 'affirms its opinion that the House of Lords must be abolished as being dangerous and unnecessary'. At the Hastings conference the following year, Sir Stafford Cripps (who received his knighthood in 1930 along with his law-officer post in the government) also called on the next Labour government to abolish the House of Lords, and the 1935 election manifesto was firmer on the position than it had been for a quarter of a century, stating that, 'Labour seeks ... power to abolish the House of Lords'. Labour recovered electorally from the disaster of 1931 but still had only a quarter of the seats in the House of Commons, and so was in no position to deliver the goods at this time.

Prior to this, however, honours controversy had raged in the trade-union movement. Walter Citrine was given a knighthood in the 1935 Birthday honours, having rejected a peerage in 1930 and a knighthood in 1933, when he had told Labour government leader and former railwaymens' union official, Jimmy Thomas,

I felt a title would be embarrassing to me. The only thing I could possibly accept would be the Privy Council. There are two reasons for that, first that I do not value honours as such – although I deeply appreciate the thought – and that there was a precedent, three trade unionists were made Privy Councillors in the First World War. (Citrine, p. 313)

Two years later, however, Ramsay MacDonald had been looking for potential knights – he had offered one to Bevin who had rejected it because 'it might create a barrier between me and the men', and one to both Citrine and Arthur Pugh, Secretary of the Iron and Steel Trades Confederation. The latter two accepted. Coincidentally, they had been respectively Secretary and Chairman of the TUC in 1926 – the year of the General Strike.

Citrine recalls the reaction in his autobiography,

> By the weekend a few chastening articles had appeared. One in the *New Leader* [Independent Labour Party weekly paper] contained a vicious attack on me by Miss Jenny Lee, the wife of Aneurin Bevan. She seemed to believe that I had been rewarded by the capitalist class for services in selling the workers.

She may well have been right – but how then was she to explain her own elevation to the peerage (as Baroness Lee of Asheridge of the City of Westminster) thirty-five years later?

The National Union of Clerks at their annual conference passed a resolution aimed at Citrine and Pugh, without naming them, deprecating the acceptance of honours by trade-union leaders and stating that they tended to bring discredit on the whole trade-union movement. Citrine noted, 'I had received, as chief official of the movement, congratulatory letters from people occupying responsible positions in the community and leaders of all the political parties (except the Labour Party).' The fact that the failure of the Labour Party to congratulate the General Secretary of the TUC on an honour only merits a mention in parenthesis is evidence of the distance that separated the man from the party to which the movement he headed owed its allegiance.

A resolution to the 1935 TUC conference was tabled in the name of the Women Clerks and Secretaries' Union which stated, 'This congress regrets that active leaders of the Trade Union Movement should accept honours at the hands of a government which is not established in the interests of the workers.' It was passed by 237 to 125 votes. The motion was moved in a stirring speech by Anne Godwin, who said:

> I want to put it to Congress that the objection we have to honours must arise not from the miscellaneous collection of letters that people put behind their names, but more particularly to the class of honours which carries with it the assumption that the recipient has passed out of the ranks of the working class, that he has gone, in some subtle way, up the social scale and away from the workers as a whole . . . It is a regrettable thing that those leaders should turn aside and play with the glittering toys of the present system, that they should have anything to do with the

outworn symbols of a system which we recognise to be obsolete. We are wasting the goodwill, the faith and the trust of the workers of the movement if we continue to accept honours on these lines.

Anne Godwin received the Order of the British Empire in 1952; as if to confirm she had not made a mistake in accepting this, she became a DBE, Dame Anne Godwin, a decade later.

The kernel of the objection to Citrine's knighthood by the Labour movement was put, later in the debate, by Mr Jack Staines of the train-drivers' union:

> I will go so far as to say that the leaders of our movement are justified in the acceptance of distinctions, they are justified in the acceptance of honours, but only such honours as were bestowed on the early pioneers of our movement like John Brown, Bob Smillie, Keir Hardie, Tom Mann and Ben Tillett – the love and appreciation of that body of men whose lives had been sweated out and whose own lives had been a living Gethsemane because of the suffering of humanity . . . The path our leader has just taken is a path which leads up to a coronet and it is a far cry from a crown of thorns to a coronet.

Citrine replied that he couldn't find any previous TUC or Labour Party decision on honours and therefore felt that the question of acceptance was a personal matter. He then adopted the Oscar-winning approach, 'The people who ought to be honoured are the General Council as a whole and not me', and ended his speech in distress, ' . . . it is desperately hard to speak. I cannot think cogently because my feelings run deep. I have tried to serve this Congress, and I hope you will permit me to go on serving it'.

Following the knighthoods that went to Citrine and Pugh in 1935, the Labour Party conference passed a resolution that

> deprecates the acceptance by members of the Party of Titles or Honours other than those which a Labour Government finds necessary for the furtherance of its own business in Parliament . . . Conference places on record its conviction that socialist participation in such functions and honours can be justified only in exceptional circumstances for the express purpose of frustrating the propaganda of the capitalist press.

The National Executive Committee was asked to consider the whole honours question and report back to the following year's conference.

The report, when it was presented in 1936, was brief to the point of absurdity, and evaded the question it was due to consider. It did not deal with the bulk of the honours system as required, but accepted the need for Labour Party members to take peerages – in order to put Labour's case in the Lords – and recognised that 'in the Civil Service the conferment of Honours is a method of establishing status'. So poorly received was the report, that it was referred back for further consideration, never again to see the light of day.

Meanwhile, Citrine's little honours saga continued. He had been a regular speaker for years at the Union of Post Office Workers' conferences. Following his knighthood, he was not invited to address the conference in 1936. It took the personal intervention of the union's general secretary to restore his invitation, and when he rose to speak a quarter of the delegates walked out of the hall. It was Bowen who, as General Secretary, persuaded his union not to reject a man because he was honoured. He clearly meant it, for he became a Commander of the British Empire in 1939 and a knight in 1953. Citrine himself continued to climb the social ladder, becoming a Privy Councillor in 1940 and a peer in 1946, both without public murmur. The established Labour Party practice of not awarding hereditary peerages to people with male heirs was dropped in Citrine's case, with the result that his son, Norman, succeeded him, not only in getting a job at the TUC, but also in becoming the second Baron Citrine of Wembley, in 1983. The question of Labour and honours seemed to fade in 1936 as quickly as it had surfaced the previous year.

Although Labour joined the Coalition government in 1940, and a truce was called on party politicking throughout the remainder of the war, the party was still desperately badly represented in the Lords. Thus, in December 1941, four new Labour peers were created in order to strengthen its speakers list in that House. One of them was William Wedgwood Benn. Benn had been a Liberal MP from 1906 to 1927, when he joined the Labour Party, and represented Labour in the Commons from 1928 until his ennoblement, serving briefly as Secretary of State for War in the postwar Labour government. Ignoring the 'no male heirs' rule caused considerable problems on his death in 1960. His son, Anthony, reluctantly became the 2nd Baron Stansgate and spent the next three years fighting in Parliament and the courts for the right not to join the

House of Lords. The result of three years campaigning led to the Peerages Act of 1963, which allowed peers to disclaim their titles and stand for the House of Commons. Tony Benn's actions then did more to change the rights of membership and non-membership of the House of Lords than all the Labour governments since 1924 have done between them.

Another 'top-up' Labour peer created at this time was Josiah Wedgwood – a strange choice, as not only did he have male heirs but he was also seventy years old and therefore unlikely to offer long active service for the party in the Lords. In the event, he died a year after his ennoblement. Josiah Wedgwood had joined Labour from the Liberals in 1919, at the age of forty-seven, and was Chancellor of the Duchy of Lancaster in the 1924 Labour government. He was made a peer in January 1942 and became the only person in recent times to have two baronies bestowed on him in a fortnight. Clement Attlee, as Deputy Prime Minister, issued a notice proclaiming the creation of 'Baron Wedgwood of Moddershall in the county of Stafford' and a warrant duly signed by the King was issued on 1 January 1942. Four days later the new baron called on the College of Arms to have his name changed, from Baron Wedgwood of Moddershall to Baron Wedgwood of Barlaston. Downing Street wasn't very enthusiastic about the change and wrote to Sir Gerald Wollaston of the College of Arms, 'I write to let you know that the King has already approved Colonel Wedgwood's title. It would be most unusual, when the King's approval has been given, for an alteration to be made.'

Wedgwood was not to be fobbed off, and knew a thing or two about getting his own way. He wrote to the King on the 9th explaining why he wished to change names. The Wedgwood pottery firm, he said, came from Barlaston and,

> although I am not a director of that firm nor the male representative of that family, the directorate and my nephew, the senior representatives of the descendants of the original Josiah Wedgwood, have asked me, I fear all too late, to have myself described as 'of Barlaston' instead as 'of Moddershall'.

As a piece of additional pressure to help him on his way, both *The Times* and the *Daily Telegraph* of 10 January announced that Wedgwood had indeed changed his name. Wedgwood apologised to the

King for jumping the gun with the announcement, but had his wish granted on the 13th.

Two years later the first of the true trade-union barons, William Westwood, entered the House of Lords, as Lord Westwood. He has been General Secretary of the Ship Constructors' and Shipwrights' Association, President of the Engineering and Shipping Trades Confederation and first President of the Confederation of Shipbuilding and Engineering Unions (the Confed.). Like his son later, he was also a director of Newcastle Football Club. By the time of Westwood's ennoblement in 1944, the 'no male heirs' policy of the Labour movement was in complete tatters – he had three sons and daughters, all married at the time. Westwood was of service to the Labour Party, becoming a whip in the Attlee government, and was a member of the House for nineteen years until his death in 1953. The danger for Labour in creating hereditary peers with heirs is well-illustrated by the cases of Lords Wedgwood and Westwood, both of whose successors currently grace the Conservative benches in the House of Lords.

Labour entered the 1945 election with a radical programme, but its manifesto promise on the Lords was considerably watered down from the version the party submitted to the electorate a decade earlier. Instead of seeking power to abolish the Lords, the 1945 manifesto stated 'we will not tolerate obstruction of the people's will by the House of Lords'.

Clement Attlee was as unflamboyant in his approach to the honours system as his general disposition indicated. Although not frugal in the award of peerages, he certainly did not use the occasion of the first majority Labour government in Britain to transform either the honours system or the House of Lords which sits at its apex. The only attempt at reform came in the shape of the 1949 Parliament Act which simply amended 1911 legislation to reduce the delaying power of the Lords from two years to one.

Attlee awarded few of the highest honours, but did ensure that due regard was paid to a proper social pecking order for those that he did create. The only dukedom created since 1900 was given to the present Queen's consort, Philip Mountbatten, in 1947. To keep the family happy his uncle, Louis, was given the only earldom that Attlee bestowed, in the same year. By the time of his death, Earl Mountbatten was a well-honoured man and had nine British honours alone. In addition to his earldom, he was a Knight of the Garter (KG), Privy Councillor (PC), Knight Grand Cross of the Bath (GCB), had the Order of Merit (OM), was a Knight Grand Commander of the Order of the Star of India (GCSI), a Knight Grand Commander of the Indian Empire (GCIE), Knight Grand Cross of the Royal Victorian Order (GCVO) and held the Distinguished Service Order (DSO).

Attlee only created three viscounts between 1946 and 1951, and two of those went to war-leaders Alanbrooke and Montgomery. His rate of viscountcy creation in that period was one every two years, on average, compared with two-and-a-half a year in the twelve years after his premiership ended. He remains, however, the only Labour Prime Minister to have appointed anybody with heirs to a rank of the peerage above the level of baron, and the last Labour Prime Minister to have sanctioned hereditary creations. It is thirty-five years since a Labour-created hereditary peerage was bestowed.

Forty-five barons, whose titles still survive, were created during the six-year premiership of Clement Attlee, a third of them in the first year. After ensuring that there were a few more Labour peers on the Lords' benches, his enthusiasm for ennoblement subsided. Fifteen peerages created in 1945 remain today, eight from each of 1946 and 1947, one each from 1948 and 1949, and six from each of the last two years of his premiership.

The forty-five surviving heirs of barons created between 1945 and 1951 have hardly brought long-term benefit and advantage to the Labour Party. Only five of them currently take the Labour Whip (Lords Crook, Lindsay of Birker, Longford, Milner of Leeds, and Shepherd), compared with thirteen who take the Conservative Whip (two of whom, Lord Lucas of Chilworth and Lord Trefgarne are currently Tory Ministers). The Alliance parties, with five peers (three SDP and two Liberal) do as well today out of the Attlee baronies as does the Labour Party. Ten of the peers describe themselves as 'independents', five give themselves no description at all, and eight, although still holding the title 'Lord', have yet to make an appearance in the House (Lords Piercy, Calverley, Wilson, Citrine, Simon of Wythenshawe, Amwell, Macdonald of Gwalnysgor, and Kirkwood). *Private Eye* for a while ran a cartoon strip, 'Focus on Fact – Britain's least-known peers', and the first issue began: 'Among the least-known peers are the descendants of those created by Clement Attlee in the postwar Labour government'. One or two examples were given but the point was later made fairly conclusively with the case of the 3rd Lord Calverley. He is perhaps better known to his friends and colleagues as Police Constable Charles Rodney Muff of Bradford, a member of the West Yorkshire Constabulary.

One of the last two peerages to be awarded by Clement Attlee went to Davie Kirkwood. It is a sad tale. He was deported in 1916 for organising a protest of Clydeside workers against increases in house rents. In the 1920s he was elected to Parliament as a 'Red Clydesider', along with such other left-wing spirits as Jimmy Maxton, and spent many a speech in his early days in Parliament denouncing the House of Lords and calling for its abolition. But he drifted steadily to the Right politically until, on his ennoblement in 1951, he was able to declare, 'I am proud to belong to this House.' (A fellow 'Red Clydesider' was Manny Shinwell; like Kirkwood he swore for many years that he would never go to the Lords, but followed in his footsteps nineteen years later.)

Quite what Attlee felt he would achieve by giving a peerage to the eighty-year-old Kirkwood is difficult to imagine. He died within four years. Perhaps it is a fitting testimony to his drift to the Right that the current Lord Kirkwood is a member of the Social Democratic Party.

The Attlee years did not dramatically affect the landscape of the honours system at the higher levels. There was some minor tinkering with the number of honours in different categories awarded to the various departments of State and armed services (as briefly referred to in Chapter 1), but these came at the behest of paid Civil Servants and not from ministers in a government committed to radical change.

The government was too busy winning the peace to concern itself with honours, and the matter did not concern the Labour Party or the trade-union movement outside Parliament in the postwar years. However, there was a brief debate at the 1948 Labour Party conference on a motion which declared, 'This conference reaffirms its belief that power must rest with a popularly elected assembly and declares that a nominated second chamber is inconsistent with the principles of democratic government.' An amendment was put calling for the establishment of a second chamber 'entirely divorced from the principles of peerage and heredity'. Both the resolution and amendment were opposed by Herbert Morrison, who said, 'The resolution and amendment before the Conference are dangerous upon their own merits.' He went on to state that, 'the heredity element is really impossible to defend'. He was, however, Deputy Prime Minister and Leader of the House of Commons at the time, and seven years later took the hereditary title of Lord Morrison of Lambeth, although he had no heirs and the title eventually died with him. Morrison was able to persuade the conference not to vote on the resolution.

Labour conferences did not concern themselves with honours and the Lords for a further thirteen years. In 1961, two resolutions were debated, both inspired by the constitutional struggles facing Anthony Wedgwood Benn in his desire to become a commoner following the death of his father, Lord Stansgate. The first resolution called upon the party's National Executive Committee and the Parliamentary Labour Party 'to state categorically that when Labour is returned to power, they will abolish the House of Lords as an hereditary chamber'. That resolution was remitted to the executive for further consideration. A second resolution was put:

> [Conference] urges all Labour Party members not to accept any honour which would mean them becoming a member of the House of Lords. Conference also instructs the National Executive Committee to prepare a policy statement calling for the abolition of the House of Lords.

This was defeated.

The Labour election manifesto of 1964 was the fifth consecutive one not to mention the House of Lords, although reference was made eighteen months later in the 1966 manifesto. The statement, however, was noticeably milder. In 1910 the message was simple – 'The Lords Must Go' – but by 1966 it had become 'legislation will be introduced to safeguard measures approved by the House of Commons from frustration by delay or defeat in the House of Lords'. That legislation was the ill-fated Parliament Bill of 1968/69.

Meanwhile, Harold Wilson was in Downing Street and tinkering around with the system. Some of his early elevations to the peerage were men and women of considerable talent with much to offer in debate. Some were former Labour MPs, who could well have been embarrassed by their earlier pronouncements about the place. Gilbert Micheson, for example, had urged, as a Labour candidate in

1934, the confiscation of all capital and privilege; eleven years later be became a Labour MP, eighteen years later a Commander of the British Empire and thirty years later, a Member of the House of Lords. Fenner Brockway had been the Labour MP for Eton and Slough throughout the 'thirteen wasted Tory years', but was defeated, against the tide, in 1964. After his defeat, he says, he was telephoned and urged to think of taking a seat in the House of Lords by Tony Benn, who gave the example of his father when showing what a peer could do. Brockway was so impressed, he says, that he became Baron Brockway of Eton and Slough, even though 'I was against the existence of the undemocratic chamber'. His wife was more principled about the matter, she declined to be called Lady Brockway, anti-establishment and egalitarian to her fingertips.

Tony Benn, who had fought to avoid joining the Lords himself in 1961 and who had encouraged Fenner Brockway to go in 1964, was by the 1970s expressing the feelings that many in the Labour movement have to the institution. In his book, *Arguments for Democracy* (Jonathan Cape, 1981), he wrote:

> The House of Lords welcomes with open arms those Labour politicians or trade-union leaders who can be induced to accept peerages and then play out an active role in mildly regretting the Conservative policies of the majority there. Labour peers actually strengthen the Lords, for the true role of the upper house is to slow down or defeat any House of Commons majority which might attempt to use the Statute Book as an instrument of reform. Labour peers give a legitimacy to the whole edifice. (p. 23)

Lord Brockway himself was able to bear testimony to this. When, in 1975, there was a conflict between the Commons and the Lords over Michael Foot's bill establishing closed shops, he wrote, 'Lord Carrington, the Tory leader, even cited me as a reason for maintaining the House of Lords . . . I think it is true that it would be easier to end the Lords if there were not radical voices within it' (Fenner Brockway, *Towards Tomorrow*, Hart-Davis MacGibbon, 1977, p. 245).

The questions of the honours system and the House of Lords were considered occasionally by Harold Wilson's Cabinet. Barbara Castle, in her diary for October 1966, noted that she had sent a letter to Wilson complaining at the social stratification of awards in the honours lists, particularly those sections dealing with Civil Servants, and calling for the system to be democratised. In his speech to the Labour Party conference in October 1966, Harold Wilson claimed credit for the fact that no hereditary peers had been created since he had entered Downing Street and that he would be announcing 'new and far-reaching changes in the Honours System'. 'They did not come,' commented Barbara Castle, tersely.

Eight months later, in May 1967, there was a discussion in the Cabinet on the reduction of the automatic award of honours to Civil Servants. Barbara Castle noted,

> The most outrageous thing about it [the honours system] was that it reflected the system of social stratification and snobbery in this country. One of my most embarrassing jobs as Minister was to present the BEMs to railwaymen and other members of the lower orders with whom the Queen did not think it was worth her while to shake hands. I was backed strongly by Wedgie [Tony Benn] and Dick [Crossman]. (*The Castle Diaries, 1964–70*, Weidenfeld & Nicolson, 1984, p. 255)

In 1968, a resolution at the Labour Party conference called for 'the immediate abolition of the House of Lords'. It was remitted to the executive for further consideration. The parliamentary leadership had no such intentions and a bill was soon published which would have had the effect of strengthening the Lords, although effectively removing the hereditary element. The parliamentary opposition to the bill was spearheaded by Michael Foot, a subsequent leader of the Labour Party, who was later to call for and get peerages conferred on a number of political colleagues. Foot called in 1968/9 and subsequently for the abolition of the House of Lords. The filibustering around the Parliament Bill was so well-organised that, on one day in March 1969, four and a half hours were spent on points of order on the question of whether the Lords' attendance records should be confidential or not. With such well-ordered opposition, Harold Wilson had little option but to drop the Bill.

Labour entered the 1970 election with an even more watered-down manifesto commitment, 'We cannot accept the situation in which the House of Lords can nullify important decisions of the House of Commons . . . proposals to secure reform will be brought forward.' Labour lost the election.

The honours question next leapt to public prominence with the

Wilson resignation list of 1976 (see Chapter 6). Tony Benn used the opportunity to revive a document on the democratisation of honours he had first drafted in 1964, and put it to Labour's Home Policy Committee. Its main proposals were that a way should be found of putting people into the House of Lords without ennoblement and that those whose public service was such that it should be recognised should receive a parliamentary medal, that awards for gallantry should be democratised and that the social stratification of awards should be ended.

However, the furore over the Wilson resignation list did not last long within the party, and the Benn proposals were not proceeded with. What was treated more seriously, though, was the House of Lords. Labour's parliamentary majority was tiny and the Conservative-dominated House of Lords frustrated and wrecked much of Labour's legislation as it passed through. In 1974–75 the government was defeated in 100 Lords divisions, in 1975–76 in 120 divisions. They suffered eight defeats on the Agriculture Bill, eleven on the Education Bill, eleven on the Race Relations Bill, seventeen on the Health Service Bill, twenty-five on aircraft- and shipbuilding legislation and twenty-eight on the Dock Work Regulations Bill.

The mood in the Labour Party was back to 1910 – 'The Lords Must Go'. In 1977, Jack Jones, then General Secretary of the Transport and General Workers' Union and the single most powerful delegate to the Labour Party conference, moved a resolution which declared that,

> the House of Lords is a negation of democracy and [Conference] calls upon the government, the Parliamentary party and the National Executive Committee to take every possible step open to them to secure the total abolition of the House of Lords, and the reform of Parliament into an efficient, single-chamber, legislating body without delay.

In the course of the debate, Lord Shinwell remarked that, 'there has been more excitement about this resolution in this Conference than there was about unemployment or any other subject'. Winding up the discussion, and speaking for the National Executive Committee, John Forrester said,

> if Conference accepts the resolution, the National Executive Committee

will gladly endeavour to have the intentions contained in the resolution included in the next election manifesto . . . the capacity of the N.E.C. to struggle for inclusion of this resolution within the framework of the next manifesto will be greatly influenced by the size of the vote which is given to the resolution at this time.

On a card vote the resolution was carried by 6,248,000 votes to 91,000. It could hardly have been more conclusive, but inclusion of the matter in the 1979 election manifesto was vetoed by Party Leader, James Callaghan.

The exclusion of this commitment caused a major row within the party and, in the midst of the acrimony that followed Labour's defeat at the election, attempts were rapidly made to reaffirm the party's commitment to abolition. Within months of the defeat of the Labour government the party held a special conference at Wembley to consider a detailed programme entitled 'Peace, Jobs and Freedom'. That document was quite explicit on the abolition issue, but said nothing about the honours system as such. It was approved by an even more comprehensive margin than the 1977 abolition resolution – 6,000,000 votes to 6,000.

James Callaghan was soon replaced as Party Leader by Michael Foot, a confirmed abolitionist. He had been primarily responsible for organising the filibuster that had scuppered Harold Wilson's attempts to reform the Lords in 1968–69 and indeed had opposed other earlier reforms of the Lords on the grounds that they gave the place increased credibility. In 1958, for example, when the Life Peerages Act was passed, he argued that Labour should have nothing to do with 'this new field of patronage' – until the party had decided its attitude to the House of Lords, no party member should accept ennoblement.

But as he climbed closer to the top of the greasy pole of Parliamentary Labour Party power, his attitude mellowed. Before becoming Leader, he called for and got a peerage for ex-MP Tom Driberg on the grounds, according to Lady Falkender, that he was getting old and going blind. He also got one for Lena Jeger, a long-serving Labour MP, on the grounds that it would be helpful in her retirement to have continued use of Westminster's library. After becoming Leader, Foot created a number of Labour peers, including John Mackie, an ex-Labour MP and colleague of both himself and Nye

Bevan, and Hugh Jenkins, a former Labour Minister and long-time comrade-in-arms in the Campaign for Nuclear Disarmament. Tony Benn clashed with Foot over these creations, both men adopting diametrically opposed attitudes to those they had expressed during the previous quarter of a century. Benn, who had urged Fenner Brockway to go into the Lords in 1964, was now arguing that no new 'working peers' should be created, because they added credibility to an anachronistic institution. For his part, Foot, who had argued precisely that in 1958, was now arguing that since only a Labour government with a good majority could abolish the Lords, the Labour Party should make the best of a bad job and strengthen its support in the chamber. On every occasion when new Labour peers were created under Michael Foot's leadership, he was at pains to point out that his decision to nominate the people in no way changed his conviction that the House of Lords should be abolished. Labour's 1983 election manifesto was firm on the question of abolition, but its defeat was comprehensive enough to ensure that the House of Lords lived to fight another day.

It is now seventy-seven years since Labour's policy to abolish the House of Lords was first developed and seventy-five since it was first proclaimed in a general election. In the intervening period there have been Labour governments for twenty years, ten of them with substantial parliamentary majorities, but Labour has done less this century to change the face of the Lords than either the Liberal or the Conservative parties. No Labour government has introduced legislation proposing abolition and when, in 1976, Dennis Skinner introduced a Private Member's Bill to do just that, he was only able to attract the support of 155 Labour MPs – about half its parliamentary strength. Within a year, a Labour conference called for the abolition of the chamber with a 700:1 majority, but twelve months on the proposal was vetoed from the manifesto by the Party Leader. Those three events illuminate most clearly the schizophrenic attitude Labour has portrayed towards the Lords since its inception at the turn of the century.

That ambivalence is reflected in the awards of honours to trade unionists. As we have seen, the general secretaries of the largest and most powerful union, the Transport and General Workers, have all rejected peerages, whereas their brothers who have sat on the TUC and led smaller unions have trod the well-worn path to ermine and red benches with private pride, albeit with public protestation and embarrassment.

An analysis of the distribution of lesser honours within the trade-union movement produces some surprising results. Table 7 is a breakdown of the award of honours to people described as officials of the country's largest unions in the twenty-two main honours lists between 1974 and January 1985. Five of the lists were compiled under Harold Wilson's premiership, six under Jim Callaghan and eleven under Margaret Thatcher. They are, therefore, half Labour and half Conservative in origin.

The table consists of people whose honours citation mentioned their union activities; it could well be, of course, that other people acting as trade-union officials received honours but were given other citations, as members of local authorities, health authorities or voluntary organisations.

The union whose members have been most honoured does not appear in any of the analysis that follows: the Association of First Division Civil Servants has a mere 7500 members but, as the top Civil Servants' union, will see about fifty of its members honoured a year. In terms of the ratios that are presented in the table, it could probably claim one gong per eleven members (not thousands of members) during the period covered and, on a weighted average (see below), it would probably work out at one point per three members. In other words, each member would have had a 2:1 chance of getting an MBE, if the distribution had been equalised to the lowest common denominator. As it is, they have a 1:11 chance of receiving something over a ten-year period.

Since 1974, four trade-union general secretaries have received peerages in major honours lists: Lord Allen (shop-workers), Lord Gormley (miners), Lord Chapple (electricians) and Lord Murray (TUC). And five have received knighthoods: Edward Britton (NUT – not affiliated and therefore not subscribing to the Labour Party) and Alf Tomkin (furniture-workers), from Harold Wilson; and John Boyd (engineers), Danny McGarvey (boiler-makers) and George Smith (construction-workers), from James Callaghan. Fourteen trade-union officials have received CBEs (5 from Wilson, 4 from Callaghan and 5 from Thatcher), 40 OBEs (3 from Wilson, 19 from Callaghan and 18 from Thatcher) and 78 MBEs (14 from Wilson, 29 from Callaghan and 35 from Thatcher). In total, then, Wilson

Table 7

Honours to Trade Unionists, 1974–85

Union	No. of members (000)	Total honours	Ratio of honours to (000) members	Weighted[1]	Weighted ratio to (000) members
Transport and General Workers	1,547	25	1:62	35	1:44
Amalgamated Union of Engineering Workers	943	12	1:79	25	1:38
General, Municipal and Boilermakers	875	14	1:63	24	1:36
National and Local Government Officers	780	5	1:156	9	1:86
National Union of Public Employees	689	0	—	0	—
Union of Shop, Distributive and Allied	403	6	1:67	26	1:16
Association of Scientific, Technical and Managerial Staffs	390	0	—	0	—
Electrical, Electronic, Telecommunication and Plumbing	365	5	1:73	25	1:15
Union of Construction and Allied Trades	260	7	1:28	17	1:12
Confederation of Health Service Employees	222	0	—	0	—
Technical, Administrative and Supervisory Staff	215	0	—	0	—
Society of Graphical and Allied Trades	213	0	—	0	—
National Union of Teachers	210	1	1:210	10	1:21
National Union of Miners	208	6	1:34	26	1:8
Union of Communication Workers	196	1	1:196	1	1:196
Civil and Public Servants Association	190	1	1:190	1	1:190
Banking, Insurance and Finance	156	0	—	0	—
National Union of Railwaymen	143	0	—	0	—
Royal College of Nursing	135	2	1:68	3	1:45
Post Office Engineers	130	1	1:130	2	1:65
National Graphical Association	129	1	1:129	1	1:129
National Association of Schoolmasters/Women Teachers	119	1	1:119	3	1:40
Association of Professional, Executive, Clerical and Computer Staff	100	0	—	0	—
	10,217	143	1:72	312	1:33

1 Peerage = 20, knighthood = 10, CBE = 3, OBE = 2, MBE = 1 – reflecting overall distribution of honours in honours list

honoured 25 in five lists, Callaghan 55 also in five lists and Thatcher 60 in eleven lists.

Jim Callaghan, the man who championed the trade-union position at the time of 'In Place of Strife', but who ignored it during the winter of discontent a decade later, offered baubles to trade-union officials at twice the rate of his predecessor as Prime Minister, Harold Wilson, and his successor, Margaret Thatcher.

The structure and recruitment patterns of trade unions follows little rhyme or reason, and is certainly not reflected in the sub-committee structure of the Main Honours Committee that makes the honours recommendations. The result is that, even in the days when trade unions nestled closest to the government – in the 1974–78 period – the honours network didn't automatically reflect that incorporation, with each committee awarding a duly prescribed number of gongs in appreciation of services rendered to the State.

There is, therefore, no sense in which the award of honours to trade unionists has followed a rational process. There is no formula for rewarding them – as there is in other spheres of economic, social and cultural activity – the award of honours depends on two independent sets of whims: those of trade-union general secretaries in forwarding names of their officials, and those of the official committees who consider the names forwarded to them from all sources. No rules of thumb apply and so the distribution is bizarre.

Table 7 lists the twenty-two largest trade unions – all bar the Royal College of Nursing being TUC-affiliated – each of whom has over 100,000 members. It gives each union's membership in thousands and the number of occasions on which officials of each union have been cited, *per se*, for honours since 1974. A ratio of honours received to thousands of members is then listed and the final two columns of the table form a weighted listing. Here 20 points are awarded for each peerage granted, 10 for each knighthood, 3 for a CBE, 2 for an OBE and 1 for an MBE, reflecting roughly the distribution of honours generally, so that the overall 'worth' attached to the union over the last eleven years by different governments can be assessed.

The ratio of honoured union officials to union membership over the eleven years is one official per 72,000 members. The major unions with significantly 'better' records are perhaps, surprising. The National Union of Miners, which has battled long and hard with Tory governments over the last decade and a half, comes out with the most 'honoured' record – one gong per 34,000 members.*

The construction-workers' union UCATT, whose employer foes are such generous funders to the Tory Party, emerge as the next most honoured – two-thirds of their six gongs coming from Mrs Thatcher. And, perhaps most surprising of all, the Transport and General Workers' Union, whose general secretaries have gone to considerable lengths to shun the House of Lords, emerges as the third most-favoured union when it comes to awards for the lesser lights.

The NUM, UCATT and the TGWU are recognised as forming the backbone of the 'Left' in trade-union terms, but between them emerge as the most-honoured bodies. Those unions normally felt to be on the Right of the movement, and who could therefore be expected to be more amenable to State largesse – the engineers, electricians and clerks – fare considerably worse.

The unions listed in the table are the largest unions still in existence. But without doubt the union whose officials have been most honoured over the last decade or so has been that of the agricultural workers, now submerged in the Transport and General (the Agricultural Workers' Union awards gained in the period of its independence have not been added to the overall Transport and General total). The Agricultural Workers' Union was an independent body for nine of the eleven years under consideration and had 70,000 members at the date of its merger with the Transport and General. In that period its officials received eight honours, which is about ten times the rate that would be expected of a union of that size; the rate of award is almost five times 'better' than that of the most honoured major union, the NUM.

* The 1985 Birthday honours list continued the long tradition of honouring mining-industry workers, but with a difference. The trade-union section was shorter than normal – only four people had their current trade-union positions cited as the reason for their honour, about half the average over the previous decade. MBEs, however, went to two miners: Roy Ottey (citation: 'lately secretary, power group NUM') and Colin Clarke ('for services to coal-mining'). They were not the kind of people who the NUM was likely to have nominated in the early months of 1985. Roy Ottey had resigned from the union's national executive half-way through the year-long strike, because of the refusal of the executive to bow to a High Court judgement, and was bitterly criticised by some of the union's activists as 'the enemy within'. Colin Clarke chaired the National Working Miners' Committee and was one of three Nottingham pitmen who took the NUM to court over its fight against pit-closures. *Labour Weekly* judged 'probably nobody played a bigger part than Clarke in destroying the hopes of miners' unity in the strike'. By such means has Margaret Thatcher dispensed baubles to some of the representatives of organised labour.

The agricultural workers undoubtedly do well from the system because their sphere of recruitment comes closest to reflecting that of the official honours committee – the one that considers agricultural awards. Such is the semi-feudal nature of much of agricultural life in this country today that an element of *noblesse oblige* tends to creep into the deliberations of the agricultural committee. After all, the president of the employer body, the National Farmers' Union, can expect to receive a knighthood when he retires. Is it not proper then that the workers' representatives should be thrown a scrap, and kept in their place – with MBEs?

Other smaller unions to have done well out of the honours system are the Communist-led furniture makers (1 knighthood and 1 MBE for its 58,000 members over the last eleven years), the hosiery and knitwear workers (2 OBEs and 1 MBE for 53,000 members), the constructional section of the engineering union (1 OBE and 1 MBE for 20,000 members) and the National Union of Journalists, whose officials have picked up an OBE and an MBE for their 32,000 members, quite apart from the dozens of NUJ members who have received their thanks in the press sections of the honours lists.

Just as the pattern of peerages going to trade-union officials, discussed at the start of this chapter, ignored the claims of the white-collar and public-sector unions, so does the distribution of minor awards. Regardless of the politics of the leadership of the white-collar unions – from the Communist-led TASS, to the right-wing Association of Professional Executive, Clerical and Computer Staffs, via maverick, politically fluctuating unions like the Association of Scientific, Technical and Managerial Staffs and such only recently TUC-affiliated bodies as the bank workers' union – officials of white-collar unions have been comprehensively ignored in the honours game. These four unions have over 860,000 members between them but do not appear to have received a single gong over the last eleven years.* If they had received honours at the same rate as the trade-union movement as a whole, 124 of their officials, past and present, could have expected to have donned a morning suit *en route* to pick up a medal from Buckingham Palace.

If the private-sector white-collar trade-union leaders have fared

---

* With the exception of Muriel Turner, Deputy General Secretary of ASTMS, who was elevated to the peerage in April 1985.

badly from the system, the greatest growth area of trade-union activity over the last two decades – the public-sector unions – have hardly fared much better. The major public-sector unions – NALGO (800,000 members), NUPE (689,000), COHSE (222,000), NUT (210,000), UCW (196,000), CPSA (190,000), NAS/UWT (119,000), the RCN (135,000) and POEU (130,000) – together have a total membership of 2.7 million. Had they received the trade-union average number of honours they could have expected to have received at least 38 major gongs between them over the eleven years under consideration. They received 12 – less than a third of the average. They could also have expected 82 MBE equivalents (as shown in the weighted average column of the table) – they actually received 27, again less than a third of the trade-union total.

It is tempting to explain the 'poor' honours performance of the officials of public-sector unions in terms of the contempt with which Mrs Thatcher appears to hold most public-sector workers and their trade-union representatives. These unions, however, fared no better in the honours stakes under Harold Wilson and James Callaghan, who was himself at one time an official of a Civil Service union and an adviser to another public-service employees' body. The truth is probably more simple. Those who are at the centre of organising the honours system are out of touch with social change; they are probably oblivious to the new topology of the trade-union movement. The growth areas, in the white-collar and public-sector unions, are therefore comprehensively ignored in the distribution of honours.

The final irony then is that those sections of the trade-union movement closest to the British establishment, like the bank workers' union (General Secretary, Leif Mills, the first Balliol-educated man to sit on the TUC General Council) don't get the establishment rewards, whereas those which are furthest removed from the *status quo*, the National Union of Mineworkers, are the most wooed.

Six

The Wilson years

The popular association of Harold Wilson with the honours system invariably revolves around his controversial resignation list of 1976. That list, according to George Hutchinson in *The Times*, 'has brought so much discredit to the honours system that it might not survive in its present form'. Publication of the list was held up from the four-week period, which is normal with such lists, to eight weeks, while the Political Honours Scrutiny Committee deliberated and questioned some of the names. The *Sunday Times* first sensed a story with the list a month before it was eventually published. The names of potential beneficiaries were well-leaked and their qualities widely written of and discussed in the following weeks. Had the recipients of other honours lists been subject to such microscopic press scrutiny over so long a period, the scandal surrounding the Wilson list may not, in comparison, have appeared so great.

If Harold Wilson is only to be remembered for his final honours list, it is a pity; for he did more than any Prime Minister in recent times to reform the honours system. Many of his achievements and attempts to change it bear the hallmarks of the general legacy of the Wilson era: he tried to modernise aspects of the system but was ultimately frustrated by the establishment and diverse political alliances; some of his reforms were essentially cosmetic and superficial, designed to give the impression of change without the corresponding substance; and twenty years after he first stepped into Downing Street almost all that he attempted to achieve has been systematically overturned by his successors.

Wilson's opening bid was a characteristically dramatic one. At one fell swoop he stopped a thousand-year-old practice: the award of hereditary titles was to cease. It was a break with the past, a sign that this new Labour government, in 1964, was more concerned with achievement than birth – the meritocracy was to replace the aristocracy as the respected class. There were to be no more dukes, marquesses, earls, viscounts, hereditary barons and baronets. Life peerages and knighthoods were to be the only handles available . . . awarded for merit and extinguished with death.

There appeared to be a strong consensus for the move, and the precedent was accepted by both his immediate successors, Edward Heath and James Callaghan, and also, it seemed, by Margaret Thatcher. But nineteen years after the principle was established, and long enough for it to be felt to be an irreversible convention, the Conservative Deputy Leader, Willie Whitelaw, and the Speaker of the House of Commons, George Thomas, were given hereditary viscountcies in 1983, following the general election. The awards re-established the position that hereditary honours were available, but cautiously, for neither recipient had a male heir and so effectively acquired the viscountcy only for life – their titles would die with them. A year later, approaching ninety, the former Prime Minister, Harold Macmillan, became the Earl of Stockton. Earldoms are there for the asking for former prime ministers; in the twentieth century, Balfour, Asquith, Baldwin, Lloyd George, Attlee and Eden have all taken one. Three of the last five earls created (Macmillan, Eden and Attlee) have been Prime Minister, the other two being Earl Woolton (close confidant and associate of Churchill), and Earl Snowdon (former husband of the Queen's sister). Harold Macmillan waited for twenty years after he left the House of Commons to re-enter Parliament as an earl at a time when he knew his son, MP Maurice Macmillan, was dying. Acceptance of an hereditary title by Harold in these circumstances would not be likely to embarrass and compromise Maurice into deciding whether to inherit a title and move to the Lords, or renounce it and stay in the Commons on his father's death. None the less, the Earl of Stockton has aided the rehabilitation of hereditary honours – the two prime ministers who followed him, Alec Douglas-Home and Harold Wilson, both contented themselves with a life peerage when they left the Commons. Earldoms for prime ministers are now back on the agenda – will Margaret Thatcher become Countess Finchley on her departure from the Commons?

Harold Wilson's bold opening gesture, then – the ending of hereditary titles – has been overturned after nineteen years. His next move came in October 1966, when he announced that he proposed to 'discontinue the practice of making recommendations concerning honours for political services of the kind which have been a feature for so many years past' – except that honours for 'public' service would remain. This reform appeared to have three advantages: it was cheap; could be popular, as it gave the impression of stamping out an objectionable form of patronage; and could, if maintained by future Conservative governments, affect Tory fund-raising.

It was, however, purely cosmetic. As has been seen in Chapter 1, Richard Crossman noted in his diary 'once you do this your announcement is merely a gimmick, because you *haven't* cut out political honours'. The award of honours for political services had always been a source of irritation for Labour Party leaders: those who received the awards were invariably the more establishment-minded members of the constituency parties. This often resulted in considerable resentment by the local rank-and-file activists, who felt that people who colluded with the opposition or trimmed the party's policies when in public office should not receive honours in the name of the party. These very same people would now receive their gongs for services to local government, the local hospital, etc. – far less contentious, politically, particularly if they had served on the authority in a senior position for a number of years. In the end, it was decided to give most of these honours to Labour people when Labour was in government, but to include about a third of such honours for Tories and Liberals – to make them less anxious to contribute to their own party funds.

So political honours for party-workers continued, under another name. Where the reform was more effective was in the House of Commons when the wholesale creation of backbench knights was ended. When Willie Hamilton attacked Harold Wilson in the Commons, just before the premier's resignation, for having fondled patronage 'as a bridegroom fondles his bride', Wilson hit back. In the seven-and-a-half years during which he had been Prime Minister, he told the Commons, 6 knighthoods had been conferred on MPs compared with 57 during the last seven-and-a-half years of Tory rule.

Harold Wilson's reform of the awarding of political honours was effective as far as Parliament was concerned, but cosmetic in the country. The distinction didn't matter to Margaret Thatcher; she told Parliament in November 1979 that she was reintroducing political honours and, as Chapter 8 shows, yet another Wilson initiative has been overturned as pre-1964 practices now prevail.

The next Wilson reform came in 1967, when he announced that there would be a reduction in the automatic awards of honours going to Civil Servants. Although, as Chapter 1 shows, they still fare better, as a group, than all others outside the magic circle of political friends, when it comes to the award of honours, the Wilson move had a clear effect. In the 1957 Birthday list, for example, 228 CBEs, OBEs and MBEs went to Home Civil Servants; nine years later this had been reduced to 180, and in the 1967 Birthday list, following the announcement, it was down to 112. Despite the fact that the numbers of Civil Servants had grown over the decade, Wilson halved the number of honours going to them. As a group they were no longer badly paid, they had secure jobs with inflation-proof pensions, and their senior members had the prospect of lucrative employment and consultancy work awaiting them after early retirement. Why, on top of all this, should they be showered with honours? This, of all the Wilson reforms, appears to have stuck, but loyal and patient Civil Servants still have, statistically, a much greater chance of an honour, simply by virtue of their employment, than any other employment group in the workforce. Wilson's reform went largely unnoticed outside Whitehall, but a decade later still rankled with those who were affected. Thus, in the wake of the resignation honours list controversy, in June 1976, an aggrieved Desmond Crawley wrote to *The Times* about how Wilson's gong-for-the-job reduction of 1967 had affected him. He said that the reform had 'reduced by two-thirds the honours conferred annually on members of the public and defence services, thus ensuring that I for one am the first of H.M.'s former ministers to the Holy See over the past 60 years not to be knighted'. Poor 'Sir' Desmond. He is still unadorned and so must content himself with his Coronation Medal (1953), CVO (1961), CMG (1964) and Knight Grand Cross, Order of St Gregory the Great (1973).

The fourth Harold Wilson reform relating to honours was essentially constitutional rather than honorific – but it had implications for the distribution of honours. This was the Parliament (No. 2) Bill of 1968–9. The Bill was designed to reform the House of Lords by taking away legislative rights from hereditary peers. It was essentially a compromise agreed by Richard Crossman and the Conservative and Liberal peers whose support it would have relied upon to ensure reasonably swift passage on to the Statute Book. Hereditary peers were to continue to have the right to take part in the Lords' debates but would be denied voting rights. These were to be restricted to 230 salaried voting peers: 105 from the government party of the day, 80 from the principal opposition party, 15 Liberals and 30 crossbenchers.

The government had its parliamentary hands full at the time with its trade-union legislation, and this constitutional reform provoked widespread opposition, from the Left of the Labour Party (personified by Michael Foot) to the Right of the Conservative Party (in the shape of Enoch Powell). Filibustering and prevarication on all sides of the House – provoked mainly by concern over the increased patronage power the measure would give to an already powerful Prime Minister, and by a fear that a modernised and more 'respectable' House of Lords would effectively reduce the influence and powers of the Commons – meant that progress on the Bill was slow or non-existent. The Bill was finally abandoned in April 1969 and with it, according to some observers, went Wilson's enthusiasm for continued reform of honours. It was soon after this that some of the more controversial figures associated with honours in the Wilson years began to find their names appearing on the lists.

One further change that Harold Wilson introduced to honours lists (it cannot be called a reform and cannot be dated by an announcement) concerns what Joe Haines calls the 'stardust'. When honours lists reach Downing Street from the Main Honours Committee, the Prime Minister and entourage do some minor tinkering of their own – usually with the higher honours, but also by inserting a popular element into an otherwise tedious list of worthies and dignitaries. The mass media must have 'names' to write and broadcast about, otherwise the lists would not receive the attention that the patronage machine requires them to get.

Before the Wilson era, the popular element had a very middle-brow, middle-class, middle-aged appeal to it. The 'stars' would be Home Service and Third Programme performers, Shakespearean actors, people from the world of opera and ballet – even the sportsmen were gentlemen: cricketers (usually batsmen, not bowlers) and

Rugby Union (not League) players. Harold Wilson knew his public and electorate, particularly the Labour voters. And as the *Daily Mirror* was as important to him as *The Times*, so *Coronation Street* and pop music found their places in his carefully prepared folksy asides – the honours lists were yet another medium for establishing his man-of-the-people appeal.

Thus, his first honours list, in January 1965, saw a knighthood for Stanley Matthews and MBEs for three medal-winners from the recent Olympic Games and six months later for all four Beatles, together with television newsreader Robert Dougall. There were also OBEs for the stars of two of TV's top long-running series: Violet Carson (Ena Sharples of *Coronation Street*) and Jack Warner (Sgt Dixon of *Dixon of Dock Green*). The next list (January 1966) saw a CBE for England cricketer Brian Statham (a bowler!) and an MBE for Welsh footballer Ivor Allchurch. June 1966 saw a knighthood for Joe Richards, President of the Football League and an MBE for Eric Ashton of Wigan Rugby League FC. Although the middle-brow talents of composer Michael Tippett and playwright Harold Pinter were rewarded with a knighthood and a CBE, respectively, the popular end saw CBEs for Peter Sellers and Harry Andrews.

January 1967 was the first opportunity to reward the victorious England World Cup football squad – so there was a knighthood for manager Alf Ramsey and an OBE for captain Bobby Moore; football administration got its reward, too, with a CBE for Denis Fellows of the Football Association. It is interesting to note that, despite Wilson's change to a more popular emphasis in honours lists, due regard was still being given to status, a 'K' for the manager, CBE for the administrator, and the lower-ranked OBE for the captain of the team that actually played the games that won the cup. June 1967 saw the award of an MBE to Walter McGowan – a professional boxer! – and a CBE to actress Vanessa Redgrave. Ms Redgrave is today probably the only British Trotskyist to be a Commander of the British Empire.

Statistically, 1968 was a low point in the 'stardust' awards: cricketer Tom Graveney received an OBE and motor-cyclist Mike Hailwood an MBE. The June list saw a knighthood for Manchester United football manager Matt Busby with OBEs for pop astronomer Patrick Moore and motor-racing driver Graham Hill.

The January 1969 list saw the by-now traditional MBEs going to the British medal-winners from the recent Olympic Games: Chris Finnegan, David Hemery, and Rodney Patterson. Other figures from the world of sport to be honoured were Henry Cooper (OBE) and Ann Jones (MBE). Reassuring television presenter, Cliff Michelmore, received a CBE.

After the failure to reform the upper echelons of the honours system, with the collapse of the Parliament Bill in April 1969, Harold Wilson appears to have launched into the 'stardust' section of subsequent lists with added gusto. Two months later, there were knighthoods for Bernard Miles and Britain's favourite poet, John Betjeman, as well as a DBE for Anna Neagle. At the more popular end of the market there were OBEs for Arthur Askey, England's best-loved footballer Bobby Charlton, and cricketer Basil D'Oliveira. England's football trainer, Harold Shepherdson, received an MBE together with squash champion Jonah Barrington.

The stardust was sprayed at twice the rate in Harold Wilson's two 1970 lists as it had been in previous years, with almost every branch of popular entertainment acknowledged. January 1970 saw a knighthood for Noël Coward and CBEs for thespians Kenneth More, Joan Plowright and Maggie Smith. Sport was well rewarded, with OBEs for John Arlott, Tony Jacklin and Don Revie and MBEs for Lilian Board, Jeff Smith and Don Thompson. Entertainers Pete Murray (subsequently a great fan of Margaret Thatcher) and Kenny Lynch (black popular performers were honoured in two successive lists) received OBEs. The final list of Harold Wilson's first premiership had the longest and most comprehensive popular appeal of any he supervised. The stars of stage and screen were honoured with a knighthood for Laurence Olivier, CBEs for Richard Burton and director John Schlesinger, and OBEs for Judy Dench, David Frost, Jessie Matthews (of radio's *Mrs Dale's Diary*) and Nyree Dawn Porter and Margaret Tyzack (of the ratings-topping *Forsyte Saga*). Music got a look in with CBEs for Janet Baker and Henry Hall, while sportsmen were honoured in such a way to keep the geographic and class divisions happy. Scotland football manager Jock Stein got a CBE and England's goalkeeper, Gordon Banks, an OBE; on horseback the darling of Hickstead, David Broome, received an OBE while the punters' pal, Stan Mellor, received an MBE.

The stardust slumped when Edward Heath entered Downing

Street. His first two lists brought rewards for the less than top of the pops: Agatha Christie, Michael Bonallack the golfer, Terence Rattigan the playwright, Alan Hardaker the football administrator, and actress Wendy Hiller. Gone were the soap-opera and pop stars; it was back to middle-brow respectability. The glitter was establishment again: January 1972 saw a CBE for yachtsman Chay Blyth and England cricket captain Colin Cowdrey, old man of golf Henry Longhurst and sports administrator Walter Winterbottom. Tinges of pandering to youth and the working class came with an OBE for forty-five-year-old Jimmy Savile, boxer Ken Buchanan and Frank McLintock, captain of the double-winning Arsenal football team. June was back to solid plod: playwright Robert Bolt, Rugby Union star Willie John McBride and women's cricket captain, Rachel Heyhoe Flint. The Heath pattern continued until he left Downing Street.

Football and family television stars re-emerged in strength on Wilson's return. In the four lists published in his second Downing Street term, ten football stars and managers were decorated: Jack Charlton, Bill Shankly, Billy McNeill, Bill Nicholson, Willie Ormond, referee Jack Taylor, Ian Callaghan, Joe Mercer, Trevor Morris and Alan Mullery – more footballers than in the next ten lists. Similarly, popular entertainers were well patronised, with honours for David Attenborough, Margaret Leighton, Sheila Hancock, Marjorie Anderson, Charlie Chaplin, George Mitchell (Black and White Minstrels), Vera Lynn, Tommy Trinder, Clive Dunn, Miriam Karlin, Roy Plomley, Harry Corbett (Sooty), Harry H. Corbett (Steptoe), Alfred Marks and Richard Attenborough. The average of four names per list was maintained by Jim Callaghan but halved by Margaret Thatcher – footballers and TV stars, like *Daily Mirror* writers, fare better under Labour (and Harold Wilson in particular) in the honours game.

To recap, the changes that Harold Wilson brought to the honours system were: the ending of hereditary honours (reversed in 1983); the partial ending of political honours (reversed in 1979); an attempt to reform the Lords powers (frustrated in 1969); the reduction in the number of honours going to Civil Servants (maintained to date); and a more popular approach to the 'stardust' element of the lists (abandoned by subsequent Conservative prime ministers).

The Wilson lists will, however, be best remembered for his resignation awards. In addition to the normal twice-yearly, New Year and Birthday honours lists, it is traditional for prime ministers, when they resign from office (or after a general election), to publish additional resignation or dissolution lists. If it is a resignation, followed by the effective retirement of the Prime Minister, the occasion is used largely to pay off various personal or political debts. When Harold Macmillan, one of the most astute manipulators of honours lists, retired in 1963 his resignation list had fifteen names on it, including a barony for John Wyndham, his private secretary (to become Baron Egremont), and baronetcies for his doctor, his press adviser and his Parliamentary Private Secretary.

Sir Alec Douglas Home's 1964 list was both a resignation list – in so far as he did not expect to become Prime Minister again, or indeed lead his party for much longer – and a dissolution list, following as it did, a general election. The personal list, of fourteen, comprised honours to those who had served him at Downing Street, and the dissolution list, of thirty, was largely for people who had served the party outside of Parliament or for former MPs who had retired from the Commons (or who had been defeated) and so were ennobled, both in recognition of their efforts and to strengthen the already overwhelming Conservative influence in the House of Lords. This list, in December 1964, included a viscount, 6 hereditary peers, 2 life peeresses, 3 baronets and 5 knighthoods, with baronetcies for the former Chief Whip, Martin Redmayne, and for Sir Alec's former Parliamentary Private Secretary, Sir Francis Pearson.

Harold Wilson's list of 1970 was unlike those of Harold Macmillan and Sir Alec, being largely a government list rather than a personal one. It came following the defeat of the Labour Party in the 1970 election, and so was supposed to be principally concerned with rewarding servants of the previous Labour government. As Mr Wilson expected to return to Downing Street the personal element was to be minimal. The list had thirty-seven names and most public attention focused on the life peerage that went to George Brown, Labour's Deputy Leader who had been defeated at the general election, and to Harold Davies, another defeated Labour MP and trusted Wilson aide.

A more careful reading of the list, however, reveals knighthoods going to three of the men who later re-emerged as peers in the much more controversial list of 1976. There was a knighthood for George Weidenfeld, founder of publishers Weidenfeld & Nicolson, who had a close personal link with the PM stretching back a quarter of a century to the time when the firm published Harold Wilson's first book, *New Deal for Coal*. There was a knighthood too, for Joseph Kagan, manufacturer of 'Gannex' coats which Harold Wilson habitually wore, and long-time financial supporter of the Labour Party. The third man to achieve the double of knighthood in the 1970 resignation list and peerage in the 1976 list was Joseph Ellis-Stone, Wilson's doctor and golf partner. Stone was the brother of the Tory Lord Ashdown, formerly Sir Arnold Silverstone, who in turn was married to one of the Conservative Party's vice-chairmen, Lady Ashdown.

A closer examination of three other names which appeared on the 1970 list would raise an eyebrow or two in retrospect. A knighthood went to John Brayley, Chairman of the Canning Town Glass Works. He had generously contributed a large number of his company's shares to the Labour Party. Later, in 1973, on Harold Wilson's recommendation, he was elevated to the House of Lords and became a Junior Minister of Defence for the first six months of Harold Wilson's second term at Downing Street (from March to September 1974). He was not popular with his colleagues on the Lords front bench who, according to Andrew Roth, urged Harold Wilson to sack him for incompetence (*Sir Harold Wilson: A Yorkshire Walter Mitty*, Macdonald & Jane's, 1977, p. 37). In the event, his ministerial term was not long and he died three years later – before, however, he was able to clear his name in court of charges that he had misused £200,000 of his company's assets.

A knighthood went to Rudy Sternberg, a German-born entrepreneur whose business career started with button manufacturing, but later revolved around an East–West export–import business. He gained monopoly rights to import potash from East Germany and to export British goods in exchange. At a time when the Cold War gave East Germany the status of a leper colony in the West, Sternberg worked hard to gain political acceptance for the country in Britain. According to Andrew Roth, 'He worked hard to free East German imports and exports from such inhibitions, putting both right-wing Tories like Brigadier Terence Clarke and Barnaby Drayson and left-wing MPs like Will Owen on his companies' pay-rolls' to represent him at international conferences (p. 29).

Sternberg was later to provide invaluable financial assistance to Harold Wilson's private office, when he was in opposition, as will be seen later. He was also able to arrange another deal of great assistance to Harold Wilson, before eventually being elevated to the peerage in 1975. The Czech government of the early 1970s was unpopular in the West following the crushing, by Soviet forces, of the Dubček government and the substitution of a puppet regime in 1968. By 1973 Harold Wilson was in the Opposition and ever grateful for the opportunity to show that he still had influence on the world political stage. The now Sir Rudy Sternberg stepped forward and, not for the first time, devised a scheme that was to please both an unpopular East European government and an ailing British politician.

Languishing in a Czech jail was a Yorkshire vicar, the Rev. David Hathaway, who had been imprisoned for smuggling Bibles into the country. Sternberg was deeply involved in organising, and possibly financing, a trip for Harold Wilson to Prague in 1973 that intended to give credibility to the Czech regime and, as a *quid pro quo*, secure David Hathaway's release. The Czechs got partial rehabilitation and Harold Wilson showed that he still had influence, even in Opposition. However, when the details of the deal eventually trickled out, none of the principals emerged with a great deal of glory; but Sternberg was at work. Two years later, after Harold Wilson's return to Downing Street, he was given a peerage and emerged as Lord Plurenden.

Like John Brayley, the other knight of the 1970 resignation list ennobled before 1976, Rudy Sternberg did not turn out to be Harold Wilson's most active supporter in the House of Lords. In May 1976, as part of the coverage of Wilson's final resignation list, the *Sunday Times* published a survey of the voting records of the 96 Wilson-created peers who were still in receipt of the Labour Whip. The paper examined 53 crucial House of Lords divisions since 1974 in which Labour had suffered a defeat in the Lords. Lord Plurenden was eligible to vote at 48 of them but did not vote once, and was described by the *Sunday Times* as 'Never speaking in the Lords'. Lord Brayley was entitled to vote at all 53 divisions but only voted once and was also described as 'Never speaking'. A third person honoured by Harold Wilson in his 1970 resignation list and ennobled before his 1976 list was his personal secretary, Marcia Williams. She received a CBE in 1970 and was, amid considerable comment, elevated to the peerage, as Lady Falkender, in 1974. That same *Sunday Times* list showed that she had not voted in any of the 50 crucial divisions she had been entitled to vote at and had never spoken in the Lords. These three close Wilson aides supplied him with less support in the Lords than 85 per cent of fellow peers ennobled by him.

Harold Wilson's early enthusiasm, in the 1964–68 period, for creating working peers who could be relied upon to put Labour's case and support the party in the division lobbies, had run out of steam. Some of his later peerages were awarded for the same old reason as they were by his predecessors: settling old obligations and flattering people with titles. The turning point in Wilson's reforming years can probably be traced to the setback he faced when attempting to reform the Lords in 1969. If he couldn't have a reformed House, he may as well enjoy the patronage powers of an unreformed House: peerages could be dished out, no matter what the attendance intention of the recipients. Andrew Roth says that after the shelving of the Parliament (No. 2) Bill in 1969, Harold Wilson lost interest in the Lords. Lord Shackleton, the Labour Leader in the Lords, repeatedly asked him to substantially increase the working Labour element in the House, and even drew up a list of over 200 names for Wilson to elevate, but he could not get the Prime Minister interested in the transfusion of new blood into the chamber.

The trauma of defeat in 1970 was compounded for Harold Wilson by the realisation that he was now deprived of the necessary resources to put his case. Opposition meant no automatic support staff and there was no money to fund research facilities and a private office. Two things characterised Harold Wilson's active political career: meticulous attention to detail (the hallmark of the former don that he was), and the effective presentation of a policy via a well-oiled publicity machine. Both needed money and staff. There wasn't any available for him to perform his task as Leader of the Opposition in the manner which he saw as necessary. Labour Party headquarters, Transport House, offered £6,000 a year to fund the office of the Leader of the Opposition – it would have paid for two secretaries. Wilson needed money to pay his personal secretary, Marcia Williams, newly appointed Press Secretary, Joe Haines and three or four other support staff – at least £20,000 a year. He had to look, not for the first time in his political career, outside his parliamentary allowance and his party's funds for the money to do his job properly.

After his resignation as President of the Board of Trade in April 1951, Harold Wilson took on consultancy work for a Labour-sympathising firm of timber merchants, Montagu Meyer. Within two years, he was receiving a salary of £1,500 a year plus a car, secretary, office and travel facilities from the firm as a foreign-trade consultant. All were invaluable to him in building his career. For example, in 1953 he achieved considerable personal acclaim by securing an hour-long interview with the Soviet Foreign Minister, Molotov, on a trip paid for by Meyer. It did his political standing at home no harm at all. He eventually publicly ended his consultancy with Meyer in 1959 – by which time he was receiving £2–3,000 per year – so that he could concentrate on his parliamentary career. The principal director of the company, John Meyer, received a CBE in 1967.

At about the time Wilson publicly gave up his Meyer consultancy, however, he privately took on another, with a long-time friend and associate. In his old Board of Trade days, Wilson had helped an Austrian refugee, Frank Schon, to finance the expansion of a detergent-making plant in Cumberland owned by his firm, Marchon Products. Much later, when Wilson was in Opposition, Frank Schon approached him to see if he could assist in a commercial transaction with the Russians. In 1958 a Wilson intervention via his old friend Mikoyan helped clinch the deal for Schon; in gratitude Schon took him on as a consultant for Marchon with a retainer of about £1,000 per year. Frank Schon received a knighthood from Harold Wilson in 1966 and a peerage in the January honours list of 1976 – six months before the controversial resignation list, but at a time when Wilson had already decided that he was going to resign.

Harold Wilson, then, had already seen the need and benefited from the practice of having a well-run externally financed private office before he became, once again, Leader of the Opposition in June 1970. His competence to judge the issue is shown by the simple fact that he is the only person to have led the Labour Party to victory in a general election over the last thirty-five years – and he did it four times. An urgent task was for him to find the money to run his office. Two channels were exploited, his memoirs and his friends. In six months he produced a mammoth tome of reminiscences, *The Labour Government 1964–70*, which he effectively wrote most of himself, often scribbling frantically at the rate of 10,000 words a day for twelve to fourteen hours. The results of his labours did not receive unreserved critical acclaim, but earnt an estimated £200,000 in a complex deal which involved the *Sunday Times* and publishers Weidenfeld & Nicolson and Michael Joseph.

The second source was a familiar one to Wilson: sympathetic businessmen. Few leaders of the business community have natural affinities with the Labour movement or socialism, but among those most likely to are mid-European Jews who fled to Britain as refugees and who in the postwar period were encouraged by Labour's attitude to, and the events in, Israel. It was from men with this background that Wilson received much financial backing. Harold Wilson's solicitor, Lord Goodman (life peer 1965) drew up the deeds of a trust fund, under which a dozen or so entrepreneurs were to contribute up to £2,000 a year and from which the expenses of the private office would be financed. The first chairman of the fund was Lord Brown, not George Brown, but a 1964 Wilson-created peer who had been a Junior Minister in the first Wilson government and who was, as Chairman of Glacier Metals, regarded as a management theoretician. He told the *Daily Mail* that the fund was low-profile and that the trustees didn't want the Labour Party to know about it because they feared the party would try to take it over. Among those who contributed to the fund were the newly knighted Sir Rudy Sternberg, Sir George Weidenfeld and Sir Joseph Kagan. A previously appointed knight, Sir Samuel Fisher (1967), who was Vice-President of the London Diamond Bourse and Chairman of the London Labour Mayors' Association (peerage 1974) was another subscriber, as was Ariel Handler, Managing Director of an Israeli-controlled finance house and the only one of the circle not to receive a Wilson honour.

This fund was subsequently complemented by a research fund established with the backing of Sigmund Sternberg (not to be confused with Rudy), a Hungarian refugee who had made a fortune from scrap metal. Sternberg's £20,000 went to service Harold Wilson and various members of the Opposition front bench – three or four graduates were hired at £2–3,000 a year to assist.

And so it was that Wilson was able to finance his private office and effectively equip the Labour front bench with research facilities. The acquisition of such debts of gratitude in order to adequately enable an Opposition to fulfil its tasks is absurd, and Wilson went some way to ensure that it was not an indignity that faced his successors. When back in government he introduced a system to fund the Opposition back-up facilities, and Mrs Thatcher was the first beneficiary of the scheme in 1975, receiving about £150,000 a year.

Harold Wilson's first resignation list, of 1970, included names which subsequently were to provoke comment and criticism. Efforts made, on his behalf, to fund and staff his support system after that list was published involved people who themselves were to figure within the controversy that surrounded his second resignation list in 1976.

The 1976 list was published some eight weeks after Harold Wilson left Downing Street for the last time – normally they are published within a month. For five of those weeks, well-informed leaks of its contents went to Fleet Street, and the backgrounds of all those named as potential recipients were dissected at great length. Members of the Political Honours Scrutiny Committee were sufficiently concerned that they challenged up to eight of the names that were originally submitted to them, and Lord Crathorne, one of the three members of the committee, was reported to have told the *Daily Express* that they objected because, 'these fellers have never done anything'.

The whole pot got a further stir in February 1977, eight months after the list was issued, with the publication of Joe Haines' memoirs, *The Politics of Power* (Hodder & Stoughton, 1977), in which he claimed that the resignation list was written out by Lady Falkender (Harold Wilson's secretary) on lavender-coloured notepaper:

> In the event, some of the names did not survive until the published list. Prudence removed a couple. One or two declined. The names added by Sir Harold improved the quality of the list, but the substantial majority of the knights and peers who were in the published list were those originally proposed by Lady Falkender. (pp. 153–54)

There were 42 names on the list, and nobody, given the system, could have objected to 32 of them. The gongs-for-the-job formula applied here. Thus there was a life peerage for former MP and manager of Wilson's political office, Albert Murray, a Privy Councillorship for TUC General Secretary Len Murray, a Companion of Honour for former Lord Chancellor Lord Elwyn-Jones, a knighthood for dying actor Stanley Baker, CBEs for Harold Wilson's constituency agent and the Labour Party's national agent, an OBE for the Chief Executive of the Borough Council which incorporated Wilson's constituency, etc. Since the list could not encompass the normal range of show-business 'stardust' Harold Wilson's lists normally had, he satisfied himself with an OBE for mimic Mike Yarwood – perhaps he was expected to do impersonations of the other people Wilson would have honoured. Various political secretaries received MBEs and then there were the also-rans – the recipients of the British Empire Medal. The four in Harold Wilson's personal list show just how thoroughly this insidious formula is applied: they went to the telephonist, the cleaner, the policeman and the messenger who serviced Number 10 – people clearly not of sufficient rank to merit a royal investiture.

The howls of outrage that greeted the list were, however, concentrated on ten people: six peers and four knights included in the list, and two others widely assumed to have at one stage been on the list and later removed. It is on occasions like this, amassing all the pomposity within its grasp, that *The Times* thunders at its most censorious. A small extract from its editorial of 27 May 1976 perhaps encapsulates the ire that publication of the list provoked:

> When one reads the role of honour: Delfont, Grade, Kagan, Rayne, Weidenfeld, Goldsmith, Hanson, Miller, Sternberg, the impression it creates with cumulative and striking force is one of unrepentant Darwinism, of the business of the survival of the fittest and of Nature red in tooth and claw. These are the very people whose lives are the contradiction of everything for which the Labour Party stands. Is it really true that they are the people he wants to thank for having helped him with his administration?

The following day, Arthur Blenkinsop MP sponsored an Early Day Motion disassociating the Parliamentary Labour Party from the list, and within hours over a hundred Labour MPs – half of those not on the government payroll – had signed it.

Who were these men to provoke so much comment? Lew Grade

and Bernard Delfont were brothers and theatrical impresarios. Although they had both been previously knighted by Harold Wilson in 1969 and 1974, respectively, they were not known as Labour Party supporters in what after all was supposed to be the political resignation list of a Labour Prime Minister. Harold Wilson's rather weak defence of the attacks made on the peerages going to these two men was,

My constituents and everyone's constituents – and I'm talking about *real* people – enjoy being entertained, entertained well and entertained professionally. And my constituents in their innocence prefer the ladies and gentlemen of showbusiness to the sanctimonious and pontificating commentators.

That was probably true of his knighthoods to John Mills and Stanley Baker and OBE for Mike Yarwood – but Messrs Grade and Delfont could hardly be thought of as central to the thoughts and hearts of the general public.

Joseph Kagan had received a knighthood in 1970 and was a long-time financial supporter of Labour, being one of those who contributed to the trust fund established to pay for the Leader's office between 1970 and 1974. He was singled out for considerable press hostility, but responded phlegmatically, 'Those who mind don't matter, those who matter don't mind.' He was later convicted of theft and false accounting. (Lady Falkender's brother married the future Lord Kagan's secretary.)

The next name to raise an eyebrow was Max Rayne. He was a property millionaire who had received a knighthood towards the end of Harold Wilson's first period in Downing Street, in 1969. Rayne was not well known as a Labour supporter and many may have felt he epitomised what Harold Wilson went to some lengths to condemn three months before becoming leader of the party, in October 1962. Talking of the Labour Party and who it sought to represent, he told Labour's Brighton conference,

It is true we cannot boast of any delegates representing some of the parasitic growth of Tory freedom – the Amalgamated Society of Share Pushers and Company Promoters is not an affiliated organisation, nor have constituency Labour Parties thought fit to send up representatives of property speculators, takeover bidders, dividend strippers, or bond washers . . .

Lord Rayne's honours citation was, in fact, 'for charitable services and services to the Arts', but it was his property dealings for which he was best known; if Harold Wilson's premiership began with disdain for people in his business, the resignation honours list would suggest he ended up more appreciative of the people it attracted.

George Weidenfeld was one of the three names to appear on both Harold Wilson's resignation lists – a knighthood in 1970 and a peerage six years later. Although Lord Weidenfeld had been a friend of Harold Wilson's since 1944 and had been his publisher from the following year, there was in fact no contractual arrangement between the two men. So, despite the fact that he published the memoirs of the leader of the 1964–70 Labour government, in an admittedly complex deal, George Weidenfeld was at arm's length from Harold Wilson when the 1976 list was published. He was also Lady Falkender's publisher and a frequent escort and host to her.

A recipient on the 1976 list who is said by Andrew Roth to have offered Lady Falkender a job was James Goldsmith. Between the announcement of Harold Wilson's resignation and the resignation taking effect, Goldsmith was a luncheon guest at Downing Street. After the lunch was over, a small number of Wilson's associates were told by him that Goldsmith had intended to offer Lady Falkender a directorship of Cavenham Foods, the company then at the centre of his complex financial empire. Goldsmith's *London Gazette* citation for his knighthood mentioned his chairmanship of Cavenham Ltd, but it also cited his 'services to ecology'. Either this was a bizarre joke in some way referring to his attempts to extinguish the satirical magazine *Private Eye* by his civil and criminal libel actions, or it was a case of mistaken identity. Sir James Goldsmith's brother, Edward, is in fact a prominent ecologist. In the month of speculation of who would or would not be in the list, most attention focused on Goldsmith. The rumour that he was to receive a peerage brought a considerable welter of protest, most notably from Lord Longford. In the event, he emerged from the resignation list as Sir James Goldsmith. The objections expressed about him came largely from Labour backbenchers and those who did not like what they saw as his vendetta against *Private Eye*, and who disliked his very close public association with the Conservative cause. He was, according to George Hutchinson in *The Times*, 'a declared contributor to Tory funds. As such he is much esteemed by party treasurers'. As an ex-party worker Mr Hutchinson was in a position to know how big a gift had to be for the donor to be 'much esteemed' by the party's fund-raisers. In 1974, for example, Goldsmith's companies gave £8,000 to the Tory coffers, in 1978 Cavenham gave £15,000 to the Conservative Centre for Policy Studies (one of its largest ever donations), in 1979 £5,000 went direct to the Tory Party and in 1982 and 1983 £1,000 a year was paid to the CPS. In addition to this generosity to the Conservative cause, Goldsmith had been an adviser on European affairs to Edward Heath during his premiership. His knowledge of matters continental, and French in particular, was considerable. So much so, that in the week of his knighthood he succeeded in persuading the shareholders of Cavenham Foods to export control of their company to France – not the kind of move that would normally have found favour with Harold Wilson.

James Hanson is an immensely rich industrialist and another Conservative funder who found himself in receipt of a knighthood in Harold Wilson's resignation list. (He has had the additional distinction of subsequently receiving a peerage (1983) from Mrs Thatcher after having become one of the Conservative Party's most generous supporters (see Chapter 7).) James Hanson had two things in common with Harold Wilson: both were born in Yorkshire and both in later life became trustees of the D'Oyly Carte opera company. One of the names that was rumoured to be appearing on Wilson's final list was David Frost but, according to Andrew Roth, his name was eventually dropped from the recommendations because it was felt that the honour might be associated in the public mind with a £100,000 television contract Harold Wilson had entered into to be hosted by David Frost, for Yorkshire TV. Ironically, James (now Lord) Hanson received his knighthood despite the fact that he was, at the time, Chairman of Trident, the company that controlled both Yorkshire and Tyne Tees TV.

The final name *The Times* listed in its 'role of honour' editorial of 27 May was that of Eric Miller. He was another property tycoon (head of the Peachey Corporation) and one-time Treasurer of the Socialist International. Miller had become a millionaire by the age of thirty-four and at the time of the 1974 general election was in a position to lend Harold Wilson his company's helicopter for campaigning purposes. When Wilson resigned in March 1976, his friends threw a leaving party and champagne costing £3,304 was supplied by Eric Miller from the Peachey Corporation's resources. Wilson thought that his friends had paid for it, but as *The Economist* was later tersely to remark, 'Most of the shareholders of the property company weren't his [Wilson's] friends at the time'. Eric Miller's inability to distinguish between his own and his company's money led to him being ousted from the board in May 1977 and for a Department of Trade inquiry to be conducted into his affairs. In the event, he shot himself in September 1977, eighteen months before the report was published. The report accused him of misappropriating vast sums of company money, misleading the company's auditors, forging documents, and trying to incriminate others in his misdeeds. Two of the many instances they cited gave an indication of his methods. He bought a necklace from Aspreys, the jewellers, with £65,000 of Peachey money and then sold it, pocketing the proceeds. He also had a personal overdraft with Keyser Ullman, the merchant bank, and used his company's money to lower it.

One name not on *The Times'* role of honour, but which certainly provoked some comment, was the peerage that went to John Vaizey, Professor of Economics and Dean of the Faculty of Social Science at Brunel University. A former member of the Labour Party, Vaizey was an outspoken and trenchant critic of Harold Wilson. He had, however, been of great service to Lady Falkender, who was the single parent of two sons: Vaizey helped fix her up with a public-school education for them, for which she was grateful.

The most widely tipped name to appear on the resignation list that didn't make it was Jarvis Astaire. There is no little irony in the fact that he, at least, was a member of the Labour Party in a list of peers and knights who were conspicuous by their antipathy to the cause. Described as a socialist for many years, Astaire joined the party in 1974, supported it financially in that year's election and may have been a contributor to the trust fund that had helped finance the Leader of the Opposition's office 1970–74. He had interests in betting (via William Hill), transmitting sporting events – particularly boxing (via Viewsport) – and a financial link with James Goldsmith (via Anglo-Continental Finance). Lord Crathorne of the Political Honours Scrutiny Committee is said to have been responsible for preventing his name appearing on the final honours list, although it had been submitted originally by Harold Wilson.

So it was that the names that appeared, and in two cases did not appear, on Harold Wilson's resignation honours list in June 1976 spoilt an otherwise carefully planned farewell and smooth transition of power. Wilson had spent the majority of his time in Downing Street attempting to inject, if not the white heat of the technological revolution, certainly a degree of reform into the honours system. In the end, he was defeated by vested interests – in itself a testimony to the strength and resilience of the system. His term of office ended with a list which provoked as much controversy as that of that other twentieth-century radical non-conformist Prime Minister who could not count on the full financial support from his nominal party – Lloyd George. Neither, in the end, beat the honours system, but both ended up exploiting it and gracing it with their own ennoblements.

Seven

Thatcher's honoured industrialists

Private-sector industrialists have received knighthoods and peerages at a faster rate under Margaret Thatcher than under any Prime Minister since Lloyd George, albeit in different circumstances. Between taking office in 1979 and June 1985, 11 private-sector industrialists were given peerages, all of whom, as shown in Table 8, directed companies which gave total donations of £1.9 million to Conservative Party funds in the first six years of the Thatcher premiership. A further 64 were given knighthoods, of whom 44 directed companies which gave, in total, £4.4 million to Conservative Party funds, as shown in Table 9.

Table 10 presents the picture in a slightly different way – it shows that ten companies gave more than £200,000 (or £33,000 per year, on average) to Conservative Party funds in the first six years of the Thatcher premiership. Nine of these companies, accounting for 89 per cent of the £2.6 million given, have had their boards of directors honoured since 1979 with, in total, 6 peerages and 5 knighthoods.

Before I examine these correlations in detail, it is necessary to say a little about Conservative Party finances, the complexities involved in discovering details of them, and the assumptions that have to be made about published information.

The Conservative Party has not published its accounts since 1980 and, even when it did, it gave no indication of the sources of its income. Commercial companies are required, under the terms of the 1967 Companies Act, to disclose all donations to political bodies of over £250 in their annual reports. But there is no central agency collecting the information like the Certification Officer. He is responsible, among other things, for drawing together details of the political funds of trade unions. Since there are only just over a

Table 8
Private-sector Industrialists Awarded Peerages by Margaret Thatcher, 1979–85

Name	Company	Date of peerage	Conservative Party donation in peerage year (£)	Total donations 1979–84 (£)
Sir Edwin McAlpine[1]	Newarthill	Jan 1980	33,000	205,000
Sir Marcus Sieff	Marks & Spencer	Jan 1980	20,500	160,000[2]
Victor Matthews	Trafalgar House	June 1980	—	210,000
Sir Arnold Weinstock	GEC	June 1980	50,000	50,000
Sir William Cayzer	British & Commonwealth Shipping	Jan 1982	95,810	410,531
Sir Charles Forte	Trusthouse Forte	Jan 1982	35,700	175,200
Sir Frank Taylor	Taylor Woodrow	Dec 1982	53,950	367,510
Sir James Hanson	Hanson Trust	June 1983	82,000[3]	217,000[4]
Sir John King[5]	Babcock International	June 1983	7,500	50,000
Alistair McAlpine[6]	Newarthill	Jan 1984	43,000	205,000
Nigel Vinson[7]	Electra Investment Trust	Jan 1985	2,500[8]	10,000
	Fleming Tech. Investment Trust		300[8,9]	1,150
			424,260	1,856,393[10]

1. Citation was for Sir Robert McAlpine Ltd, Newarthill is its parent company
2. Money mainly to British United Industrialists
3. Includes £2,000 to Centre for Policy Studies
4. Includes £7,000 to Centre for Policy Studies
5. Also Chairman of British Airways and Secretary of City and Industry Liaison Council
6. Also Joint Treasurer of Conservative Party
7. Founder of Centre for Policy Studies
8. Latest figure available
9. Money to Centre for Policy Studies
10. Newarthill figure only counted once

Table 9

Private-sector Industrialists Awarded Knighthoods by Margaret Thatcher, 1979–85

Name	Company	Date of knighthood	Conservative Party donation in knighthood year (£)	Total donations 1979–84 (£)
Austin Bide	Glaxo	Jan 1980	26,250[1]	288,500[3]
Robert Clayton	GEC	Jan 1980	50,000	50,000
Eric Sisson	Smiths Inds	Jan 1980	6,600[4]	56,400[5]
Graham Wilkins	Beecham	June 1980	21,000[6]	140,000[7]
Patrick Meaney	Thomas Tilling	Jan 1981	—	—
	Rank Organisation[2]		31,000[6]	190,000[8]
Reginald Smith	Wimpey	Jan 1981	25,000	170,175
Owen Aister	Marley	June 1981	—	45,000
James Duncan	Transport Development Group	June 1981	4,500[9]	31,200[10]
Alistair Frame	RTZ	June 1981	—	—
	Plessey[2]		5,000[6]	190,000[8]
Ernest Harrison	Racal	June 1981	30,000	200,000
Peter Macadam	BAT	June 1981	2,000[11]	11,000[11]
Keith Showering	Allied-Lyons	June 1981	71,500	424,025
Lawrence Barratt	Barratt Development	Jan 1982	—	20,000
James Cleminson	Reckitt & Colman	Jan 1982	20,000	132,000
	United Biscuits[2]		33,000	217,000
Trevor Holdsworth	GKN	Jan 1982	11,000[6]	97,750[8]
Christopher Laidlaw	ICL	June 1983	—	—
	Commercial Union[2]		25,000[12]	121,000[12]
Alan Smith	Dawson International	June 1982	1,500	10,500
John Baring	Baring Brothers	Jan 1983	25,050	120,800
Terence Conran	Habitat/Mothercare	Jan 1983	—	—
Adam Thompson	Caledonian Aviation	Jan 1983	—	26,500[3]
	MEPC[2]		7,500	50,000
Basil Blackwell	Westland	June 1983	10,000	28,340
Duncan Macdonald	NEI	June 1983	45,000	202,500
Joseph Nickerson	Nickerson Group	June 1983	—	1,100
Clive Sinclair	Sinclair Research	June 1983	27,000	39,000
Richard Bailey	Royal Doulton[14]	Jan 1984	16,000[6]	107,200[8]
Timothy Bevan	Barclays Bank	Jan 1984	—	—
	Commercial Union[2]		—	121,000
John Robert Carter	Distillers	Jan 1984	50,000	50,000

Name	Company	Date		
Alan Veale	Royal Insurance	Jan 1984	35,000	185,000
	GEC	June 1984	—	50,000
George Bowman-Shaw	Lancer Boss	June 1984	—	18,253
Nigel Broackes	Trafalgar House	June 1984	40,000	210,000
Robert Lickley	Fairley Holdings[14]	June 1984	16,000[6]	107,200
Thomas Risk	Bank of Scotland		—	—
Gordon Brunton	Merchants Trust[2]	Jan 1985	750	2,750
	Sotheby Parke Bernet		—[15]	20,000
	Bemrose Printing[2]		—[15]	2,575
William Coats	Coats Patons	Jan 1985	10,000[15]	48,000
Robert Haslam	Tate & Lyle	Jan 1985	10,250[15]	67,875
Peter Reynolds	Rank Hovis McDougall	Jan 1985	20,000[15]	130,000
Jeffrey Sterling	Sterling Guarantee Trust	Jan 1985	10,000[15]	10,000
	P & O Shipping[2]		20,000[15]	77,500
George Bernard Audley	AGB	June 1985	50,000[15]	150,000
Leonard Gow	Christian Salvesen	June 1985	20,000[15]	45,200
Ronald Halstead	Beecham	June 1985	35,000[15,8]	140,000
Martin Jacomb	Kleinwort Benson	June 1985	20,015[15]	112,515
Eric Pountain	Tarmac	June 1985	20,000[15]	93,500
	Glynwed	June 1985	20,000[15]	105,000
			870,915	4,303,458[17]
Total of Tables 8 and 9 (excluding duplications)			1,255,175[18]	5,899,851[19]

1. Includes £1,250 to Centre for Policy Studies (CPS)
2. Not principal company with which director associated
3. Includes £8,500 to CPS
4. Includes £600 to CPS
5. Includes £1,800 to CPS
6. Includes £1,000 to CPS
7. Includes £10,000 to CPS
8. Includes £5,000 to CPS
9. Includes £2,000 to CPS
10. Includes £10,700 to CPS
11. All to CPS
12. Includes £2,500 to CPS
13. Donation made by Mothercare before Conran became a director
14. A subsidiary of S. Pearson that made the donations
15. Latest figures available
16. Amec is an amalgamation of the Fairclough Group and William Press Construction; the donations were made by William Press before the 1982 amalgamation
17. The figure excludes duplication of the donations of Royal Insurance, Commercial Union, S. Pearson, GEC
18. Less one of two GEC entries
19. Less one GEC entry and one Trafalgar House entry

hundred TUC-affiliated unions, the task is not a huge one, and the Certification Officer is able to provide an annual account of the state of health of trade-union political funds. The 1984 Trade Union Act put further restrictions on trade unions' abilities to fund the Labour Party by requiring unions to hold ballots at least every ten years to legitimise the continuation of the funds. There is no such requirement on companies to ballot over gifts of money to the Conservative Party, and there is no central government-appointed agency responsible for publishing annual details of those donations. Nor is there any means of tracing corporate donations of less than £250.

Table 10
Top Ten Conservative Party Funders, 1979–84

Company	Donations 1979–84 (£)	Director honoured	Honour	Year
Allied-Lyons	424,025	Keith Showering	Knight	1981
British & Commonwealth Shipping	410,531	Sir William Cayzer	Baron	1982
Taylor Woodrow	367,510	Sir Frank Taylor	Baron	1982
Guardian Royal Exchange	296,000	None		
Glaxo	288,500	Austin Bide	Knight	1980
Hanson Trust	217,000	Sir James Hanson	Baron	1983
United Biscuits	217,000	James Cleminson	Knight	1982
Trafalgar House	210,000	Victor Matthews	Baron	1980
		Nigel Broackes	Knight	1984
Newarthill	205,000	Sir Robert McAlpine	Baron	1980
		Alistair McAlpine	Baron	1984
Northern Engineering Industries	202,500	Duncan Macdonald	Knight	1983

The task of tracing donations is left to outside bodies. The Labour Research Department, a trade-union-funded research body not connected with the Labour Party, is the chief supplier of that information. The job is a daunting one. There are 600,000 currently trading registered companies in the UK, each of which is required to file details of its trading with Companies House in Cardiff every year. Copies of these accounts are available to the public – at £1 each. A proper annual search would thus cost at least £600,000, plus an enormous amount of time. Unfortunately, the problem is even more complex. In 1983, 406,000 companies broke the Companies Acts by failing to file their accounts on time. These failures weren't taken very seriously by the government – only 871 of them, or 0.2 per cent, were prosecuted with an average fine of only £40.

Given these problems, the Labour Research Department simply examines the published accounts of the 2,000 major public companies each year. In the years when the Conservative Party did publish some form of accounts it gave a company-donations figure that was fairly consistently about 50 per cent above the total discovered. It seems fair to assume, therefore, that about two-thirds of company donations to Conservative Party funds can be traced in these searches. It does seem bizarre in the extreme that a party that is so concerned about the source of the Labour Party's funds is so secretive about its own.

The next problem facing the diligent researcher is the Tory Party's use of a number of 'front' organisations. The best known, and most commonly used, is British United Industrialists (BUI). Until recently BUI had a small suite of offices in Park Lane, but in 1984 it became a tenant of the Economic League in Wine Office Court, off Fleet Street. An estimated £500,000 per year is given by companies to BUI, but when I tried to find out why BUI was used and where its money went, I was stonewalled. According to its current Director, Captain Tom Briggs, the organisation consists of him and his secretary and their job is to collect money and 'give it to organisations that work for free enterprise'. An academic authority on Conservative Party finance, Michael Pinto-Duschinsky, was told by Conservative Party headquarters that 80 per cent of BUI's money goes to them (*British Political Finance 1830–1980*, p. 229).

British United Industrialists was itself a limited company until 1968, but it then dissolved itself to become an unincorporated association, which meant that it was not covered by the 1967 Companies Act and therefore did not have to disclose in its annual accounts how much it passed on to Conservative Party headquarters.

Captain Briggs said that his work was overseen by 'a council of prominent industrialists' (who he was not prepared to name), which was self-perpetuating. BUI provides records of where its money goes for its donors, but for nobody else. When I asked a number of major BUI-funders for details of where the money went I was given evasive answers. Mr Silver of Sun Alliance and London Assurance, when asked why the company gave money to British United Industrialists, felt the topic was 'not a fruitful source of discussion' and put the phone down. Reckitt & Colman, despite at the time employing 14,000 people in Britain, could not find a single person to discuss their gift of £20,000 a year to BUI. Chairman Sir James Cleminson was not prepared to speak directly, but gave the message via his secretary that he had to 'rush out' but that the company gave its donation 'in the interest of free enterprise'.

Allied-Lyons is BUI's largest financial backer. Its Public Relations Officer, Mr Marquis, was not prepared to tell me why the company gave money to BUI or where that money went, but he did say, 'If any shareholder wants to know, they only have to ask and they shall be provided with information.'

A pension-fund administrator of a major British trade union, with shares in Allied-Lyons, took up Mr Marquis's offer, but received an uninformative response from Company Secretary, F. H. Fearn:

> The company has chosen to contribute to British United Industrialists because it considers it a reputable organisation and is satisfied that the money donated to it will be applied in accordance with BUI's objectives to support bodies which serve the cause of free enterprise. We do not feel it is for us to respond or comment on your other requests for information, as these concern matters which ought to be raised with BUI itself.

The manager of a charitable trust with shares in Reckitt & Colman wrote to the company asking why they gave money to BUI and what they got from it. He was told:

> BUI disburses its funds in a variety of ways. Support is given to the Conservative Party as well as to other organisations of varying types and sizes. All of them have as their prime factor the wish to support free enterprise. If you would like to have further information on BUI, I would suggest that you telephone them and ask for Captain Tom Briggs, the Director-General.

The charity trust-fund manager did one better, he wrote to Tom Briggs and received the reply, 'I confirm that BUI's aim is to promote and defend Free Enterprise. However, as an Unincorporated Association, we are not required to publish our accounts and it is not our policy to issue them publicly or the names of the organisations that receive our support. I regret I am unable to be more helpful.'

I have included this discourse on BUI to indicate some of the difficulties in tracking down who actually gives money to the Conservative Party. Since BUI's accounts are not published and they won't say how much of their funds they pass on to Conservative Central Office, and since the academically respectable Pinto-Duschinsky was told by the Conservative Central Office that it was 80 per cent, I have included donations to British United Industrialists in the sums of Tory Party funds in the tables in this chapter.

BUI is, however, only the largest of the organisations which pass money over to Tory funds; there are also nine regional bodies, known as 'regional industrialists' councils'. Over forty companies a year declare a political donation to one or other of the following: Northern Industrialists' Protection Association (NIPA); North-West Industrialists' Council (NWIC); Humberside Industrialists' Council (HIC); West Yorkshire Industrialists' Council (WYIC); South Yorkshire Industrialists' Council (SYIC); Midlands Industrial Advisory Council (MIAC); East Midlands Industrial Council (EMIC); South-Western Industrialists' Council (SWIC); the City and Industrial Liaison Council (CILC). None of these bodies appears in the telephone directories, yet a phone call to the Newcastle Central Area Conservative Party Office asking to speak to someone from NIPA will be put through, without question, to Lt-Col. J. M. Barton, the NIPA secretary. Similarly, phone calls for NWIC to Conservative Area HQ in Manchester, HIC to Conservative offices in Grantham, WYIC to Conservative offices in Leeds, SYIC to Conservative offices in Grantham (again), MIAC to Conservative headquarters in Birmingham, EMIC to Conservative offices in Grantham (yet again), SWIC to Tory Exeter offices and CILC to Conservative Central Office in Smith Square, Westminster, will be answered by someone from the appropriate industrialists' council.

On average, Labour Research is able to trace about £140,000 a year going to these bodies, rising to £250,000 in election years. As with BUI, they are unincorporated associations and nobody at either the individual industrialists' councils or the companies giving money to them is prepared to say where the money goes and why it is channelled through these organisations. In an apparently unguarded moment, one-time Secretary of the NIPA, Colonel Knight, told the *Newcastle Journal* (16 June 1976): 'basically the money goes to the Conservative Party as an instrument in fighting for free enterprise'. When the then Trade Minister, Gerard Vaughan, was asked in Parliament in December 1982 whether he would consider introducing legislation requiring these bodies to publish accounts showing the sources and destination of their money, he replied simply, 'No'. When I asked Conservative Central Office whether the industrialists' councils simply passed their money directly to Tory Party funds, they refused to comment. When I asked the various regional secretaries for comments I was referred to Conservative Central Office. One, Michael Hankinson of WYIC, said, 'We've heard that you've been making enquiries among industrialists about us. I have to tell you that I'm an employee and I have been given very clear instructions not to talk to you. Thank you and good-bye.'

The central figure in the industrialists' councils network is Major-General Sir Brian Wyldebore-Smith (knighted by Margaret Thatcher in 1980), who doubles up as Director of the Conservative Board of Finance. He is Secretary to the CILC and oversees the activities of three other councils (HIC, EMIC and SYIC) from his home town of Grantham. When contacted, he said, 'I never discuss either donations or industrialists' councils with the public.' The Major-General, like his co-fund-raiser, Conservative Party Treasurer, Lord McAlpine of West Green (Thatcher peerage 1984), is well connected to generous companies. In 1944, he married Molly Cayzer, sister of two vice-chairmen of British and Commonwealth Shipping. In 1982, the firm made a donation of £95,810 to Tory Party funds. British and Commonwealth's Chairman, and their cousin, Sir William Cayzer, was elevated to the peerage in the same year.

Given the total unwillingness of those associated with the industrialists' councils to discuss their finances, and the public unavailability of their accounts, together with overwhelming circumstantial evidence, I have assumed for the purposes of indicating a destination of political donations that money declared to be going to the industrialists' councils goes, in fact, to Conservative Party coffers.

Reading the almost tea-leaf-like evidence of Conservative Party finance, it is clear that the party has in recent years experienced financial hardship. Pinto-Duschinsky, in his authorative book on the history of British political finance, writes:

Conservative finances have come under strain since the 1960s ... the party suffered considerable financial losses in the general elections of 1964, 1974 and 1979. Normally the Central Office has relied on making sufficient profit on its election-year appeals to carry it through the years between elections ... After three years (1975/76–1977/78), during which income balanced expenditure, the Central Office has suffered further serious deficits in the past two years (1978/79 and 1979/80). During this time, spending exceeded income by £1,966,000. That a loss of this magnitude should have been incurred at the time of the 1979 general election – when a surplus could normally have been hoped for – indicates that the Conservative Party treasurers will be hard-pressed to raise funds for the routine expenses of the Central Office in the lean period that normally follows a campaign. Unlike most previously published Central Office accounts, those for 1978/79 and 1979/80 do not include information on the state of the party's reserves. The magnitude of the deficits incurred between 1978 and 1980 and the low level of the reserves at the start of the period suggests that the central organisation has exhausted its funds and that it has been obliged to seek bank loans to cover its day-to-day operations. (*British Political Finance 1830–1980*, American Enterprise Institute, p. 153)

The trends that Pinto-Duschinsky noted seem to have continued in the period after he wrote, although the Conservative Central Office press desk refuses to discuss the matter with even such respectable newspapers as the *Sunday Times*. In 1981, for example, forty-one Central Office staff were made redundant. A third of the companies that were still in existence which had regularly given money to the Conservative Party until 1979 had stopped their donation in the four years after the general election of that year.

In December 1983, *Labour Research*, reviewing the first eight Thatcher honours lists, found that 8 peers and 33 private-sector industrialist knights had been created. 28 of the 41 men were associated with companies that had given the Conservative Party £2.75 million since 1979, 'that is 34% of the total donations traced in searches of 2,000 sets of company accounts'. The article further stated that although 41 per cent of the top 100 British industrial companies gave money to Tory Party funds and only 15 per cent of the top 2,000 did, 78 per cent of the companies associated with men who had received honours had given money over the previous four years. Eighteen companies had given £90,000 or more to the Conservative Party over the previous four years, fourteen of which, the article stated (in fact, it was fifteen – Lord Taylor of Taylor Woodrow was omitted), had had one of their directors honoured during Mrs Thatcher's premiership. 'Companies that have dominated Tory fund-raising have been honoured at twice the rate of companies that have dominated the economy,' concluded the analysis.

Publication of the research findings resulted in considerable publicity in *The Times* and dominated a Ten Minute Rule Bill debate in the House of Commons. The *Daily Telegraph*, on the day of publication, noted: 'To allay any criticism of the present system of honours arising from the report, there has been a Whitehall-inspired "leak" in the past few days that there has been a tightening up of the security that ensures that there can be no suggestion of impropriety.'

After quoting extensively from the findings, Austin Mitchell, in his speech to the Commons introducing the Ten Minute Rule Bill which sought to control political donations, said, 'What is happening is totally contrary to the spirit and intention of the Honours (Prevention of Abuses) Act 1925 and merits a full and independent enquiry.'

Ten Minute Rule Bill procedure normally dictates that there is one speech in favour of a motion and one in opposition. The Tory Party opposed the Mitchell Bill. According to the *Daily Mail*'s then parliamentary sketch-writer, Andrew Alexander:

> Their champion yesterday was Mr Cranley Onslow, a Foreign Office junior minister until June, a veteran Tory MP, and a man of whom one expects little and is rarely disappointed. Yesterday he did not answer the argument but spent most of his time assailing the Labour Research Department, an organisation 'once proscribed by the official Labour Party'. Tories shouted 'Aha' expectantly ... BUT were the LRD's figures actually wrong? Mr Onslow skirted round this aspect of the argument, preferring the more generalised scoff.

It is interesting that it should have been Cranley Onslow who was chosen to oppose Austin Mitchell. Mr Onslow subsequently, quite properly, disclosed that he was employed as a consultant to Bristow Helicopters. Bristow Helicopters is a subsidiary company of British and Commonwealth Shipping – the contributor of the largest single donation to Tory Party funds. In the autumn of 1984, Cranley Onslow defeated Edward du Cann to become Chairman of the 1922 Committee. That committee was established in the latter days of the Lloyd George Coalition government by dissident Conservative backbenchers who were unhappy at their party's continued membership of the Coalition; they disliked being tainted with the Lloyd George brush.

Cranley Onslow, as Andrew Alexander indicated, did little to challenge the figures presented by Austin Mitchell. Instead he attacked their source using information published in a *Wall Street Journal* article written by Mr Douglas Eden, exposing the 'Communist infiltration' of those connected with the Labour Research Department. At that time the Press Council was considering a complaint brought by Robert Hughes MP against the *Daily Express*. The Press Council report on the case, dated 28 February 1984, gives the details: 'A story headlined "Spot the Trots" by John Warden, political editor, was accompanied by a table compiled by election analyst Douglas Eden purporting to show the political interests and involvement of the Labour candidates in 70 constituencies.' The Press Council, a body not known for the ferocity of its language, passed judgement:

> The *Daily Express* should have checked the accuracy of its information before publishing their attack on Mr Robert Hughes MP and other Labour parliamentary candidates. The information was inaccurate and the Press Council agrees that the published reference to him constituted a politically malicious and unjustified slur on Mr Hughes which should have been withdrawn. The newspaper failed either to substantiate or withdraw its allegation that most of the 70 Labour candidates it named were 'cold doctrinaire advocates of the all-powerful one-party state'.

Having quoted Mr Eden's *Wall Street Journal* article, Cranley Onslow explained the safeguards against abuse of the existing Political Honours Scrutiny Committee and how Mrs Thatcher had issued guidelines tightening it up in 1979. 'What we have before us today is a shabby and scurrilous attack on the members of the Political Honours Scrutiny Committee . . . This is a sordid little proposal and it should be voted down without further ado.'

Unusually for a Ten Minute Rule Bill debate, a third MP rose to speak, Norman Atkinson, veteran Labour MP and former Party Treasurer. He said that when he had been Treasurer, the party took a decision never to accept donations from limited companies or from any other group that could be interpreted as trying to obtain favours from the government. He went on to say that James Callaghan had asked him 'to scrutinise the matter to ensure that not one person who appeared on his list or on any recent list had made a donation of any type to the Labour Party; and the fact that no one had done so was verified'. At that point he was shut up by the Speaker. However, Atkinson later returned to his feet: 'Under the 1925 Act the charges made by my honourable friend the Member for Greater Grimsby [Mr Mitchell], which I believe to be true, could, if proved, mean imprisonment for the Prime Minister.' The House divided and Austin Mitchell's Bill was defeated, by 271 votes to 172.

Anthony Bevins of *The Times* sought out Atkinson after the debate, and the paper reported:

Mr Atkinson said afterwards that Mr Callaghan had cited the Honours (Prevention of Abuses) Act 1925 and had given a warning that if a person honoured had signed a contribution cheque or otherwise authorised payment there would be a *prima facie* offence . . . Mr Atkinson said 'Jim Callaghan was very fastidious about this'. Asked by *The Times* whether Mr Callaghan had not honoured leaders of unions which had made donations to Labour, Mr Atkinson said: 'They do not personally give donations.'

Following the debate, there was a minor flurry of press attention, including a leader column in the *Daily Mirror*, written by Harold Wilson's former Press Secretary, Joe Haines, in which he cited, without naming them, six dubious honours awarded in recent times:

Countless thousands of people have been deservedly decorated. But others have bought their way into ermine or towards lesser titles. Of that there is no doubt. Only the libel laws and the difficulty of proof prevented private scandals from becoming public ones . . . That is why the Commons was wrong to reject a Bill aimed at curbing honours for those who contributed money – their own or their company's – to political funds. Taint one honour and all are tainted. MPs should have seized the chance to make the Honours Lists honourable.

If the figures correlating honours awarded with donations to Conservative Party funds were dramatic in December 1983, the following four honours lists did little to diminish the extent of the coincidences. In December 1983, Labour Research reported that 8 private-sector industrialists had been made peers and 33 had been knighted, of whom 28 were directors of companies which had contributed £2.75 million to Conservative Party funds since 1979 – 34 per cent of the money traced by Labour Research. By the summer of 1985, those figures could be updated: 11 peerages and 64 knighthoods had been awarded to private-sector industrialists since 1979. Fifty-five of the 75 men were or still are associated with companies that have given the Conservative Party £5.8 million since 1979 – 43 per cent of the money Labour Research has traced in donations going to the Conservative Party.

All eleven of the industrialist peers created since 1979 are, of course, very successful and distinguished businessmen whose contributions to the strength of their companies have been immense. All eleven have taken the Conservative Whip in the House of Lords, according to the government whip's office, and could well have been elevated to the Lords to strengthen the Conservative Party in that House.

The two peers who direct companies with the smallest donations in the list, Lord King and Lord Vinson, have less of a personal family connection with or controlling interest in the companies they direct and have other major qualities which would have made them attractive additions to the Conservative benches in the House of Lords. Lord King of Wartnaby, as well as chairing Babcock International, is Chairman of British Airways. It is traditional that the chairmen of nationalised industries receive honours. He has done much to make British Airways a practical proposition for privatisation, a cause dear to the heart of the present administration. He is also Chairman of the Conservative fund-raising organisation, the City and Industrial Liaison Council.

When Lord Vinson received his peerage, the *London Gazette* citation was that he was Chairman of the Development Corporation and President of the Industrial Participation Society – both the kind of posts that a distinguished holder could normally expect to receive a knighthood for. He is on the board of Barclays Bank and two investment trusts that give to Tory Party funds. Margaret Thatcher will have greater cause for gratitude for another of his activities: it was he, along with Thatcher and Keith Joseph, who established the Centre for Policy Studies in 1974. This organisation, which will be considered in more detail in the next chapter, provided a foundation upon which she was able to build her bid to become Leader of the Conservative Party the following year. Thatcher, as will be seen, rewards her ideological backers well. Lord Vinson had to wait ten years for his reward, but he jumped from plain Mr to Lord in one leap – not for him an interim period as a knight.

All the other nine peers, or their families, dominate, or have dominated, the firms on whose boards they sit as much by their competence as by their shareholdings – their positions as eminent industrialists cannot be denied. The fact that Mrs Thatcher has awarded life peerages to the father and son McAlpines is an indication of how highly she values the family. Lord McAlpine of Moffat, the father, has an interest in five million shares in the family building concern, Newarthill. Lord McAlpine of West Green, the son, is not on the main board of Newarthill but on the boards of seven of its subsidiary companies. He is also Treasurer of the Conservative Party.

Of these nine, only Lord Sieff of Marks & Spencer is not associated with a company that gave the Conservative Party, or its front organisations, a donation of £30,000 or more in the year before or the year of his elevation to the peerage – but even Marks & Spencer gave £20,500. Lord Sieff of Brampton holds 438,000 shares in Marks & Spencer and is a trustee for 750,000 more.

Lord Matthews, like Lord Vinson, did not experience the intermediary status of knighthood before he was ennobled the year after the 1979 election. Perhaps his peerage should be considered as much in the chapter on the press as in this section on private-sector industrialists, for at the time of the 1979 election the *Daily* and *Sunday Express* newspapers were both wholly owned by Matthews' company, Trafalgar House, and were wholly favourable to the Conservative cause. Victor Matthews received his peerage a year later, the only year in the last five when Trafalgar House did not make a donation of £40,000 or more directly to Tory Party funds.

Although Lord Weinstock has subsequently fallen out with the Thatcher administration, most notably over its privatisation of British Telecom – a company with which his own firm GEC did much business – and over his own appointment of prominent Thatcher critic James Prior as GEC's Chairman, he was an early applauder of her brand of Conservatism. He dominates his company much as she dominates her Cabinet, although he has the additional advantage of thirteen million of its shares as backing. The £50,000 that GEC gave to the Conservative Party in the year of Lord Weinstock's peerage is the only donation the firm has made to the party in recent years. Mrs Thatcher's appreciation of the work done by the industrial giant, GEC, was further expressed in the knighthoods she gave to its directors Robert Clayton (January 1980) and Alan Veale (January 1984).

Lord Cayzer of St Mary Axe in the City of London was elevated to the peerage in 1982, the same year that the company of which he is chairman, British and Commonwealth Shipping, made the largest single donation ever recorded by a company to Conservative Party funds, £95,810. British and Commonwealth Shipping's latest accounts show Lord Cayzer to hold 55,000 shares directly in the company and a further 354,000 in the company which owns half of British and Commonwealth. Sir William Nicholas Cayzer, as he was before his elevation, had no need of the interim honour of knighthood as he succeeded to his father's baronetcy in 1943. That baronetcy was originally bestowed at the end of the Lloyd George era – in 1921.

Lord Forte of Ripley is very much the man at the centre of the Trusthouse Forte empire, with an interest in twenty-five million of the company's shares, and having been either the company's Chairman or its Chief Executive continuously since 1971. Trusthouse Forte is a steady donor to Conservative Party funds and the £175,200 it has given them since 1979 makes it about the fifteenth largest industrial contributor. Lord Forte, himself, has picked up a number of honours in his seventy-seven years, some of which show his Italian origins. He is an Honorary Consul-General for the Republic of San Marino, a Grand Officer, Ordine al Mento della Repubblica Italiana, and Cavaliere di Gran Croce della Repubblica Italiana. He was created a knight in 1970 and a peer in 1982.

Lord Taylor of Hadfield was founder, in 1921, of the Taylor

Woodrow Group, was its Managing Director 1935–79, Chairman 1937–74 and he has been its president since 1979. It is difficult to think of how much more dominant one person could be in the affairs of a company over half a century. He was created a peer in December 1982, not in a normal honours list, but as one of nine new 'working peers' appointed because they were expected to play a full and regular part in the affairs of the House of Lords – he was seventy-seven at the time. Taylor Woodrow is the third most generous contributor to Conservative Party funds – although it does split its contribution between money going straight to Conservative Central Office and money to British United Industrialists. The year following his elevation, which was an election year, Taylor Woodrow gave a total of £79,035 to the Conservative cause, the fourth-largest donation traced by Labour Research.

Lord Hanson of Edgerton controls the Hanson Trust – a far from household name – which he has propelled over two decades to become the fifty-fifth largest industrial company in Britain. The firm regularly features in takeover battles in the City pages of newspapers, although the then plain James featured more in the gossip columns of the same newspapers thirty years ago for his friendship with Audrey Hepburn, Jean Simmons and Princess Margaret. Lord Hanson's ascendancy within the company is indicated by his holding of three million shares in the firm and his receipt of £490,000 in pay and dividends from the company in the year ending September 1984. He was created a knight in Lord Wilson's controversial resignation honours list of 1976, although he is a committed Conservative. He, for example, welcomed the 1983 general election result as one 'in favour of clear leadership, determined resistance to inflation, return of freedom to the individual and of the policy of shrinking the bureaucratic state' (Hanson Trust's annual report). His appreciation of modern-day Conservatism has been expressed by donations totalling £217,000 to Conservative Party funds since Mrs Thatcher entered Downing Street. The Hanson Trust's largest contribution, £82,000 – at the time the second-largest single donation publicly recorded as going to the Conservative Party – was made in the year of his peerage, 1983.

All of the eleven private-sector industrialists to have received peerages since 1979 are clearly men of distinction who have made a significant contribution to the affairs not only of their companies but, more generally, to the economy as a whole. The fact remains, however, that there is a coincidence between the peerages that these men have received and the contributions to the Conservative Party made by the companies that they direct.

Six of the eleven men direct companies which are in the top ten institutional donors to Conservative Party funds. Four of them direct companies which have made the largest recorded donations to the funds of the Conservative Party and its allies.

The £1.9 million in total donations given between 1979 and 1984, as shown in Table 8, accounts for 14 per cent of the £13.5 million Labour Research has traced in donations to Conservative Party coffers over the same period. However, only one of the top eleven United Kingdom companies, as defined by the Times 1000 1984–85, has made a contribution directly to Conservative Party funds since 1979 – and that was GEC, whose £50,000 accounts for less than half of one per cent of the party's central income. Peerages have gone to six directors on the boards of the top ten institutional investors to Conservative Party funds but to only one of the top ten UK companies (GEC). Although the companies that are directed by the men who have received peerages are important, they cannot be said to dominate the economy. In rank order in the Times 1000 they are GEC (number 9), Marks & Spencer (18), Hanson Trust (55), Trafalgar House (68), Babcock International (82), Trusthouse Forte (89), Taylor Woodrow (134), British and Commonwealth Shipping (198) and Newarthill (259). The Electra Investment Trust is not classified by the Times 1000 in the same way as industrial companies, but rates as number 15 in their listing of investment trusts.

Sixty-four private-sector industrialists have been awarded knighthoods in the twelve Birthday and New Year's honours lists published since Mrs Thatcher entered Downing Street. 44 of them (69 per cent) are directors of companies which have given a total of £4.3 million to the Conservative Party since 1979 – that represents 32 per cent of the money Labour Research traced in corporate donations to the Conservative Party over the same period. To put these figures into perspective, the companies directed by those 44 account for a third of the income donated by 2,000 companies analysed. Over two-thirds of the men receiving knighthoods direct companies that give money to the Conservative Party, yet only a third of the top fifty UK companies give money to the Conservative Party and its allies.

Table 9 gives an indication of the scale. In addition to the 44 listed, the 20 men associated with companies which did not donate to the Conservative Party and received knighthoods are: William Shapland (of Blackwood Hodge), Eric Weiss (Foseco Minsep), the late Maxwell Joseph (Grand Metropolitan), Norman Macfarlane (Macfarlane Group), Ronald Owen (Prudential Assurance), John Sainsbury (J. Sainsbury), Austin Pearce (Esso), Peter Baxendell (Shell Transport and Trading), Kenneth Corfield (STC), Leslie Porter (Tesco), William Duncan and John Harvey Jones (ICI), Peter Walters (BP), Peter Thompson (National Freight), Owen Green (BTR), Eric Sharp (Cable & Wireless), Kenneth Durham (Unilever), Christopher Hogg (Courtaulds), Phil Harris (Harris Queensway) and Peter Main (Boots). All 20 had their industrial directorships mentioned on the citations for knighthood – in four cases the men had made other large contributions of a kind that are often rewarded by the bestowal of an honour. Both Kenneth Durham of Unilever and Peter Walters of BP are prominent members of at least half a dozen significant quangos and charities, and Eric Sharp (Cable & Wireless) and Peter Thompson (National Freight) eased their companies through privatisation. Had the companies remained in public ownership, the two men could have expected to have received a knighthood as a traditional reward for heading a nationalised industry; as it is they received their reward after overseeing the fulfilment of a major piece of Conservative government policy – privatisation.

There is a much closer relationship of knighthoods being awarded to directors of major companies than there is of peerages, and some of these knighthoods have gone to men who directed companies that have not given money to the Conservative Party.

Nine of the top ten UK companies have had a board member knighted since Mrs Thatcher entered Downing Street. Six of these men – Austin Pearce, Maxwell Joseph, William Duncan, Peter Baxendell, Peter Walters and Kenneth Durham – direct companies that have not given money to the Conservatives or their allies in recent years. BAT's donation of £9,000 to the centre for Policy Studies over a five-year period hardly registers as a major donation to Tory Party funds, yet Peter Macadam received his peerage in

1981. The only company in the top ten with a director yet to receive a knighthood from the Thatcher administration is the Imperial Group (Chairman and Chief Executive Geoffrey Kent).

Twelve of the top thirty companies have had a director honoured; in addition to the nine already mentioned, John Sainsbury (J. Sainsbury), Leslie Porter (Tesco) and Christopher Hogg (Courtaulds) have all been knighted. None of the three companies that employ these men make donations to Conservative Party funds; nor does BTR, whose Chairman, Owen Green, received a knighthood in 1984. These thirteen men all direct companies larger than those of nine of the eleven men who received peerages from the Thatcher government.

The correlation of knighthoods to industrialists of leading companies is therefore a close one; but so is the correlation of knighthoods to directors of companies which give money to the Conservative Party. Table 10 lists ten companies that have given over £200,000 each to the Conservative Party between 1979 and 1984. The total given by the ten is £2,635,566. All but one of them had directors honoured during the Thatcher government, and in total they have received 6 peerages and 5 knighthoods between them. The as yet unhonoured board is Guardian Royal Exchange.

The next ten most generous donors to Tory funds, each having given £150,000 or more since 1979, have given £1,602,100 in total. Eight of them have had directors honoured, mainly in the early days of the Thatcher premiership before the correlation of honours and donations was commented upon. The as yet unhonoured boards are: Consolidated Goldfields (total donations 1979–84 £200,000) and the holding company London and Northern (£166,925). In 1980 Marks & Spencer (£160,000) saw Sir Marcus Sieff receive a peerage; the following year knighthoods went to Ernest Harrison of Racal (£200,000), Alistair Frame, non-executive director of Plessey (£190,000), Patrick Meaney, Director and future Chairman of the Rank Organisation (£190,000) and Reginald Smith of Wimpey (£170,175). A year later, Trusthouse Forte (£175,000) saw Sir Charles Forte elevated to the peerage. In 1984 Edwin Nixon, who in addition to being Chairman of IBM sits on the board of Royal Insurance (£185,500), was knighted. Finally, in June 1985, George Bernard Audley of Audits Great Britain received a knighthood; this came after three successive annual donations of £50,000 to Tory

Party coffers. The top twenty donors to Tory Party funds have given £4,237,666 since 1979 and between them have received 8 peerages and 11 knighthoods.

A number of remarkable coincidences stand out from Table 9. In July 1983, when writing of the Birthday honours list, *Labour Research* alleged, 'Rank Hovis McDougall's ... chief executive, Peter Reynolds, is clearly being punished for the company's failure to make a donation. His is, however, a name to watch out for in the future.' That future was just eighteen months in coming – he received his knighthood in the 1985 New Year honours list.

In addition to building houses, Lawrie Barratt built one of the fastest-growing and most successful house-building companies in Britain. It was most fitting, therefore, that his efforts should be recognised, and they were with a knighthood in 1983, which was the year in which Barratt Developments, his company, made the first of its two £10,000 donations to the Conservative Party.

The Distillers Company is one whose board of directors has been well honoured in the past, particularly in the Lloyd George era (see pp. 67–68), but it is not a company that had declared a donation to the Conservative Party in the first four years of Mrs Thatcher's premiership. In the 1984 New Year's list, however, a knighthood was granted, to quote the *London Gazette*, to 'John Robert Carter, lately chairman, the Distillers Company plc'. Distillers' financial year ends in March and its directors' report for the year ending three months later shows the company to have made a donation of £50,000 to the Conservative Party in the previous year.

Clive Sinclair's firm, Sinclair Research, first began giving money to the Tory Party in 1982, when it donated a modest £7,000. The following year it gave £5,000, but the accounts for the year ending March 1984, nine months after his knighthood, reveal a donation over five times as much, £27,000. As the *New Statesman* was later to comment, tartly, 'He must be the only Thatcherite industrial knight who has been formally admonished by the Advertising Standards Authority for advertising which continued to quote delivery dates he had no hope of meeting' (14 June 1985).

In order to put the Thatcher years into perspective, it is necessary to look at how other prime ministers, particularly Conservative ones, distributed honours to industrialists and how far that distribution coincided with substantial donations to party funds. What makes the investigation of the Thatcher years possible is the Companies Act 1967, which for the first time made it obligatory for companies to declare in the directors' report section of their annual accounts their donations to political bodies, even if the spirit of the Act has been broken by those who donate to British United Industrialists and Regional Industrial Councils. Because the Act was not passed until 1967 the only previous Conservative Prime Minister whose activities can be examined is Edward Heath (the records of Harold Wilson and James Callaghan have been looked at in earlier chapters).

As far as Conservative Party funds in the Heath era (1965–75) are concerned, Pinto-Duschinsky, although denied access to the figures for the first two years of the period, showed that Central Office had a surplus of income over expenditure of £750,000 between 1967 and 1974. Finances were not a major matter of concern to party organisers at that time. However, disaster then struck, and it was a disaster Margaret Thatcher was to inherit. According to Pinto-Duschinsky,

> In 1974 the reserves suffered a second blow [second, that is, to a drain on income 1960–64] from which they have not recovered. In 1973 the party conducted its normal pre-election appeal which enabled Central Office to finance the February 1974 general election and to make an adequate profit, but no extra money seems to have been gathered for the second general election held in October 1974. Consequently, the Central Office ran a huge loss of nearly £1.3 million during the financial year 1974/75 and the reserves had fallen by March 1975 [two months after Thatcher's election as Leader of the Party] to £649,000, which was equivalent to only four months' routine running costs of the central party organisation. (p. 152)

For the greater part of the Heath years, therefore, there was no need to look for other than normal means of party fund-raising. The last financially disastrous year of his leadership of the party provided considerable headaches for those who followed him to run the organisation.

As far as his treatment of private-sector industrialists in the honours stakes was concerned, Edward Heath could be described as a frugal dispenser. In his eight honours lists, no private-sector industrialist peers were created, and only 23 knights (about 50 per cent of the Thatcher rate), and half of that number's citations said that their awards were for export achievement.

Political donations records of the years of Mr Heath's premiership, 1970–74, are less comprehensive than they are for the more recent period, but the indications are that only 11 of the 23 honoured men were directors of companies that gave money to Conservative causes over that four-year period, and only eight of those donations could be considered significant. All 23 were, however, directors of major British public companies, which (with the exception of three which have subsequently been taken over) remain household names today.

Table 11 covers the entire Heath era, and shows total company donations for the 1970–74 period. In addition, twelve other private-sector industrialists were knighted: David Barron (Shell), Alexander McDonald (Distillers), Alan Baker (Baker Perkins), Donald Barron (Rowntree Mackintosh), Montagu Pritchard (Perkins Engines), Sidney Ryder (Reed International), George Butterworth (English Calico), Eric Eastwood (GEC), Ernest Woodroofe (Uni-

Table 11
Donations and Knighthoods in the Heath Era, 1970–74

Director honoured	Company	Date of knighthood	Total donations[1] 1970–74 (£)
Raymond Brookes	GKN	Jan 1971	167,750
Marcus Sieff	Marks & Spencer	Jan 1971	30,000
John Clark	Plessey	June 1971	70,450
John Davis	Rank Organisation	June 1971	127,000
John Lindbury	Hawker Siddeley	June 1971	500
Samuel Sewar	Stone Platt Industries	June 1971	3,000
Kenneth Corley	Joseph Lucas	Jan 1972	48,000
Kenneth Barrington	Morgan Grenfell	Jan 1973	15,020
Gerald Thorley	Allied Breweries	Jan 1973	25,000
James Menter	Tube Investments	June 1973	1,000
Frank Taylor	Taylor Woodrow	Jan 1974	41,825
			519,545

1. These sums are likely to be an underestimate because the figures for some companies' years are unavailable

lever), Alexander Alexander (Imperial Foods), Jan Lewando (Carrington Viyella) and Herbert Mathys (Courtaulds).

Only 11 of Heath's 23 knights' companies gave to the Conservative cause (47 per cent), and the donations of 2 of these 11 were what in retrospect Edward Heath would consider to be in very poor taste. The £500 of Hawker Siddeley and £1,000 of Tube Investments were both destined for the Thatcher-created Centre for Policy Studies and not the then Heath-controlled Conservative Party.

A brief run through the knights created in the Heath era would show that the three associated with the party's most generous backers on the list (Raymond Brookes of GKN, John Davis of Rank and John Clark of Plessey), along with sixth-placed Marcus Sieff of Marks & Spencer, all received their knighthoods within a year of Edward Heath entering Downing Street. The Rank Organisation gave over £50,000 to Conservative Party funds in the year prior to John Davis's knighthood, and GKN gave £33,000 in each of the years before and during the year of Raymond Brookes' knighthood. Plessey gave £11,500 in the year before John Clark's knighthood and Marks & Spencer £10,000 in the year before Marcus Sieff's. Kenneth Barrington's Morgan Grenfell gave the Conservative Party £15,020 in the year he was honoured and Frank Taylor's Taylor Woodrow gave £20,000 to British United Industrialists in the year of his knighthood. Kenneth Corley's Joseph Lucas gave a steady £12,000 a year to the Conservative Party throughout the Heath years.

In total, the companies whose directors were honoured by Heath contributed less than £520,000 to the Conservative cause in his period in office – or less than 10 per cent of the £5.4 million Pinto-Duschinksy shows the party to have received in donations in the 1970–74 period. In comparison, the companies of the industrialists honoured by Mrs Thatcher have accounted for 43 per cent of the corporate donations Labour Research has traced going to the Conservative cause. Even if account is taken of the fact that Labour Research is not able to trace the total amount of company donations to the Conservative Party but that it is usually about a third under, the companies of the Thatcher-created knights and barons have contributed 28 per cent of the corporate income to the Conservative Party – two-and-a-half times as much, in real terms, as those knighted by Heath. Only a third of the industrialists honoured by Heath were directors of companies that made significant donations to the Conservative Party whereas three-quarters of those honoured by Thatcher are, despite the fact that fewer companies donate money to Tory Party funds now than they did a decade ago.

Eight

Thatcher's political honours

There is a long tradition of honours being awarded for political service – the 1922 Royal Commission on the honours system noted that they had been continuously granted since the establishment of party government. It also recorded that political honours fell into two categories: those awarded to MPs and those going to others. The MPs were recommended by the party whips to the party leader, and the non-parliamentarians had their names forwarded by the head of the party organisation. It was these honours that most concerned the Royal Commission and that led them to call for the establishment of the Political Honours Scrutiny Committee, which was to examine the names submitted by the Prime Minister and make observations on their suitability.

A typical modern Conservative honours list is likely to contain 45–50 names of people receiving awards for 'political service'. The June 1985 list, for example, had one dame, 10 knights, 7 CBEs, 12 OBEs and 18 MBEs. Mrs Thatcher's lists, in addition, have featured another category of people who although not described as 'political' have done much to promote her and her own particular brand of Conservatism: her ideologues. A sprinkling of these may be found in most of her twelve lists to date. The political lists and lists of ideologues provide an insight into the forces at work in the patronage game.

As long ago as 1908, radical MP Hugh Cecil Lea complained in the Commons that the honours system was being abused by political patronage. He said that he had examined the honours lists over the previous five years, covering a period of both Conservative and Liberal rule, and concluded that between November 1903 and December 1905 the Conservative Party had awarded 138 major honours (knighthoods and above) and that 36 of the recipients, or 28.1 per cent, were members of the House of Commons. Similarly, over the next two years, December 1905 until November 1907, the Liberals created 167 major honours, 37 of which, or 22.1 per cent, went to members of the House of Commons.

When the Royal Commission on the honours system was sitting in 1922, *The Times* turned its attention to Lloyd George's record, not simply in elevating businessmen and press owners, but to the other awards made in his era. It concluded: 'Lloyd George is not only pre-eminent as a peer-maker but he may fairly be described as having been most profuse in the distribution of honours among his supporters in the House of Commons'. In 1918, 533 Coalition supporters had been elected to the Commons; by November 1922, 17 of them had become peers, 25 Privy Councillors, 26 baronets, 33 knights and 13 had been awarded orders of distinction. In addition, 14 had been appointed to major posts outside Parliament. That record of 130 titles or offices distributed over the four-year period meant that one in four of Lloyd George's supporters had received his patronage during this period (quite apart from those who were given government office), at the rate of 33 awards per year.

Criticism of the frantic rate of political honours bestowed seemed to abate until the onset of the Macmillan era, in 1957, although an average of 17 Conservative MPs per year had received an honour over the previous five years, compared with only 2 Labour MPs over the whole period (and one of these was the traditional earldom that went to former Prime Minister, Clement Attlee). James McMillan in his book *The Honours Game* (Leslie Frewin, 1969) quoted Jeremy Thorpe as saying that 'Under Macmillan we seem to be reverting – at least in the lower echelons – to something not far removed from the sale of honours. Though the honours are not actually sold, cheques are signed by honorary chairmen and treasurers in the confident expectation of favours to come. And the Tory Party acquires a lot of funds as a direct result' (p. 131). No names were mentioned, of course, and no evidence offered.

McMillan's own analysis of the political honours of Harold Macmillan showed that his first honours list, the Birthday one of 1957, gazetted 4 baronets for political service, compared with 1 in the previous list. Both lists had 10 'political' knights. In 1958, the two honours lists showed politicians receiving 1 barony, 2 baronetcies and

17 knighthoods for political service. One of them went to Tory MP Henry 'Chips' Channon, father of the present Rt Hon. Paul Channon, who was a wealthy society entertainer. Such was the impact and contribution Sir Henry made to political life that *Hansard* records him as having spoken for a total of twenty-one minutes in five sessions of Parliament. In the 1959 Birthday list, 2 of the newly created barons were Tory MPs, and after the dissolution of Parliament in 1959, 3 life peerages were awarded to Tory politicians, including a viscountcy for James Stuart. The 1st Viscount Stuart of Findhorn was Harold Macmillan's brother-in-law. He had also presided over the Scottish Conservative Party in a lamentable way – the party had been eclipsed in Scotland, losing a number of seats, while Conservatives made considerable advances in England and Wales.

Safely returned to power after the 1959 general election, 4 Conservative MPs received baronetcies and 3 more got knighthoods. In 1960, 3 viscountcies, 2 more baronetcies and 7 additional knighthoods were awarded to Tory MPs. 1961 saw a lull in Macmillan's endeavours. A single earl, 2 life peers, 1 baronet, 6 knights and 1 dame were created for political services.

Writing of the 1962 list, Richard Crossman had this to say:

> In the higher echelons, nearly 20%, and in the lower, just under 1%, of the honours awarded this year have been given to help the Tory Party. Here is my breakdown of the political honours at the top of the Prime Minister's list:
>
> | | |
> |---|---|
> | Barons | – 2 out of 4 |
> | Baronets | – 1 out of 2 |
> | Knights | – 6 out of 28 |
> | KBE | – 1 out of 3 |
> | CBE | – 12 out of 89 |
> | OBE | – 17 out of 180 |
> | MBE | – 29 out of 320 |

Crossman said that the 17 OBEs and 29 MBEs had been allocated to Tory Central Office. In addition, 14 further MBEs had been awarded to female Tory voluntary workers.

Macmillan's final year in office, 1963, saw the creations of 1 viscount, 2 barons, 2 life peers, 6 baronets and 6 knights from the massed ranks of Tory MPs.

That scourge of honours, Willie Hamilton MP, summarised the

Macmillan era in his book on the monarchy: 'Between coming to office in January 1957 and leaving it in October 1963, he wielded his patronage like a political Casanova. Knighthoods or peerages were given to every Tory MP who showed signs of life, and averaged one a month throughout his premiership' (*My Queen and I*, Quartet, 1975, p. 136). A year later, thirteen years of continuous Tory rule ended. In that period, 207 honours went to Tory MPs, which, allowing for the turnover of MPs during the years, amounts to over a third of those who served on the Tory benches. Over the same period, a total of 23 honours were given to Labour MPs – an imbalance of 9:1.

The question of honours has always been a difficult one for Labour. Harold Wilson's first four years in office displayed a crusading zeal in his attitude to honours and the system supported by them. That, however, proved to be more of a gimmicky piece of window-dressing than a reality, although it has been partially effective so far as the Labour Party is concerned. The Crossman diaries entry for 22 September 1966 makes the point neatly:

> This afternoon we had a meeting at No 10 about political Honours. Harold was in the chair and . . . again repeated his determination to get rid of political Honours. I had thought this a good idea at first but after I'd talked to Len Williams at Transport House and heard the reaction of our regional offices and party agents I realised that excluding political Honours really meant excluding party agents and regional organisers and virtually no one else. When Harold heard this he replied, 'We'll include them all under public Honours.' But of course once you do this your announcement is merely a gimmick because you *haven't* cut out political honours. (Anthony Howard, ed., *Selections from the Diaries of a Cabinet Minister 1964–1970*, Magnum, 1979, p. 241)

Political honours were finally scrapped, but people who previously would have been given an honour for 'political' service now found themselves, particularly at the lower levels of OBE and MBE, receiving it for 'public service' or local government or health service duties. The recipient was unlikely to be too bothered what the citation was for as long as the bauble was in place.

Harold Wilson continued to recommend Labour MPs and ex-MPs for elevation to the peerage in order to boost the ranks of the Labour benches there. It is, of course, a fine definition that regards these as not being political appointments. However, the biggest impact of the Wilson reform was felt in the Commons itself. No baronetcies were created after 1964 and only 5 backbenchers received knighthoods (and one of them was a Conservative) between the announcement in 1966 and Labour leaving office in 1970. That average of one per year is in very marked contrast to the dozen-a-year average award of knighthoods and baronetcies in the ten years before Labour took office in 1964. The precedent set by Harold Wilson was largely continued by Edward Heath – only 8 knighthoods were awarded to Conservative MPs during his four years as Prime Minister, and none to Labour. Harold Wilson's second term in Downing Street, 1974–76, saw the publication of five main honours lists, but only 2 MPs received knighthoods – Peter Kirk for services to the European Parliament and William Williams for services to the Inter-Parliamentary Union. Nobody received a knighthood for political services, not even in the controversial resignation list of June 1976.

James Callaghan continued the tradition – not a single MP received a knighthood for political or any other services in the five New Year and Birthday honours lists he supervised. It was not until his resignation list of June 1979 that Callaghan so rewarded Judith Hart with the female equivalent of a knighthood to become a Dame of the British Empire. Today she is the only dame or knight among the 200 Labour MPs. This is a fact that would embarrass most left-wing Labour MPs, but not, apparently, Dame Judith.

Within six months of gaining office, Margaret Thatcher over-turned the thirteen-year-old convention of not awarding honours for political service when she told the Commons, 'I have accordingly recommended that the forthcoming New Year Honours List and subsequent lists should include a number of awards to members of parties for their political and public service. Her Majesty the Queen has approved my recommendation.' She invited leaders of Opposition parties to submit names to her. Speaking for Labour, Jim Callaghan replied, 'The Prime Minister will remember that this system was discontinued in 1966 to some extent because of – I do not wish to use too strong a word – abuse of the system in the conferment of knighthoods and baronetcies by previous Tory Chief Whips ... I regret that the Right Honourable Lady is introducing this partial change – I shall, therefore, not be making any nominations.'

Mrs Thatcher has fulfilled her promise. In every honours list since January 1980, an average of 8 knighthoods have been awarded for 'political and public service' – approximately half have been MPs, the others party officials in the country. The result is that 56 of the almost 400 Conservative MPs now have a handle and a further 21 have a lesser honour – CBE, OBE or MBE.

Scanning an eye over the names of those backbenchers nominated for knighthoods by Mrs Thatcher, it is difficult to escape the conclusion that the major qualifications for 'political and public service' for MPs is patience and a preparedness to await the outcome of Buggins' Turn.

There is no doubt that few senior politicians (of all parties) hold the attainment of a knighthood as a very suitable reward for their service. It is noticeable, for example, that former prime ministers Harold Macmillan, Edward Heath and James Callaghan have never taken a knighthood, although one was surely available for the asking for each of them. The elevation to the peerage poses problems for active politicians who would rather spend their time in the Commons than the Lords, but it is also not highly regarded by some of the most senior politicians who have retired from active life. Winston Churchill never took a peerage and Harold Macmillan waited until he was ninety – twenty years after resigning as Prime Minister – before taking up his earldom.

For politicians, the real distinction, the honour that matters, is membership of the Privy Council – that prestigious but anachronistic body that pre-dates the Cabinet as the central committee of political power. At a time when the prefix 'Sir' can mean a title inherited as a baronetcy or acquired for services semi-competently rendered, the title 'Right Honourable' usually confers status and acknowledges that the possessor has made a mark on public life. Many of the most distinguished of today's political leaders and elder statesmen who still sit in the Commons content themselves with their Privy Councillorship. Since Labour MPs are no longer knighted, by the party's choice, they have little option in the matter – but such long-serving and eminent Conservative MPs as Julian Amery, Humphrey Aitken, Edward Heath, James Prior and Margaret Thatcher have not become knights or dames.

The knighthood has become the reward for the 'nearly' men, and a parting gift for displaced Ministers. In the House of Commons a knighthood is second-best. Nevertheless, it has been assiduously used by Margaret Thatcher to keep the old-stagers happy. Its conferment has been applied with less regard to the ability of the recipients than to the length of service on the green benches. Since its reintroduction by Mrs Thatcher in 1979, it has become very much the long-service award of modern politics.

There are presently 29 MPs with continuous membership of the House of Commons who were first elected as Conservatives in 1959 or before. In 1979, before Mrs Thatcher entered Downing Street, less than half of them were either Privy Councillors (9) or knights (4). She has spent the last six-and-a-half years filling in the gaps. All 29 are now either Privy Councillors or knights. Buggins' Turn has run its course among the generation of '59 and its predecessors. There were 2 knighthoods for their number in 1980 (David Price and William Clark), 4 in 1981 (John Biggs-Davidson, Anthony Kershaw, John Osborn and William van Straubenzee), 1 in 1982 (Peter Emery) and 2 in 1983 (Edward Gardner and Kenneth Lewis). The last of the class of '59 with continuous Commons membership to be honoured were John Farr and John Wells, who had to wait a full twenty-five years – until 1984 – before their gongs came.

By 1985 all 29 had *either* a knighthood or a Privy Councillorship – only 2, Keith Joseph and Ian Percival, appeared to have both, but special circumstances explain the double honours. Sir Keith's handle is not a knighthood but an inherited baronetcy, and therefore the Privy Council membership is the only honour he received in his own right, and Ian Percival got his knighthood automatically with his job as Solicitor-General in 1979. The Privy Council membership that came his way in 1982 was the only honour that was his true recognition of service.

The allocation of an honour apiece had been fulfilled by 1984, but restlessness still prevailed. A clever solution emerged, publicly unnoticed in the New Year's list of 1985 – doubling up! Both a knighthood and a Privy Councillorship were to be bestowed on the old brigade, any would-be dissension in the ranks could be quelled by the prospects of two honours. And it was done three times in one list.

Edward du Cann had recently been defeated as Chairman of the 1922 Committee of Tory backbenchers, and clearly deserved a reward for the long stint he had put in. But he was already a Privy

Councillor, he clearly didn't want to be dispatched to the Lords, and common knighthoods are a bit second-rate for distinguished politicians. The options were thus limited. One temptation for Mrs Thatcher, who had already turned the clock back as far as the award of both hereditary peerages and political honours was concerned, must have been to revert to the creation of hereditary baronetcies – abandoned by Harold Wilson twenty years earlier. She demurred. Du Cann was to become a Knight of the British Empire – not a hereditary baronet, but a knight regarded by the *cogniscenti* as a cut above your ordinary Knight Bachelor. He now adorns the benches of the Commons as Colonel the Right Honourable Sir Edward Dillon Lott du Cann, KBE, PC, MP.

Privy Council membership is usually only extended among politicians to Cabinet Ministers or very senior and distinguished backbenchers. Sir Frederic Bennett, MP for Torbay, was welcomed to the ranks of the Privy Council in January 1985. He had never risen above the rank of Parliamentary Private Secretary in the government and he was almost as known for his business interests, including those in the Cayman Islands, as for his government service. Sir Frederic is clearly a man to be honoured. He received his knighthood in 1964 and is also a Commander of the Order of Phoenix, Greece, holder of the Sithari Star of Pakistan, Commander Polonia Restituta, Poland, a member of the Order of Al-Istiqlal, Jordan, and a member of the Order of Hilal-i-Qaid-i-Azam, Pakistan. In addition, Sir Frederic was the second-longest-serving Conservative backbencher not to be a member of the Privy Council, until January 1985. He was suitably rewarded and is now to be known as the Right Honourable Sir Frederic Mackarness Bennett Kt, PC, MP. Quite how popular his appointment to the Privy Council is with those who feel that membership of that august body is a symbol of considerable parliamentary status and achievement, we do not know.

The only Tory backbench MP not in the Privy Council with a (then) longer continuous House of Commons membership than Sir Frederic is Sir Bernard Braine, who first entered the House in 1950. The highest government office he has achieved in his thirty-five years was that of Junior Minister in the early 1960s – before even Edward Heath's premiership. He too was made a member of the Privy Council in January 1985, becoming the third member of the pre-1959 club to 'double up' in that one honours list.

If, as it appears, membership of the Privy Council is being used as the second long-service medal for those on the Tory benches who are already knighted, look out for the status being conferred on Sir Raymond Gower (first elected in 1951), Sir John Biggs-Davidson, Sir Paul Bryan, Sir Anthony Kershaw and Sir David Price (all elected first in 1955).

The last gesture in the direction of the class of '59 to be made in the 1985 New Year's list went to Fergus Montgomery. He was first elected to Parliament in 1959, but a fickle electorate ensured that his membership has not been continuous ever since. None the less, he received his knighthood in January 1985. The class of '59 are all now suitably rewarded.

What of the next generations? There are currently 36 Conservative MPs who were first elected to Parliament in 1964. Fourteen of them are Privy Councillors – half nominated by Margaret Thatcher (Michael Alison, Peter Blaker, Alick Buchanan Smith, Mark Carlisle, Terence Higgins, Michael Jopling and Norman St John Stevas). Ten of the 36 are 'Sirs', and 8 of the 10 owe their knighthoods to Mrs Thatcher, one (Sir Geoffrey Howe) to Edward Heath, when he was Solicitor-General, and the other (Sir Anthony Meyer) to an inherited baronetcy first created in 1910.

Now that the class of '59 is satisfied, those first elected in 1964 can expect the rate of knighthoods bestowed on their number to be speeded up in the next few honours lists. None of the 1964 entrants received a knighthood in 1980, only 1 did in 1981, 2 did in 1982 and 4 did in 1983 (including Anthony Berry, killed in the October 1984 Brighton bomb). John Page got his in 1984 and Paul Dean his in the 1985 New Year list. Eldon Griffiths and Peter Hordern both received theirs in the June Birthday list of 1985.

There are only 10 Conservative survivors of the 1964 election yet to be honoured, three of them (Peter Griffith, Patrick McNair Wilson and Teddy Taylor) have had a gap in service and one other, Charles Morrison, has the courtesy title of 'Honourable' as the second son of a peer. Of the remaining 6, 2 were elected at by-elections before 1964 – Robert Maxwell Hyslop (1960) and Norman Miscampbell (1962) – and therefore must feel that their time for honours must be fast approaching. The other 4, each with twenty years' continuous service, could, given the distribution pattern of political honours under this government, expect with confidence a knighthood before the next general election. Ian Lloyd, David Mitchell, Cranley Onslow and David Walters will have the right to be disappointed men if they are not campaigning under the title of 'Sir' in 1987.

1966 was a landslide victory for Labour. It was also, nevertheless, the occasion of the first general election victory for 12 currently serving Conservative MPs. Three of their number are Privy Councillors – Geoffrey Rippon, David Howell and Michael Heseltine, the latter two owing their appointment to Mrs Thatcher – and 6 are knights or dames, all honoured during the Thatcher years (Michael Shaw, 1982; Walter Clegg, 1983; Hugh Rossi, 1983; Reginald Eyre, 1984; Peter Tapsell, New Year 1985; Jill Knight, June 1985). Another elected for the first time in 1966, Nicholas Scott, already had an MBE before Mrs Thatcher's premiership and can expect further advancement when he leaves the government. Of the 12 of '66 only Richard Body and David Crouch remain unhonoured. The *Guardian* described the knighthood awarded to Peter Tapsell in January 1985 as 'a tribute to the Prime Minister's charitable instincts'. Of a parliamentary party of almost 400, only 8 Conservative MPs have been in the Commons longer, continuously, and remained unhonoured.

The same long-service reward principle seems to be creeping into the Liberal/SDP benches. Two of the longest-serving Alliance MPs are Party Leaders David Steel (entered Parliament in 1965) and David Owen (1966). They have both become Privy Councillors – Owen in 1976 and Steel a year later. Russell Johnston has, however, been in Parliament longer than both of them, first entering in 1964. He too has received his long-service reward, a knighthood in the Birthday list of 1985 – twenty years on. Richard Wainwright, first elected in 1966, is probably next in line for a Liberal 'K'. But he did have a break in service between 1970 and 1974, so he might just have to wait until 1990 for his reward. As far as the SDP is concerned, elder statesman Roy Jenkins already has his PC from his days in Labour government and his wife Mary became a Dame of the British Empire in June 1985. The next SDP MP in line for an honour is Robert Maclennan, who has represented Caithness and Sutherland since 1966. A 'K' in the New Year's list of 1987 would not seem amiss. Mrs Thatcher's political supporters and promoters are not, of course, limited to her House of Commons colleagues. Outside

Parliament, there is a whole variety of think-tanks and pressure groups that have had the ear of Thatcher and have been rewarded with honours for their leading lights. The most obvious of these centres of influence are the policy units and advisers that spring up in Downing Street. Ex-ICI director John Ibbs went to Downing Street in 1980 to head the Central Policy Review Staff; when he left in 1982 he received a knighthood, but was retained by Mrs Thatcher as her adviser on 'efficiency and effectiveness in government'. In taking on his new post he effectively succeeded Derek Rayner, a director of Marks & Spencer, who had been on secondment to Mrs Thatcher from 1979 until 1983 in order to advise the Prime Minister on 'improving efficiency and avoiding waste in government'. When his secondment ended, he was rewarded with a peerage and returned to Marks & Spencer as Chief Executive.

Another Downing Street aide was John Hoskyns. Brought in from ICL in 1979 to head the Prime Minister's policy unit, he stayed for three years and left with a knighthood. He promptly joined the board of the social research company Audits Great Britain (AGB Ltd), which in that year began making political donations of £50,000 a year to the Conservative Party and whose Chairman, Bernard Audley, in turn received his knighthood in June 1985. In 1983, Alan Walters finished a two-year stint on secondment from Johns Hopkins University, Maryland, as Mrs Thatcher's personal economic adviser. He received a knighthood and continued to advise the Prime Minister on economic matters in a part-time capacity.

Two years later, according to the *Economist* (somewhat astonishingly for so establishment a publication), 'Mrs Thatcher continues her habit of consoling with knighthoods the string of political advisers who leave Whitehall frustrated by their exclusion from influencing the inner sanctum of Downing Street. Mr Adam Ridley (Treasury) and Mr Jeffrey Sterling (Industry and also Chairman of P & O) are this year's crop' (5 January 1985).

Quite the most influential source of political inspiration and policy initiated for the Thatcher government outside both Downing Street and Whitehall, has been the Centre for Policy Studies. This was founded in 1974, three months after the first election defeat of the year for the party. Its founders were Margaret Thatcher, Sir Keith Joseph and Nigel Vinson. They installed Alfred Sherman as the first Director of Studies. Sherman is a born-again Conservative;

he came from a socialist family in Hackney, joined the Communist Party and fought in the International Brigade in the Spanish Civil War, then drifted away from Marxism after the Second World War and spent time writing editorials for the *Daily Telegraph* and serving as a Conservative councillor in Kensington. The man has subsequently been dubbed – by the *Sunday Times* – as Mrs Thatcher's favourite intellectual.

Among those who have sat on the board of the Centre for Policy Studies in its ten-year existence have been Caroline Cox, Director of the Nursing Education Research Unit at Chelsea College, Max Beloff, founder of the private University of Buckingham, Sir William Cayzer, Chairman of British and Commonwealth Shipping, Frank Taylor of Taylor Woodrow, David Young, later of the Manpower Services Commission, and Hugh Thomas, historian of the Spanish Civil War. Apart from their directorship of the CPS, what all six of these people have in common (together with seventh board member Nigel Vinson), is that they have all been elevated to the peerage by Mrs Thatcher. It is difficult to imagine a more greatly appreciated centre of influence during the Thatcher years than this. Lord Beloff received a knighthood in 1980 and a peerage the following year, Lord Thomas received his peerage in 1981, and Lady Cox and Lord Taylor theirs in a special peerage list in December 1982 – the same year as Lord Cayzer. In 1983, Alfred Sherman, the Director of Studies, received a knighthood, and David Young was ennobled in 1984 when Margaret Thatcher brought him into her Cabinet. The only non-MP in the triumvirate of founders, Nigel Vinson, got his peerage in January 1985. The Centre's current Treasurer, Ronald Halstead, a director of Beecham, received a knighthood in the Birthday honours list of 1985. One of the most recent additions to the board of the Centre for Policy Studies is Ferdinand Mount, political columnist of the *Daily Telegraph* and literary editor of the *Spectator*. He landed on the board of the Centre in March 1984, having spent two years heading Mrs Thatcher's policy unit at Downing Street. His honour cannot be long in appearing.

The Centre for Policy Studies is a limited company whose aim, according to its articles of association, is to 'engage in research into methods available for improving the standard of living, quality of life and freedom of choice for the British people, with particular attention to market forces'. The general tenor of its publications has been to argue the case for less 'government' and more monetarism. Centre for Policy Studies publications from the late 1970s and the early 1980s greatly influenced later policy decisions of the Thatcher government. Among the early 'successes' were: *Second Thoughts on Full Employment* (1975), *Myths and Magic in Economic Management* (1976), *Stranded in the Middle Ground* (by Sir Keith Joseph in 1976), *The Litmus Papers* (by Institute of Economic Affairs advisory director Arthur Seldon, in 1980) – calling for privatisation in the National Health Service – and *NEB: A Case for Euthanasia* (1980).

More recently, the Centre has published books calling for the abolition of the Inner London Education Authority, a move unsuccessfully attempted by Education Secretary and Centre for Policy Studies founder, Sir Keith Joseph, in 1984. A book entitled *The Right to Strike in a Free Society*, which argued for outlawing of strikes in essential services, was published by the Centre in 1982. *Telecommunications in Britain*, also published in 1982, called for a 'competitive free market in telecommunication' – steps carried out by the government with the establishment of Mercury Communications in the same year and the privatisation of British Telecom in 1984. Another title, *BL: A Viable Future*, called for the privatisation of the car firm – very much on the agenda of the present government.

Lord Cayzer resigned from the CPS board in August 1984. His son-in-law, Michael Colvin MP, continued to make his contribution to the Centre with his recent publication for them entitled *British Shipping – The Right Course*. And among other recent Centre for Policy Studies authors have been Lord Harris of High Cross (Thatcher-created peerage 1979), Sir William Rees-Mogg (Thatcher knighthood 1981), Sir Alan Walters (Thatcher knighthood 1983) and Sir Adam Ridley (Thatcher knighthood 1985).

The high regard in which Mrs Thatcher holds the Centre for Policy Studies can be gauged by the fact that she hosted a dinner in honour of the Centre at 10 Downing Street on 12 December 1984. Among the 46 guests were 5 peers and 6 knights of her creation.

The Centre is not, however, a huge body. Its latest set of published accounts for 1983 show it to have had an income of only £123,000, the great majority of which goes to subsidise the publication of its literature (should not uneconomic publications be closed down?) which made a loss over the year of £77,000. The Centre only employed seven staff in 1983. Like the Conservative Party itself, the Centre for Policy Studies does not publish a list of its sponsors, nor is there a central registry where details of donations made can be inspected. Those interested in finding out which companies give money must make the same trawl through company accounts as is necessary to investigate Conservative Party funding. The Labour Research Department does that and is usually, through its searches, able to account for about a quarter of the Centre for Policy Studies' finances. Much of the rest of the money may, of course, come either from companies who feel they do not have to declare their donation (the 1967 Companies Act definition of politi-cal donations is a very narrow one), or because it is less than £250, or from individuals.

Nevertheless, Labour Research has discovered seven companies which have made donations in excess of £2,000 in the last year of their published accounts. Six of those companies have had directors honoured by Mrs Thatcher. The companies are: Beecham, £5,000 (Graham Wilkins, knighthood 1980, Ronald Halstead, knighthood June 1985); Hepworth Ceramics, £5,000 (Peter Goodall, CBE 1983); Transport Development Group, £2,500 (James Duncan, knighthood 1981); Commercial Union Assurance, £2,500 (no known honour); BAT Industries £2,000 (Peter Macadam, knight-hood 1981); Glaxo, £2,000 (Austin Bide, knighthood 1980) and Hanson Trust, £2,000 (Lord Hanson, peerage 1983).

In 1982, a charity – the Institute for Policy Research – was estab-lished. In addition to sharing the Centre for Policy Studies' address at 8 Wilfrid Street, Westminster, it also shares one of its directors, Simon Webley. It published its first (and only, to date), set of accounts in September 1983, showing an income of almost £48,000. The Centre may feel that the Institute could take on some of its work which the Charity Commissioners would consider to be educational. This would have two advantages, there would be benefits accruing to those who donated to the Institute and as their donations would not be classed as political they therefore would not have to be declared in companies' annual reports. If such arrangements were to be made it would become even more difficult to discover the sources of income of 8 Wilfrid Street, and impossible to know whether the companies sending money there were fortunate enough to have their directors honoured by the present or future prime ministers.

If the Centre for Policy Studies has been a key source of inspiration for much of the policy initiatives of the Thatcher government, a second influential body has undoubtedly been the Institute of Economic Affairs (IEA). When the IEA's journal, *Economic Affairs*, was revamped and relaunched in the autumn of 1983, Mrs Thatcher provided it with a positive endorsement: 'All policies are based on ideas. Our policies are firmly founded on those ideas which have been developed with such imagination in the *Journal*.'

The IEA, a registered charity, was formed in 1956 and is based at 2 Lord North Street in Westminster. Its Director since its foundation, Ralph Harris, received a peerage from Mrs Thatcher in 1979 and its Advisory Director, Arthur Seldon, a CBE in 1983. The Institute's trustees include Nigel Vinson (ennobled in 1985), Ronald Halstead (knighthood in June 1985) and Kenneth McAlpine (Director of Newarthill) who has seen two of his relatives ennobled by Mrs Thatcher.

However, the Institute has not always been well received by the establishment: 'We were voices crying in a hostile wilderness . . . Journalists used to lambast us as "Impractical . . . old fashioned . . . right wing . . .". Our ideas emerged from disillusionment with Keynes and Beveridge and Titmus,' Seldon told Geoffrey Hodgson of the *Sunday Times* (4 March 1983). Their anti-Statist message was at a particularly low point in the mid-1960s, although they enjoyed the patronage of Tory MPs Enoch Powell and Sir Keith Joseph. In the late sixties they succeeded in getting arch-monetarists Friedrich Hayek (Companion of Honour from Margaret Thatcher in 1984) and Chicago guru Milton Friedman to write for them, and from that moment began to attract the attention of Conservative economic thinkers. Currently, according to the *Sunday Times*, they have 'achieved just the sort of audience in the seats of power that Fabians had sought for a quarter of a century and never quite achieved'. That influence has been rewarded not simply by the Conservative Party's enactment of many of the IEA-inspired thoughts, but also in the way in which its leading lights have been honoured since Mrs Thatcher entered Downing Street.

Closely allied to the Institute is another charity, the Social Affairs

Unit. It was founded in 1980 as an offshoot of the IEA, whose offices it shares. According to its articles of association, it exists to 'publish vigorous, readable and scholarly studies of controversial social issues in order to encourage informed public debate'. Although a tiny concern, with an annual income of less than £40,000, the message of its publication will be music to the ears of many of the present government. Its first book, *Breaking the Spell of the Welfare State*, published in 1981, argued for a large reduction in public expenditure and in the role of government. In a section that will have pleased, in particular, the monetarist hawks in the administration, it took the government to task for not having made any 'significant cuts' in welfare spending since 1979. *The Pied Piper of Education*, its next publication, called for the introduction of education vouchers, short-term contracts for teachers, and an end to 'the anti-business bias taught to teachers during training by the sociologists of education'. Late in 1984, it produced a report that would have given comfort to those in the Conservative Party – including its former Chairman, John Selwyn Gummer – who were concerned at the involvement of the churches in general, and some bishops in particular, in social matters. Entitled 'The Kindness that Kills: The Churches' Simplistic Response to Complex Social Issues', it received considerable press attention for its central thesis that the churches have too many left-wing do-gooders betraying the essentials of Christianity. Two of the Social Affairs Unit's trustees have been honoured by Mrs Thatcher. Caroline Cox received a peerage in December 1982 and Arthur Seldon a CBE in 1983.

Many of the names of these ideologues recur in a number of different settings which have the ear and sympathy of Downing Street. Another such body is Aims of Industry, a limited company founded in 1942 with the object of 'Campaigning for freedom and free enterprise and against the extension of nationalisation and state control'.

Few could doubt the Prime Minister's adherence to these objectives, which she spelled out on the occasion of Aims' fortieth birthday celebration: 'For 40 years Aims has been a tireless crusader for our great liberties. Long may it continue.' Aims' past or present directors have included the Thatcher-honoured Lord Vinson (although he resigned in 1973, shortly before moving to set up the Centre for Policy Studies) and Lord Taylor of Hadfield as well as Kenneth McAlpine, of the twice-honoured McAlpine family.

Crystal-ball gazers might look for a future bauble to be bestowed on Nigel Mobbs – Director of Slough Estates, a company that generously supports the Conservative Party and Aims. (Nigel has recently taken the chair of Aims.)

Aims has given free-enterprise awards, sometimes in ceremonies attended by Mrs Thatcher, to the following Thatcher-honoured people: Lord Forte, Sir Alfred Sherman, Lord Sieff, *Daily Telegraph* Deputy Editor T. E. Uttley CBE, economist F. A. Hayek CH, Norris McWhirter CBE and Arthur Seldon CBE, and has published material written by Sir Alfred Sherman and Lord Harris of High Cross as well as former Thatcher PPS and now Minister of Housing Ian Gow.

Some of the same honoured ideologues crop up in two other Conservative think-tank/pressure groups whose thoughts have the sympathy of Mrs Thatcher. The Adam Smith Institute was established in Britain in 1981 for 'the advancement of learning by research into public policy options, economic and political science and the publication of such research'. It is a registered charity and has produced a large array of material supporting privatisation of services in the NHS and local government and calling for the reduction of Government intervention over a whole range of activities. Like its fellow charity, the Social Affairs Unit, the Adam Smith Institute's income is small but the distinctions awarded to its leading lights by the Thatcher government are considerable. Its academic board is chaired by Friedrich Hayek and includes T. E. Uttley, while its authors include Thatcher-created peer Lord Bellwin and at least three Conservative MPs. One current Conservative MP and Adam Smith Institute supporter, Christopher Chope, was awarded the OBE by Mrs Thatcher in 1981 – two years before he entered Parliament.

Finally, in this run-around of the honoured Right, there is the Freedom Association, a body which has spent a considerable amount of time and money in legal fees, campaigning against the closed shop and trade-union power. Its deputy chairman, Norris McWhirter, is Thatcher-honoured, as is fellow management committee member and financial backer, Lord Taylor of Hadfield. Contributors to its publications include the almost ubiquitous T. E. Uttley, Baroness Cox, Lord Harris of High Cross and Arthur Seldon CBE, and one of its council members is Anthony Quayle (cited for services to acting), the actor who does voice-overs for Conservative Party political broadcasts and who received a knighthood in January 1985.

When the honoured ideologues are added in number to the promoted MPs and other recipients of honours for 'political and public service' and to them are added the names of the directors of companies who have contributed to Conservative Party funds, almost a half of those who have received major honours from the Thatcher government have provided it with ideological, voting or financial sustenance.

Epilogue

I wonder people do not begin to feel the distinction of an unadorned
name.

Sir Robert Peel

The Thatcher honours controversy comes at the end of half a millen-
nium of honours-touting and -trading. Reforms have been proposed
and tried but the temptations that the system offers to insecure, vain
or just plain corrupt dispensers of patronage are enormous. Many
Civil Servants, politicians, businessmen, newspaper-owners, trade-
union officers and whole swathes of public officials and voluntary
workers are controlled and kept in their place by the honours
system.

It is part of the cement that binds together the edifice of society
and is taken very seriously, indeed run by, those who care most
about its continued stability. After every major scandal – or even
whiff of one – this century, the establishment closed ranks rapidly,
proposed cosmetic reforms and ensured that the process continued
largely unabated.

The honours system provides the beautiful simplicity for prime
ministers of being able to repay favours at almost no cost. Just a little
sprinkle of a couple of dozen names twice a year on an otherwise
innocuous-looking list pays off accumulated debts and gives the nod
and the wink to other would-be recipients. A few more hopefuls are
kept in order and will continue to provide long, loyal and in some
cases lucrative service in the expectation of gongs to come.

This book has only looked at the tip of the iceberg: the small percentage of nationally known and infamous characters who owe their
elevation or honour to the political masters. Who is to say that a
similar story is not available to the assiduous researcher enquiring
into the nominations of the other 90 per cent or so who owe their
rewards to the mysterious official machinery of the honours system?

Appendix

The Honours (Prevention of Abuses) Act, 1925

An Act for the prevention of abuses in connection with the Grant of Honours. [7th August 1925.]

Be it enacted by the King's most Excellent Majesty, by and with the advice and consent of the Lords Spiritual and Temporal, and Commons, in this present Parliament assembled, and by the authority of the same, as follows:—

1.—(1) If any person accepts or agrees to accept or attempts to obtain from any person, for himself or for any other person, or for any purpose, any gift, money or valuable consideration as an inducement or reward for procuring or assisting or endeavouring to procure the grant of a dignity or title or honour to any person, or otherwise in connection with such a grant, he shall be guilty of a misdemeanour.

(2) If any person gives, or agrees or proposes to give, or offers to any person any gift, money or valuable consideration as an inducement to reward for procuring or assisting or endeavouring to procure the grant of a dignity or title or honour to any person, or otherwise in connection with such a grant, he shall be guilty of a misdemeanour.

(3) Any person guilty of a misdemeanour under this Act shall be liable on conviction on indictment to imprisonment for a term not exceeding two years or to a fine not exceeding five hundred pounds, or to both such imprisonment and such fine, or on summary conviction to imprisonment for a term not exceeding three months or to a fine not exceeding fifty pounds, or to both such imprisonment and such fine, and where the person convicted (whether on indictment or summarily) received any such gift, money, or consideration as aforesaid which is capable of forfeiture, he shall in addition to any other punishment be liable to forfeit the same to His Majesty.

(4) The Vexatious Indictments Act, 1859, as amended by any subsequent enactment, shall apply to offences under this Act as if they were included among the offences mentioned in section one of that Act.

2. This Act may be cited as the Honours (Prevention of Abuses) Act, 1925.

Index